"At a time when debates about the quality of our liturgical life often degrade into instrumentalizing liturgical styles in order to score 'traditionalist' points or 'progressive' points, Marx offers us a better way. Through reflections on Scripture, the history of the liturgy, the documents of the church, and his own pastoral conversations, he presents a profound exposition of what allows us to engage in worship that is truly 'authentic.'"

— Rev. Mark R. Francis, CSV
President
Catholic Theological Union

"Marx revisits the complex issues of liturgical reform by applying a brilliant new hermeneutical key: authenticity. Everyone wants an authentic liturgy; everyone wants to do liturgy authentically. But what could that possibly mean? Marx tells us in this discriminating book by providing historical and theoretical background and arriving at an irenic conciliation."

— David Fagerberg
University of Notre Dame

"Acknowledging that the concept of authenticity has been derided as a 'thin cover for narcissism and moral relativism,' the author convincingly argues that 'authentic liturgical participation requires worshippers to cultivate and enact a duplex virtue . . . *magnanimity* and *humility*.' Cultivating this dynamic virtue over time and through practice is the foundation for authentic liturgical celebration. I cannot recommend this book highly enough for all those who preach and preside, sing and serve—for all who enact liturgical worship under the guidance of the Holy Spirit."

— Fr. Jan Michael Joncas
University of St. Thomas
St. Paul, Minnesota

"In part historical and ritual study, what Marx gives us here is a liturgical theology of authentic Christian worship. I highly recommend this not just for students of liturgy, but for communities, parish groups, worship committees, and in short, for all of us concerned about authenticity and integrity in our worship. It is simply excellent!"

— Maxwell E. Johnson
University of Notre Dame

"Nathaniel Marx is an important fresh voice in matters liturgical and theological today. The breadth of his erudition in the sources used, the way he contextualizes such a breadth of them, and the invitational style through which he makes his arguments makes Marx someone to read and savor now, as well as someone to watch and learn from, hopefully for decades to come."

— Monsignor Kevin W. Irwin
The Catholic University of America

# Authentic Liturgy

## Minds in Tune with Voices

*Nathaniel Marx*

**LITURGICAL PRESS**
**ACADEMIC**

Collegeville, Minnesota
www.litpress.org

1     2     3     4     5     6     7     8     9

**Library of Congress Cataloging-in-Publication Data**

Names: Marx, Nathaniel, author.
Title: Authentic liturgy : minds in tune with voices / Nathaniel Marx.
Description: Collegeville, Minnesota : Liturgical Press Academic, 2020. |
    Includes bibliographical references. | Summary: "Nathaniel Marx argues
    that the defining characteristic of authentic liturgy is harmony. He unfolds
    the meaning of the call to authentic worship through scriptural exegesis,
    liturgical history, anthropology of ritual, and philosophy of action"—
    Provided by publisher.
Identifiers: LCCN 2020003268 (print) | LCCN 2020003269 (ebook) |
    ISBN 9780814684696 (paperback) | ISBN 9780814684931 (epub) |
    ISBN 9780814684931 (mobi) | ISBN 9780814684931 (pdf)
Subjects: LCSH: Benedictines—Liturgy. | Benedict, Saint, Abbot of Monte
    Cassino. Regula. | Catholic Church—Liturgy. | Authenticity
    (Philosophy)—Religious aspects—Catholic Church | Divine office.
Classification: LCC BX2049.B4 Z75 2020 (print) | LCC BX2049.B4 (ebook) |
    DDC 264/.02—dc23
LC record available at https://lccn.loc.gov/2020003268
LC ebook record available at https://lccn.loc.gov/2020003269

*For my parents,*
Alice and Paul,
*who taught me to pray*
*with my voice and with my mind*

# Contents

**Introduction**   ix

*Chapter One*
**The Quest for Authentic Liturgy**   1

*Chapter Two*
**Authentic Worship in the Bible**   33

*Chapter Three*
**Harmony and Authentic Prayer**   71

*Chapter Four*
**The Authentic Performance of Prayer**   111

*Chapter Five*
**Authenticity and Liturgical Reform**   153

*Chapter Six*
**Tuning Adjustments**   189

*Chapter Seven*
**Authentic Liturgy and the Virtue of Authenticity**   219

**Bibliography**   245

**Name Index**   260

**Subject Index**   262

# Introduction

Chapter 19 of the Rule of Benedict instructs the monks in the right way to pray when they come together for the Liturgy of the Hours: "Let us stand to sing the psalms in such a way that our minds are in harmony with our voices."[1] St. Benedict's articulation of the authentic way of participating in liturgical prayer encapsulates the ideal not just for monks but for all Christians. Paraphrasing Benedict's Rule, the Second Vatican Council's Constitution on the Sacred Liturgy says that when the people participate in the liturgy, it's necessary "that their minds be attuned to their voices."[2] In this way, they cooperate with grace and receive the full benefit of what God freely offers them in the liturgy. The following pages are partially the result of a hunch that one could write an entire book on the meaning and history of these few words. More than that, though, this study is the product of a conviction that the desire for authenticity isn't limited to these words or to the Roman Catholic tradition. Authentic liturgy is, and has always been, a central aspiration of all Christians.

I am asking readers of this book to embrace the moral and religious value of *authenticity*, an ideal frequently derided as a thin cover for narcissism and moral relativism. Authenticity is a "vitally important

---

[1] Timothy Fry, ed., *Rule of Saint Benedict 1980* (Collegeville, MN: Liturgical Press, 1981). Unless otherwise noted, all translations are from this edition and are cited as RB.

[2] Second Vatican Council, Constitution on the Sacred Liturgy (*Sacrosanctum Concilium*), December 4, 1963, in *Vatican Council II: Constitutions, Decrees, Declarations; The Basic Sixteen Documents*, ed. Austin Flannery (Collegeville, MN: Liturgical Press, 2014). Unless otherwise noted, all translations are from this edition and are cited as SC.

addition to any conversation concerning what it means to be fully human," but as Brian Braman observes, "the current debate that swirls around this ideal fails to see beyond its cultural caricature" as shallow and selfish.[3] Over the past thirty years, Charles Taylor has offered a sustained and compelling response to the "knockers" of the modern culture of authenticity. Though its defenders often "degrade" authenticity by taking it to mean "a kind of soft relativism," Taylor maintains that "authenticity should be taken seriously as a moral ideal."[4] More recently, Daniel Dahlstrom has argued, as I do here, that authenticity is "a new name for an old virtue."[5] Its renewal in worship and ethics would contribute much to human flourishing today.

In their finely detailed ethnography of a young, racially diverse evangelical church in downtown Chicago, Jessica Barron and Rhys Williams adopt a sociological understanding of authenticity. They exclude the possibility that anyone can prescind from particular cultural constructions of authenticity and definitively say what things are *correctly* believed to be authentic:

> Leaders of Downtown Church are eager to create an authentic urban establishment in order to attract authentic urban members. Thus, we conceptualize authenticity as a cultured understanding of what is real and true, in contrast to what is faked, put on, or superficial. Authenticity is informed by a collective imagination; it is not itself objective but simply a more-or-less shared set of beliefs about the nature of things we value in the world because they can be relied upon to be "real." . . . Authenticity is alluring to outsiders due to its status as something that is not readily accessible to the mainstream public—in a sense, a privileged mystique. However, the search for authenticity as true and not consciously created will always be a failing prospect as authenticity is always manufactured.[6]

[3] Brian J. Braman, *Meaning and Authenticity: Bernard Lonergan and Charles Taylor on the Drama of Authentic Human Existence* (Toronto: University of Toronto Press, 2008), 28–29.

[4] Charles Taylor, *The Ethics of Authenticity* (Cambridge, MA: Harvard University Press, 1992), 17, 22–23.

[5] Daniel O. Dahlstrom, *Identity, Authenticity, and Humility* (Milwaukee, WI: Marquette University Press, 2017), 136.

[6] Jessica M. Barron and Rhys H. Williams, *The Urban Church Imagined: Religion, Race, and Authenticity in the City* (New York: New York University Press, 2017), 14.

Sociologists who study authenticity have a point; authenticity is a culturally constructed concept, from top to bottom and from individuals to whole societies. But *how* is authenticity constructed, and *to what ends*?

I claim that authenticity can be constructed in wrong ways and to wrong ends—or in right ways and to right ends. In the former case, authenticity is the vice that its critics say it is, but in the latter case, authenticity is a virtue. I know that authenticity, which purports to stand in contrast to artifice, "is ironically always fabricated."[7] Yet I insist on distinctions between fabrication and faking, construction and deception, art and artificiality—between the deep cultivation of a virtue and the superficial donning of a mask. Although this book offers much neutral analysis of various ways that the concept of authenticity can be constructed, it also argues for a right way of constructing authenticity as a virtue.

As it pertains to liturgy, authenticity is rightly constructed when it aims at the glorification of God and the sanctification of human beings. *Sacrosanctum Concilium* affirms this duplex goal of the church's activities, all of which have the liturgy as their "summit and source." In its next paragraph, the Constitution on the Sacred Liturgy speaks about the right way to construct authenticity, both as an intellectual concept and as an embodied virtue. Authenticity is built up by bringing "minds" and "voices"—interior activity and exterior activity—into harmony, concord, or "tune," as most English translations have it (SC 11). If this musical metaphor is apt—and a tradition reaching back to the Rule of Benedict and beyond suggests that it is—then an unexpected conclusion follows. Authenticity is dynamic, not static. The quest for authentic liturgy doesn't confront us with the dichotomy of true or false, but with the challenge of cultivating a virtue, over time and through practice.

Chapter 1 will propose some terminology helpful in approaching authentic liturgy as a quest. I will distinguish two meanings of authenticity—a *genealogical* meaning and a *performative* meaning—whose careless or deliberate elision hinders agreement about what makes a liturgical celebration authentic. Although the rest of the book will more often explicitly address the performative meaning of authentic

---

[7] Barron and Williams, *Urban Church Imagined*, 15.

liturgy, the chapters are arranged to demonstrate that the genealogical meaning of authentic liturgy is fulfilled only by satisfying the perennial requirement for the participants in liturgical prayer to have their minds in tune with their voices.

The demand for authentic performance of divine worship is no modern invention. For Christians, the requirement is deeply rooted in the Hebrew Scriptures and the New Testament. Chapter 2 will show that the authentic performance of prayer is a point of major importance in the preaching of the Hebrew prophets, the teaching of Jesus, and the ministry of Paul. Scripture also supplies the basic metaphors that generations of Jews and Christians have used to articulate the necessity of harmonizing minds and voices in prayer.

Chapters 3, 4, and 5 are mainly historical. They supply the deep genealogical background for the Second Vatican Council's understanding of the people's authentic performance of their part in the sacred liturgy. Chapter 3 relies on early Christian pastors and ascetics to demonstrate the close alliance between integral prayer and ecclesial communion. Individual Christians sought harmony of mind and voice in prayer so the whole church could harmoniously offer God one pure sacrifice of praise. Chapter 4 traces the endurance and transformation of this ideal of authentic prayer across the centuries that separate the Rule of Benedict from Vatican II. It aims to show how the traditional emphasis on the interior prayer of the heart could become disconnected in both Catholic and Protestant practice from the full ideal of harmony between interior and exterior prayer. Chapter 5 argues that authenticity is central to the modern liturgical movement's efforts to renew the church's capacity to perform what Romano Guardini calls "the integrated liturgical act," which embraces "not only a spiritual inwardness," but the minds and voices of all the faithful, joined in one harmonious song of praise.[8]

Chapter 6 describes the *tuning adjustments* that individuals, congregations, and even the universal church must make to bring minds and voices into harmony. These adjustments proceed in two directions, *inside-out* and *outside-in*, and both are essential to authentic liturgy. To illustrate the integrity of both kinds of tuning adjustments, I rely on the voices of contemporary free church evangelicals and

---

[8] Romano Guardini, "A Letter from Romano Guardini," *Herder Correspondence* 1, no. 8 (August 1964): 237–39.

Latin Mass Catholics. Seeking harmony rather than dichotomy between these two approaches to authentic liturgy, chapter 7 claims that authentic liturgical participation requires worshippers to cultivate and enact a duplex virtue. Following Thomas Aquinas's pairing of the virtues of *magnanimity* and *humility*, Dahlstrom explains that both are necessary to realize the modern ideal of "being true to ourselves."[9] That ideal—though degraded by its "boosters" and dismissed by its "knockers"—is the virtue of *authenticity*, and it is the key to authentic liturgy.

Chapter 7 closes with an "examination of conscience for liturgists," which I offer to all Christians—not just those who hold professional responsibility for a congregation's worship—whether or not they identify their worship as "liturgical." *Leitourgia* is first of all the work of Jesus Christ on behalf of his people, the church. By inviting worshippers to examine the authenticity of their participation in Christ's liturgy, I hope to offer a modest return on the help that fellow "liturgists"—colleagues, students, editors, friends, and family—have given me in reflecting on the tuning adjustments that would make my own liturgical participation more authentic. I am especially grateful to my coworkers and students at Saint Meinrad Seminary and School of Theology, who have generously offered encouragement, feedback, and time to write. While working on this book, I learned that the seminarians had chosen "authenticity" as the theme for their final year of studies before ordination to the priesthood. I applaud the choice even as I reflect that the same word can signal openness or rigidity, vulnerability or defensiveness, accountability or insularity. Which will it be for them and which will it be for all who seek to offer God authentic worship?

---

[9] Dahlstrom, *Identity, Authenticity, and Humility*, 112–36.

*Chapter One*

# The Quest for Authentic Liturgy

The reform of the Roman Catholic liturgy is the most visible and best-known outcome of the Second Vatican Council. Catholics and non-Catholics can be wholly unaware of what Vatican II said about the interpretation of the Bible, the church's self-understanding, and reconciliation with other Christians, other religions, and the modern world. Yet most know that decisions made by the council directly or indirectly changed how Catholics pray the Mass. The switch from Latin to vernacular languages, the sweeping revisions of liturgical books, and the flourishing of local variety in church music, art, and architecture all look like major changes, at least in external forms. The goal of these changes to the liturgy's exterior is also broadly familiar, even if fewer Catholics could quote the council's hope that all of God's faithful people would be "led to take that full, conscious, and active part in liturgical celebrations which is demanded by the very nature of the liturgy" (SC 14). The liturgical reform can be considered a success only if the exterior renewal has been accompanied by an interior renewal of the understanding and devotion with which the laity participate in liturgical celebrations.

## Minds in tune with voices

The council's clearest expression of the desired harmony of interior and exterior activity that constitutes full, conscious, and active participation appears near the beginning of the Constitution on the Sacred Liturgy. The document affirms that the liturgy is principally the work of God in Christ. From it, "grace is poured forth upon us as from a fountain, and our sanctification in Christ and the glorification of God to which all other activities of the church are directed, as toward their end, are achieved with maximum effectiveness" (10). Any activity that humans undertake in the liturgy is only by way of cooperation with the activity of God's grace.

> But in order that the liturgy may be able to produce its full effects it is necessary that the faithful come to it with proper dispositions, that their minds be attuned to their voices, and that they cooperate with heavenly grace lest they receive it in vain (see 2 Cor 6:1). Pastors of souls must, therefore, realize that, when the liturgy is celebrated, their obligation goes further than simply ensuring that the laws governing valid and lawful celebration are observed. They must also ensure that the faithful take part fully aware of what they are doing, actively engaged in the rite and enriched by it. (11)

If liturgy is to glorify God and sanctify worshippers, it must be authentic: the interior activity of participants' minds and hearts must be in tune with the exterior activity of their voices and bodies. Only then is the liturgy truly the *corporate* activity of the whole Body of Christ.

Authenticity in liturgy includes sincerity, but it goes beyond the absence of an intention to deceive others. Authentic liturgy seeks a harmony of interior and exterior participation that excludes mindlessness as much as hypocrisy, self-deception as much as dissemblance. Authenticity is not the decision of a moment. According to the council, which borrows the image of minds in tune with voices from the Rule of Benedict, authenticity must be grown and tended by the faithful and their pastors. Each layperson is like a monk who never stops learning to pray the hours with greater understanding and devotion, long after the words of the Psalms have been memorized and the routines of standing, sitting, kneeling, and bowing have become automatic.

As the Rule of Benedict shows, authenticity in the liturgy is not a uniquely modern value. It comes to the fore whenever prophets, preachers, or pastors call for the invigoration and purification of a people's worship. For the same reason, authenticity especially characterizes the goal of modern liturgical renewal. Authenticity is embraced as an ideal, however, by groups of Christians who take different approaches to realizing that goal. If "authentic liturgy" strikes us as a mere label that partisans apply to diametrically opposed visions of public prayer, this only proves the shared attraction that authenticity holds for people who disagree about how to find it. I argue that authenticity is not an empty concept and that authentic liturgy does exist. It happens when the minds of participants are attuned to their voices, coordinated with their movements, and ready to cooperate with the grace that approaches them through their senses.

When liturgy fails to be authentic, calls to restore its integrity usually emphasize either interior changes ("minds") or exterior changes ("voices"). Either emphasis raises questions. How can worshippers internalize a liturgy whose exterior forms are unintelligible? How can they conform themselves to the liturgy's spirit when its external expressions keep changing? How can people give voice to heartfelt prayers and beliefs in a foreign language? How can incorporating new words and gestures into the liturgy avoid introducing something foreign to its spirit? The pastoral wisdom and durability of the council's liturgical constitution lies in its willingness to keep these questions in view simultaneously. Passage after passage of *Sacrosanctum Concilium* declines to exclusively focus on either interior or exterior changes, seeking instead the renewal of harmony between minds and voices.

If the liturgical constitution's commitment to authenticity is one of its enduring strengths, it also underlies many struggles over the right interpretation and implementation of the liturgical reform. Everyone desires authentic liturgy, but how to evaluate authenticity, how to nurture it in the liturgy, and how to restore it when lacking are disputed questions that regrettably divide Christians into camps. "Liturgical churches" versus "free churches," "traditional worship" versus "contemporary worship," "transcendent liturgy" versus "immanent liturgy"—all claim the mantle of authenticity.

The conclusion to draw from this contest isn't that authentic liturgy is whatever one wishes it to be. Rather, authentic liturgy is one thing with two distinct yet inextricable meanings. This is because the authenticity sought in the liturgy is not only the harmony of one worshipper's mind and voice. Nor is the only goal the harmony of several minds and voices gathered at a single time and place. The quest for authentic liturgy seeks the symphony of all minds, hearts, voices, and bodies that have ever participated or will ever participate in the worship offered to God in Christ. This chorus is eternal, and it acclaims God's glory with "one voice," as the eucharistic prayers of many traditions testify. Authentic liturgy requires two kinds of authenticity: a *correspondence of the interior with the exterior*, and a *continuity of the present with the past*. While we can distinguish them in theory, in practice these two meanings of authenticity are inseparable.

## Two meanings of authenticity

The word "authentic" appears to be an all-purpose synonym for adjectives that name disparate concepts, including "true," "real," "sincere," "original," "identical," and "traditional." This makes claims about authentic liturgy difficult to compare, since different authors—and different readers—often have different meanings of authenticity in mind. Still, there is an important reason to continue using "authentic" to name liturgies that possess the quality of *authenticity*. The noun and the adjective both pinpoint the desire to *verify* or *authenticate*—to put something to the test by observing the presence or absence of authenticating characteristics. Claims about authenticity assert not simply that a liturgy *is* true, real, sincere, or traditional, but that it is *verifiably* so. Even when the claim of authenticity is advanced by legislators and officials, it isn't a naked assertion of authority, but an argument or testimony that offers evidence.

The evidence testifying to a liturgy's authenticity falls into two broad categories that can be distinguished from one another, even if they are normally intertwined. One category of evidence testifies to *genealogy* or *origin*, while the other testifies to *correspondence* or *integrity*. This distinction follows one made by anthropologist Charles Lindholm in his analysis of authenticity as a modern cultural value: "There are two overlapping modes for characterizing any entity as authentic: genealogical or historical (*origin*) and identity or correspondence (*content*). Authentic objects, persons, and collectives are original, real, and pure; they are what they purport to be, their roots are known and verified, their essence and appearance are one."[1]

People demanding authentic liturgy aren't demanding two things, but one thing with two meanings. For convenience, we can call these the *genealogical meaning of authenticity* and the *performative meaning of authenticity*. The genealogical meaning of authenticity refers to the

---

[1] Charles Lindholm, *Culture and Authenticity* (Oxford: Blackwell, 2008), 2.

claim that the present liturgical assembly is celebrating the same liturgy that their spiritual ancestors celebrated. Such genealogical claims may be based on interior or exterior sameness, and sameness can mean identity, continuity, or some combination of the two. Before the modern era, these claims didn't depend on the work of expert genealogists such as liturgical historians, but instead relied on judgments about the correct approach to receiving and handing on the liturgical tradition, whole and intact, from one generation to the next. Inevitably, these genealogical judgments overlap with judgments about authentic formation and performance. One effect of modernity, however, is that genealogical judgments are increasingly seen as a task for the historical sciences, even as judgments about performative authenticity ignore or reject communal tradition as a point of reference.

The performative meaning of authenticity refers to the claim that the minds and voices of the people gathered for worship are in tune—that their exterior participation in the liturgical celebration is accompanied by corresponding interior participation in the mystery that the liturgy celebrates. Although the adjective "performative" is the most convenient shorthand for this meaning of authenticity, it's potentially misleading. Beginning in the early modern period, performance came to imply the *opposite* of authentic expression, along with a cluster of terms including "show," "play," "theater," "ritual," and "act." This prejudice should not keep us from seeing that liturgy *is* a performance. Liturgy *enacts* the work of salvation and the glorification of God in Christ; it doesn't merely narrate or represent these realities.[2] As a species of performance, liturgical enactment possesses

---

[2] See SC 5, 10. For a definition of "enactment" as "the specifically liturgical manner" of performance, see Richard D. McCall, *Do This: Liturgy as Performance* (Notre Dame, IN: University of Notre Dame Press, 2007), 86–89. McCall often speaks of "enactment" of the liturgy "to avoid the theatrical overtones" of performance (6). Nicholas Wolterstorff, in his philosophical reflections on liturgy as a type of action, similarly prefers to use the term "enactment" "because of the misleading connotations of the term 'performance.'" *Acting Liturgically: Philosophical Reflections on Liturgical Practice* (Oxford: Oxford University Press, 2018), 3 n. 8. While sharing these reservations about the word "performance," I also see a benefit in continuing to speak of human participation in the liturgy as a performance whose intended audience is God. While examples of Christian disapproval of theatrical performances exist in every era, it is also a scripturally rooted commonplace to encourage performing for a divine audience

interior elements (dispositions, motivations, intentions, and meanings) and exterior elements (speech, gestures, and movement). In an authentic liturgical act, these elements of performance form an integrated whole, with minds attuned to voices.

As Nicholas Wolterstorff argues, the "performative dimension of liturgy" can and should be understood in distinction from "the *expressive* function of liturgy and the *formative* function." A liturgical performance isn't reducible to its functions of expressing and forming "beliefs, commitments, habits, emotions, and so forth."[3] Liturgical performance is first an act of worshipping God. We should understand the performative authenticity of the liturgical act as valuable in itself, apart from any contribution authenticity might make to liturgy's adequate expression of orthodox beliefs or successful formation of Christian habits. As important as the expressive and formative functions of the liturgy are, they are not the primary purpose of liturgical action. "Christian liturgical enactments are for the purpose of learning and acknowledging the excellence of who God is and what God has done."[4] *Worship* is the fundamental purpose of liturgy. Liturgy isn't just a way of expressing beliefs *about* who God is and what God has done, nor is it only a means to the formation of commitments and habits of living that acknowledge God's excellence.

Still, both the expressive and formative functions of liturgy affect the performative dimension of liturgy in ways that can't be set aside, because the expressive adequacy and formative influence of liturgical activity impact the authenticity of the liturgical performance. Minds and voices don't come into tune accidentally, but as the result of individual worshippers faithfully following communal prescriptions for "correct enactment" of a particular liturgy—prescriptions that Wolterstorff calls a "script" and that Nathan Mitchell compares to a musical "score."[5] The prescriptions of the liturgical score are subject to interpretation, adaptation, and adjustment. Participants adjust in

rather than a human audience (see especially Matt 6:1-18, which will be examined in detail in the next chapter). The theatrical metaphor plays an important and recurrent role in the Christian call to performative authenticity in the liturgy.

[3] Wolterstorff, *Acting Liturgically*, 5. Emphasis in original.

[4] Wolterstorff, *Acting Liturgically*, 29.

[5] Wolterstorff, *Acting Liturgically*, 12–19; Nathan D. Mitchell, *Meeting Mystery: Liturgy, Worship, Sacraments* (Maryknoll, NY: Orbis Books, 2006), 38.

response to different circumstances of culture and history, but also because liturgy requires that the participants mutually respond to one another and to God. Therefore, "pastors will be fulfilling one of the chief duties of a faithful dispenser of the mysteries of God" when they "see to the liturgical instruction of the faithful and their active participation, internal and external, in the liturgy, taking into account their age, condition, way of life and standard of religious culture" (SC 19). *Sacrosanctum Concilium* assumes that much of this formation for active internal and external participation takes place within the celebration of the liturgy itself, so the rites "should be within the people's powers of comprehension, and normally should not require much explanation" (34). Even though the people should come to the liturgy with the right interior dispositions, they acquire those dispositions primarily through participation in the liturgy. In the case of the sacraments, "the very act of celebrating them is most effective in making people ready" to receive sacramental grace "to their profit" (59). Authentic formation for liturgy takes place through celebrations of the liturgy that are authentic in the performative sense. The effect is circular. By celebrating the liturgy with minds attuned to voices, the people learn to make adjustments that bring their minds and voices even more perfectly into tune with one another.

The necessity of these *tuning adjustments* brings the genealogical meaning of authenticity back into view. It's neither possible nor desirable for one enactment of the liturgy in time and space to be the exact duplicate of a celebration that preceded it. However, any adjustments from one celebration to the next must allow the present assembly to celebrate the same liturgy as their ancestors in faith. Because of the performative meaning of authenticity, neither an exclusively interior sameness nor an exclusively exterior sameness will preserve a liturgy that is authentic in the genealogical sense. Continuity and adjustment must be sought both internally and externally. This is why *Sacrosanctum Concilium* allows "innovations" in the external forms of the liturgy if "the good of the church genuinely and certainly requires them," yet insists that "any new forms adopted should in some way grow organically from forms already existing" (23). Authentic liturgical development is "organic" because it seeks to preserve the living ensemble of minds and voices, not disembodied ideas or mindless gestures. For the liturgy to remain true to what it is, minds *and* voices have to change.

In the realm of liturgical development, the two meanings of authenticity overlap in one further way. Although interior *and* exterior adjustments are required to bring minds and voices into tune, it seems necessary in practice to hold one steady while adjusting the other. But where does the reference tone originate: in the internal activity of minds and hearts or in the external activity of voices and bodies? Do the words and gestures of the liturgy first have to be adjusted to the capacities and dispositions of the people? Or must the people first try to conform their minds to the external rites handed down to them?

On the one hand, preserving genealogical continuity in the liturgy's external forms appears essential to enabling each successive generation of worshippers to bring their minds into tune with the tradition of prayer handed down to them. Those entrusted with handing on the liturgy's external forms must do all they can to ensure that "sound tradition may be retained" (SC 23). The imperative has more to do with changing hearts in the present than with preserving voices from the past. Tradition is retained for formation, which occurs as the things that people hear, say, and do slowly work their way into their minds and hearts. Stability of these external forms over time facilitates the interiorization of the "true Christian spirit" that pastors of souls should seek above all else for themselves and for the people entrusted to their care (14).

But the unity that the liturgy enacts across generations and among all the peoples of the world is a unity of understanding and charity that has expressed itself, from the first Pentecost, in many tongues and actions, each conditioned by a people's culture and way of life. At least some of the liturgy's external forms are "subject to change," and "these not only may be changed but ought to be changed with the passage of time, if they have suffered from the intrusion of anything out of harmony with the inner nature of the liturgy" (SC 21). Also, the "various races and peoples" to whom the gospel comes possess "qualities and talents" that the church "preserves intact" and even admits into the liturgy "so long as they harmonize with its true and authentic spirit" (37). From this perspective, the retention of "sound tradition" means changing external forms to hand on the liturgy to new generations and new peoples with its "inner nature" and "authentic spirit" intact.

In seeking to hand on the authentic liturgical tradition, external forms are not the only or even the most important of the liturgy's

*original* elements. The liturgy originates in the work of God, "principally in the paschal mystery of [Christ's] blessed passion, resurrection
from the dead, and glorious ascension" (SC 5). The church's participation in Christ's work originates in the gift of the Holy Spirit, and
it is "through the power of the Holy Spirit" that the church "has never
failed to come together to celebrate the paschal mystery" (6). The
church relies on the Holy Spirit's aid in faithfully handing on the
liturgy from generation to generation. The Spirit guides the church's
discernment of the "unchangeable elements divinely instituted" from
"elements subject to change" (21). But there are other ways that the
Holy Spirit moves in the church, including by inspiring in the hearts
of its members "enthusiasm for the promotion and restoration of the
sacred liturgy" (43). And when elements of a newly evangelized
people's way of life are found to "harmonize with [the liturgy's] true
and authentic spirit," this is no accident, but the result of the Holy
Spirit's preparatory work. The Spirit influences the minds of individuals and the customs of nations to receive the gospel and to enrich
the church with new "qualities and talents" (37). Whatever the historical or cultural origins of a new form of external participation, it
is *original* to the liturgy if it proceeds from the Holy Spirit's prompting
of hearts and minds.

Authentic liturgy is rightly described as original, traditional, sincere, true, and real. It isn't, however, simple or obvious. Authenticity
is a complex quality, in part because judgments about it rarely isolate
the genealogical and performative modes of authentication from each
other. These two meanings of authenticity "are not always compatible
nor are both invoked equally in every context, but both stand in
contrast to whatever is fake, unreal, or false, and both are in great
demand."[6] Many battles about liturgical change and continuity since
Vatican II have been waged on the ground of authenticity by opponents who elide the genealogical and performative meanings of authenticity instead of working through the complex ways they overlap.
The debate over maintaining the pre-Vatican II liturgy as an "extraordinary form" of the Roman Rite is one such battle. Conflicts over
liturgical music, art, and architecture could also be illuminated and
perhaps ameliorated by analyzing how opposing sides invoke the

[6] Lindholm, *Culture and Authenticity*, 2.

genealogical and performative meanings of authenticity in their arguments. For now, I will illustrate this analysis by turning to another vigorously contested topic in liturgical reform: translation.

## An illustration: translating the liturgy

Different approaches to liturgical translation since Vatican II allow us to distinguish the two meanings of authenticity and observe how emphasizing one or the other leads to different practical decisions. Authentic liturgy requires much more than a well-composed and well-translated text, but liturgical translation has been the site of much controversy since the council. This controversy has been usefully explained as a clerical struggle between bishops' conferences and the Roman Curia, or as a scholarly disagreement about strategies of translation (*dynamic equivalence* versus *formal correspondence*).[7] However, the competing claims about how to translate and authorize liturgical texts also reflect tension between the two meanings of authenticity.

The Vatican's 2001 instruction on translation, issued by the Congregation for Divine Worship and the Discipline of the Sacraments, demonstrates the potency of claims to authenticity in its very title: *Liturgiam Authenticam*.[8] Since its promulgation, the document has governed new translations of the Roman Catholic liturgy into several major languages, drawing to itself praise and criticism for the successes and shortcomings of those translations. *Liturgiam Authenticam's* opening paragraph reiterates the council's central interest in authenticity, but it describes authentic liturgy as a means to an end, not the goal itself.

---

[7] See Peter Jeffery, *Translating Tradition: A Chant Historian Reads* Liturgiam Authenticam (Collegeville, MN: Liturgical Press, 2005); Gerald O'Collins, *Lost in Translation: The English Language and the Catholic Mass* (Collegeville, MN: Liturgical Press, 2017).

[8] Congregation for Divine Worship and the Discipline of the Sacraments, *Liturgiam Authenticam*, Fifth Instruction on the Right Implementation of the Constitution on the Sacred Liturgy of the Second Vatican Council, March 28, 2001, trans. in *The Liturgy Documents, Volume Three: Foundational Documents on the Origins and Implementation of Sacrosanctum Concilium* (Chicago: Liturgy Training Publications, 2013), 527–62. Hereafter cited as LA.

> The Second Vatican Council strongly desired to preserve with
> care the authentic Liturgy, which flows forth from the Church's
> living and most ancient spiritual tradition, and to adapt it with
> pastoral wisdom to the genius of the various peoples so that the
> faithful might find in their full, conscious, and active participa-
> tion in the sacred actions—especially the celebration of the Sacra-
> ments—an abundant source of graces and a means for their own
> continual formation in the Christian mystery. (LA 1)

*Liturgiam Authenticam*'s way of framing the goals of liturgical reform make it appear as though the council was trying to balance the
imperative of preserving the authentic liturgy *against* the desire to
make changes that allow "various peoples" to participate in the liturgy
more fully, consciously, and actively.[9] In such a framework, the question for the church is how much pastoral adaptation it can endorse
without diluting or adulterating the authentic liturgy. Authenticity
appears throughout *Liturgiam Authenticam* as a preexisting quality of
the liturgy that must be preserved, safeguarded, secured, and maintained.[10] The document rightly calls liturgical texts a "patrimony"
(20), but it rarely speaks of authentic liturgy as the *activity* that happens when minds are in tune with voices. It treats the quest for authentic liturgy almost exclusively as the preservation of genealogical
continuity between an original model and a reproduction. It under-
emphasizes the desire expressed in *Sacrosanctum Concilium* for performative correspondence between the internal dispositions of minds
and the external expressions of voices. *Liturgiam Authenticam* opens
its general principles of translation with a warning that too much
accommodation to the interior dispositions of the people can threaten
the authenticity of the liturgy. According to the instruction, the words
of the liturgy "are not intended primarily to be a sort of mirror of the
interior dispositions of the faithful; rather, they express truths that
transcend the limits of time and space" (19).

When performed authentically, however, the liturgy's expressions
of eternal truth *should* reflect what the participants feel and believe
most deeply. The participants should "cooperate with heavenly grace

[9] On the falsity of this opposition, see Peter Jeffery, *Translating Tradition*, 58–87.
[10] See LA 1, 4, 5, 7, 50, 52, 55, 57, 61.

lest they receive it in vain" (SC 11). *Liturgiam Authenticam* doesn't say this with the same clarity and urgency that is heard in *Sacrosanctum Concilium*. Still, *Liturgiam Authenticam* recognizes that the external words of the liturgy are not ends in themselves, but instruments with which "the Holy Spirit leads the Christian faithful into all truth and causes the word of Christ to dwell abundantly within them" (19). By calling for stability in the exterior forms of liturgical prayer, *Liturgiam Authenticam* hopes to facilitate the interior participation of the people. This approach to harmonizing minds with voices has considerable merit.

The emphasis is very different in the instruction on liturgical translation that *Liturgiam Authenticam* replaces, *Comme le prévoit* (CP), which was issued in 1969 by the Consilium charged with the initial implementation of *Sacrosanctum Concilium*.[11] *Comme le prévoit* begins with the assumption that a liturgical translation is no longer just a written aid to understanding Latin. Instead, vernacular translations have become " 'the voice of the Church,' "[12] part of the exterior activity whose purpose is "to proclaim the message of salvation to believers and to express the prayer of the Church to the Lord." In proclamation and prayer, the voice of the church expresses the gospel message that lives in the minds and hearts of believers today, so "it is not sufficient that a liturgical translation merely reproduce the expressions and ideas of the original text" (6). For *Comme le prévoit*, the ultimate criterion of a translation's accuracy and value is whether it can "serve the particular congregations who will use it" (14). Although the truths voiced by the church in the liturgy transcend any single congregation, the voice that expresses those eternal truths is always particular:

> The prayer of the Church is always the prayer of some actual community, assembled here and now. It is not sufficient that a formula handed down from some other time or region be translated verbatim, even if accurately, for liturgical use. The formula translated must become the genuine prayer of the congregation,

---

[11] Consilium for Implementing the Constitution on the Sacred Liturgy, *Comme le prévoit*, Instruction on the Translation of Liturgical Texts for Celebration with a Congregation, January 25, 1969, in *The Liturgy Documents, Volume Three*, 417–25. Hereafter cited as CP.

[12] *Comme le prévoit* quotes Paul VI, address to participants in the congress on translations of liturgical texts, November 10, 1965.

and in it each of its members should be able to find and express himself or herself. (20)

Although the people must adapt their own interior dispositions to find and express themselves authentically in the liturgy, a translated liturgical text also "often requires cautious adaptation" to bring minds and voices into tune (21).

*Comme le prévoit* recognizes that new liturgical translations "should in some way grow organically from forms already in existence" (SC 23, quoted in CP 43). The liturgical texts in existence have been transmitted for centuries in the Latin language, and the connection to this lineage must be maintained. Unlike *Liturgiam Authenticam*, however, *Comme le prévoit* usually avoids speaking of the Latin liturgical texts themselves as a patrimony or treasury to be preserved. The handing on of exterior words through the tradition of the church is ancillary to the transmission of the interior meaning that the words communicate. Thus, "a translation must faithfully communicate to a given people, and in their own language, that which the Church by means of this given text originally intended to communicate to another people in another time" (6). For *Comme le prévoit*, the givenness of a people's language, history, and culture is a fact as important as the givenness of the liturgy's traditional text. "Modern words" must be found so that what the priest and people say with their voices is "suited to the contemporary mind." Without this present correspondence of minds and voices, genealogical continuity with the past is disrupted. If a liturgical text "no longer expresses the true original meaning" that it did for an earlier generation, then it must be cautiously adapted in translation to "express true doctrine and authentic Christian spirituality" (24). For *Comme le prévoit*, the two meanings of authenticity are deeply intertwined.

Despite an otherwise robust understanding of authentic liturgy, *Comme le prévoit* does not mention the usefulness of external stability, reiteration, and uniformity as vehicles for bringing minds into tune with voices. This may be unfair criticism of a document written during a comprehensive overhaul of the Roman Rite's external liturgical forms. Only six years before *Comme le prévoit* was issued, the council declared its preference for a liturgy "free from useless repetition," and it disavowed any desire to "impose a rigid uniformity" (SC 34, 37). *Comme le prévoit* therefore doubts the wisdom of preserving certain

repetitive and stylized features of liturgical Latin in vernacular translations. The "piling up" of adjectives, the "routine addition of *sanctus*
or *beatus* to a saint's name, or the too casual use of superlatives" may
"weaken the force of the prayer" or cause it to sound "pompous and
superfluous" in languages other than Latin (12, 34). *Liturgiam Authenticam* directs translators to retain the original Latin text's "stylistic
elements," including "repetition" and "recurring and recognizable
patterns of syntax." The persistent use of these elements, along with
words and expressions that "differ somewhat from usual and everyday speech" supposedly have an effect "in the mind of the hearer"
that goes beyond transmission of the "conceptual content" and allows
the texts to "become truly memorable and capable of expressing
heavenly realities" (27, 59).

Debates over liturgical translation don't simply pit the genealogical
meaning of authenticity against the performative meaning of authenticity. Although *Liturgiam Authenticam* emphasizes the former and
*Comme le prévoit* the latter, both documents invoke continuity *and*
correspondence, origins *and* integrity. Both hold that authentic liturgy
requires interior and exterior participation, and both assume that
unity with past congregations is essential to authentic liturgy in the
present. The documents diverge in the approach each takes to authentic liturgical formation and authentic liturgical reform.

*Comme le prévoit* focuses on the *creative* activity that moves *outward*
from minds and hearts to find expression in the external forms of the
liturgy. For the people to do their work of tuning their minds to their
voices, they should be able to "find and express" themselves in texts
that "must become the genuine prayer of the congregation" (20). In
*Comme le prévoit*'s approach to authentic liturgy, creative expressions
that emerge from the minds and hearts of participants form an essential part of the people's growth in closeness and conformity to the
liturgy's true spirit. By extension, the work of liturgical revision and
translation assumes that "in many modern languages a biblical or
liturgical language must be created by use" and that in addition to
translations, "the creation of new texts will be necessary" (19, 43).

*Liturgiam Authenticam* discourages creativity and emphasizes instead the *repetitive* activity that allows the liturgy's words, gestures,
and external signs to become familiar and work their way *inward* to
imprint themselves on the minds of the people. The instruction assumes that the work of creating new texts was essentially completed

in the years following Vatican II, with the promulgation of the Latin "typical editions" (*editiones typicae*) of the Roman Missal, the sacramental rites, the Liturgy of the Hours, and other liturgical books. Further creative revision of this "rich patrimony" is not anticipated. So that it "may be preserved and passed on through the centuries, it is to be kept in mind from the beginning that the translation of the liturgical texts of the Roman Liturgy is not so much a work of creative innovation as it is of rendering the original texts faithfully and accurately into the vernacular language" (LA 20). While vernacular translations will need to be updated periodically, *Liturgiam Authenticam* cautions against revising too frequently the translations of Scripture, eucharistic prayers, and other texts that people learn by hearing or speaking repeatedly (36, 64). Overall, "a certain stability ought to be maintained whenever possible in successive editions prepared in modern languages. The parts that are to be committed to memory by the people, especially if they are sung, are to be changed only for a just and considerable reason" (74).

Since *Liturgiam Authenticam*, not *Comme le prévoit*, now governs most aspects of liturgical translation in the Roman Rite, the inward-moving activity of repetition and iteration has been emphasized over the outward-moving activity of creation and innovation in recent translations. It is noteworthy, however, that Pope Francis's 2017 *motu proprio* on liturgical translations, *Magnum Principium*, revives some of *Comme le prévoit's* perspective, sometimes borrowing its ideas almost word for word. *Magnum Principium* affirms, for example, that vernacular languages are "the voice of the Church," that "it is necessary to communicate to a given people using its own language all that the Church intended to communicate to other people through the Latin language," and that "fidelity cannot always be judged by individual words but must be sought in the context of the whole communicative act."[13]

Most important, *Magnum Principium* aligns itself with an approach to authentic liturgy that takes the minds of the people as a starting point. It assumes, as Pope Paul VI did in 1967, that "peoples' deepest and sincerest sentiments can best be expressed through the vernacular

[13] Pope Francis, Motu Proprio *Magnum Principium*, September 3, 2017, http://www.vatican.va/content/francesco/en/motu_proprio/documents/papa-francesco-motu-proprio_20170903_magnum-principium.html. Compare with CP 6.

as it is in actual usage."[14] So, while *Liturgiam Authenticam* begins with a claim about the council's desire to "preserve with care the authentic liturgy" (1), *Magnum Principium* opens by reaffirming "the great principle, established by the Second Vatican Ecumenical Council, according to which liturgical prayer be accommodated to the comprehension of the people so that it might be understood." *Sacrosanctum Concilium* enshrines this "great principle" in the preamble to the section that establishes general norms for liturgical reform: "In this renewal, both texts and rites should be ordered so as to express more clearly the holy things which they signify. The Christian people, as far as is possible, should be able to understand them easily and take part in them in a celebration which is full, active and the community's own" (21).[15]

The council's purpose here was well explained in 1964 by Cipriano Vagaggini, OSB, a key member of the preparatory commission for the liturgical constitution, a *peritus* at Vatican II, and the primary shaper of texts that would become Eucharistic Prayers III and IV. Vagaggini writes, "In a word one can say that the fundamental wish of the Council in this material is once more to make the liturgy wholly unadulterated and *authentic*. . . . Having an *authentic liturgy* means to have a liturgy in which the texts and rites, which are signs, clearly express for the people the sacred reality they signify and which the people, without unnecessary difficulties, can be fully immersed without unnecessarily obscuring the transcendence of the divine."[16]

---

[14] Paul VI, "Address to the Members and *Periti* of the Consilium," April 19, 1967, repr. in *Acta Apostolicae Sedis* 59 (1967): 419, trans. in *Documents on the Liturgy, 1963–1979: Conciliar, Papal, and Curial Texts* (Collegeville, MN: Liturgical Press, 1982), 228. I am indebted in this paragraph and the following one to Mario Lessi Ariosto, "Rights and Duties Arising from the Nature of the Liturgy: Considerations in the Light of the Motu Proprio *Magnum Principium*," published on the official website of the Congregation for Divine Worship and the Discipline of the Sacraments, December 22, 2017, http://www.cultodivino.va/content/cultodivino/it/documenti/motu-proprio-/-magnum-principium---3-settembre-2017-/articoli/mario-lessi-ariosto--s-j-/english.html.

[15] Although *Magnum Principium* does not supply a citation, Paul VI is responsible for first calling the accommodation of liturgical prayer to the understanding of the people the "great principle" (*magnum principium*) of the liturgy constitution. See Paul VI, "Address to the Members," 419 (trans. 228). Ariosto, "Rights and Duties."

[16] Cipriano Vagaggini, "Fundamental Ideas of the Constitution," in *The Liturgy of Vatican II: A Symposium*, ed. William Baraúna and Jovian Lang, vol. 1 (Chicago: Franciscan Herald Press, 1966), 116. Emphasis added.

*Magnum Principium*'s reaffirmation of this "great principle" represents a resurgence of the performative meaning of authenticity that may be more significant than the change the document makes to the process for approving liturgical translations. While it would be hasty to infer so much from a single *motu proprio*, the future may bring new openness to creative, exterior adjustment of texts so the people can immerse their minds and hearts in the words they say and hear.

In any case, it is certain that vernacular translations will continue to cause controversy. Besides playing a central role in modern liturgical reform, translations are an important proxy that participants use to make judgments about the genealogical and performative authenticity of the whole liturgy. Still, using the "mother tongue" is among the "secondary problems" of liturgical renewal, according to another one of the liturgical movement's twentieth-century giants, Romano Guardini.[17] More fundamental than the authenticity of a liturgical translation is the authenticity of the liturgical act itself. To this problem we now turn.

## The liturgical act: a "forgotten way of doing things"

The adjective "authentic" is regularly applied to a wide variety of objects (e.g., documents, paintings, and recordings) and subjects (e.g., people, institutions, and churches). In *authentic liturgy*, however, the adjective modifies an *activity*. Above all, as the first paragraphs of *Sacrosanctum Concilium* assert, liturgy is the activity of Jesus Christ, the Son of God, offering himself completely and eternally to God the Father, in union with the church that has become Christ's body through the outpouring of the Holy Spirit. The church's participation in this eternal, trinitarian liturgy is likewise an activity, as is each worshipper's participation in that same liturgy. The quest for authentic liturgy therefore can't be reduced to a search for authentic liturgical texts, music, art, or architecture. Neither can authenticity describe only an intellectual or emotional state in the people who are, individually and collectively, the subjects of liturgical prayer.

The quest for authentic liturgy is the quest for an authentic liturgical act. Guardini succinctly described this goal and the major ob-

<hr>

[17] Romano Guardini, "A Letter from Romano Guardini," *Herder Correspondence* 1, no. 8 (August 1964): 237–39.

stacle to it in 1964, just as work was about to begin on revising the liturgical books according to the norms laid out in *Sacrosanctum Concilium*.[18] Guardini believed that the revision could do much to rectify "ritual and textual problems" arising from a Mass whose prescribed form had remained virtually unchanged since 1570. The modern techniques of comparative liturgiology had revealed the history of such prescribed forms—their sources, diversity, and evolution over time—in ways that could allow a deeper connection to the church's heritage of liturgical prayer. But in his letter, Guardini argues that this can happen only if a solution is found to a more "central problem," the problem of "the cult act or, to be more precise, the liturgical act." To be even more precise, Guardini speaks of "the integrated liturgical act," which embraces "not only a spiritual inwardness, but the whole man, body as well as spirit." There must be a joining of the "spiritual" to the "corporal"—an "expression of the inward through the outward"—for participation in the liturgical act to be "genuine and honest." Such liturgy is *corporate* prayer because the individual's "self-expression" and that of the communal "corpus" are incorporated into one another in a performance authentically "done by every individual, not as an isolated individual, but as a member of a body in which the Church is present."[19]

The contemporary "problem" is that it is difficult "to get modern man to 'perform' the act without being theatrical or fussy." Theatricality is the enemy of authentic liturgy because it assumes a picture of the human person in which "body and spirit, outward and inward personality" do not "form an integrated whole." When the temporal and material particulars of worship are considered "merely external decorations," when prayers uttered and gestures made in common are "dismissed as artificial and officious," and when those interested in liturgical renewal are perceived as "aesthetes" who lack "Christian sincerity," then a deep suspicion of corporate liturgy has taken hold.[20] The church can't afford to ignore the widespread misunderstanding

---

[18] Guardini, "Letter from Romano Guardini," 237–39. The responses to Guardini's "open letter" are many and varied, but one that is particularly helpful in relating Guardini's concerns about liturgical renewal to issues in the anthropological study of ritual can be found in Nathan Mitchell, *Liturgy and the Social Sciences* (Collegeville, MN: Liturgical Press, 1999).

[19] Guardini, "Letter from Romano Guardini," 237–38.

[20] Guardini, "Letter from Romano Guardini," 237–39.

of the liturgical act that such criticism reveals. As Guardini writes elsewhere, there is a real risk of the liturgical act becoming "dead and superficial":

> It is true that it is the Church which is responsible for the sacred functions, but the Church becomes actual and real in the individual: in the faithful and in the priest. It is true that it is the act of the Church which carries out the liturgy, but this act passes through the souls of the individuals present. But if the individual has not learnt to face God, if his ear is not opened to hear nor his tongue loosened to speak, then the liturgical act does not pass through his living soul but only through his outer organs; and he who is listening, speaking and acting there, is no real person but an impersonal thing. In such a case the whole act loses its truth and its solemnity. Only when the individual prays as an individual too, can the great prayer of the Church come into the freedom and truth which is its own.[21]

Guardini doesn't claim to have a solution to this problem. "Quite a number of people" think that liturgy is a relic of the past, and that "it would be more honest to give it up altogether" because liturgy has become inimical to sincere Christianity. Guardini wonders, "Instead of talking of renewal ought we not to consider how best to celebrate the sacred mysteries so that modern man can grasp their meaning through his own approach to truth?" This is a "hard saying" for those who think that "liturgy is indeed fundamental." Still, Guardini identifies hopeful trends, especially in how religious educators are approaching the liturgical formation of the people. They are no longer satisfied with "giving better instruction on the meaning of ceremonies and liturgical vessels," for they realize that even in this "industrial and scientific age," people need "more than mere talk, intellectual explanations, and formal organizing. The faculties of looking, doing, and shaping must be fostered and included in the formative act."[22] Only then can the people "be brought to participate

---

[21] Romano Guardini, "Personal Prayer and the Prayers of the Church," in *Unto the Altar: The Practice of Catholic Worship*, ed. Alfons Kirchgaessner, trans. Rosaleen Brennan (New York: Herder and Herder, 1963), 40–41.

[22] Guardini, "Letter from Romano Guardini," 237–39.

in the act of worship without turning this act into a theatrical performance and empty gestures."[23]

In the half-century since Guardini's letter was published, the educational trends he praised appear to have gained widespread acceptance, at least in theory. It's now a commonplace to insist that catechesis, religious education, and seminary training should go beyond dispensing intellectual explanations and aim to shape the whole person. In these settings, liturgical instruction and participation are considered essential to integral Christian formation of minds *and* voices, spirits *and* bodies. Unfortunately, there is far less agreement about how to answer other questions Guardini raised: "What is the nature of the genuine liturgical action, as opposed to other religious actions, such as individual devotions or the loose communal act of popular devotions? How is the basic liturgical act constituted? What forms can it take? What might go wrong with it? How are its demands related to the make-up of modern man? What must be done so that he can really and truly learn it?"[24]

The last three questions are especially contentious because they invite reconsideration of the need for modern liturgical reform. Authentic liturgy is a permanent right and duty of every Christian, and the imperative to attune minds with voices is not unique to any period of Christian history. According to Guardini, however, something has gone wrong in modernity, and the result is that people have forgotten how to perform an integrated liturgical act. But is the problem with the people or with the liturgy? Why is it necessary to change external forms of liturgical celebration that generations of Catholics have used to glorify God and grow in holiness? Could the exterior changes actually inhibit interior transformation? Guardini is convinced that "the Council has laid the foundations for the future." Yet he worries that if the liturgical movement contents itself with "reforms of rites and texts" alone, it may happen that "people with a genuine concern for real piety come to feel that a misfortune is happening." Exterior reforms are insufficient in themselves to restore authenticity to the liturgical act. However carefully liturgical scholars may labor to recover forgotten texts, symbols, and ritual orders, their

---

[23] Guardini, "Letter from Romano Guardini," 237. These last words are not Guardini's, but those of the editors who printed his open letter in the *Herder Correspondence*.

[24] Guardini, "Letter from Romano Guardini," 239.

work will be in vain unless modern worshippers can "relearn a forgotten way of doing things."[25]

Guardini's way of framing the contemporary problem of authentic liturgy is helpful because he refuses to simplistically pit adaptation against preservation, exterior reform against interior transformation, or the genealogical meaning of authenticity against the performative meaning. Instead, Guardini's call to "relearn a forgotten way of doing things" points to a complex task with three interlocking facets. The contemporary problem of authentic liturgy is a problem of *memory*, of *performance*, and of *formation*. Something that was known to past generations of Christians has been "forgotten" in the present, and this calls for a historical investigation. Without anticipating the results, we can say that the thing forgotten is a manner of performance—a "way of doing things." And without prematurely defining the authentically liturgical manner of performance, Guardini indicates that it is a learnable behavior.

Before examining these facets of the problem further, we should emphasize that they demarcate a *human* problem. God's prevenient activity in the liturgy is not in question. The work of Christ's passover, which the liturgy makes present, is already perfect praise and fullness of redemption. From God's side, the liturgical act is complete and sufficient. But Christ's self-offering for the life of the world has also won him a people, the church, which Christ "always associates . . . with himself in this great work in which God is perfectly glorified and men and women are sanctified" (SC 7). The church's definitive participation in Christ's work is by way of liturgical *anamnesis*—a performative, ritualized remembering of the mystery of Christ. Liturgical anamnesis is not the only activity of the church, but it is the "summit" and "source" of all other activities, because "no other action of the church equals its effectiveness by the same title nor to the same degree" (SC 7, 10). To be precise, the "forgotten way of doing things" that Guardini would have modern Christians "relearn" is human participation, by means of liturgical anamnesis, in the fully divine, fully human activity of Jesus Christ.

Since liturgical *anamnesis* is a human activity, it is subject, both individually and corporately, to human imperfections, including

---

[25] Guardini, "Letter from Romano Guardini," 238.

inauthentic performance. The ideal is described in *Sacrosanctum Concilium* as "full, conscious, and active" participation in the liturgical act (14), but the ideal may be realized to greater or lesser degrees. From the side of human participation, one performance of the liturgical act may be more or less authentic than another, even though God's activity and invitation to participation remain the same. To convey this idea, *Sacrosanctum Concilium* borrows language from scholastic sacramental theology and applies it to all liturgical participation. The liturgy is always an effective "fountain" of grace because it makes the already-accomplished work of Christ present to the faithful (10). This is analogous to saying that a valid sacrament unfailingly confers grace *ex opere operato*, in the very performance of the sacramental action. For a sacrament to be not only administered validly, but also received *fruitfully*, the recipient of the external, sacramental sign must not inwardly block the activity of grace. To receive the *res* of the sacrament, the "spiritual effect intended by Christ," a person "must belong to Christ, be joined to Christ by the faith and love that Christ seeks. Those who are not members of Christ's body act fictively when they receive the sacrament; by their action, they are claiming what is not in fact the case."[26] For Thomas Aquinas, those who are most guilty of "lying to the sacrament" are those who have separated themselves from Christ through refusal of faith or through mortal sin, which ruptures the bond of love.[27] However, even those whose interior devotion is hindered by venial sin or who otherwise approach the sacraments "with mind distracted" don't benefit from their reception as fully as they could.[28] Analogously, *Sacrosanctum Concilium* claims that the "full effects" of the liturgy depend not only on the external observance of "laws governing valid and lawful celebration" but on what goes on in the "minds" of the people. Participants in the liturgy must perform the liturgical act "with proper dispositions" and "cooperate with heavenly grace lest they receive it in vain" (11). So, authentic performance of the liturgical act is like fruitful reception of the sacraments: both demand internal disposi-

[26] Joseph P. Wawrykow, *The Westminster Handbook to Thomas Aquinas* (Louisville, KY: Westminster John Knox Press, 2005), 131.

[27] Thomas Aquinas, *Summa Theologiae* III q. 80 a. 4 resp., trans. in St. Thomas Aquinas, *Summa Theologica*, trans. Fathers of the English Dominican Province, rev. ed. (1920). Hereafter cited as ST.

[28] ST III q. 79 a. 8.

tions and actions in tune with the visible, tangible, and audible signs that comprise the external rite. Fruitful reception of the sacraments is a specific, exemplary case of authentic celebration of the liturgy in general.[29]

If performance of the liturgical act is something that modern Christians have forgotten how to do authentically, then the comparison to fruitful reception of the sacraments suggests what it would mean to relearn authentic liturgy. Fruitfulness, unlike validity, depends on the interior disposition and cooperation of the recipient, and different degrees of cooperation with grace result in a sacrament bearing more or less spiritual fruit. Similarly, authenticity is not a binary property of a person's or a congregation's participation in worship. Liturgy is not simply authentic or inauthentic. Performance of the liturgical act can become more authentic through practice and formation. Worshippers can cultivate proper dispositions and nurture interior cooperation. Through internal and external adjustments, whole congregations can attune their minds more closely to their voices and to the minds and voices of their ancestors in the faith. Modern Christians can relearn the *habit* of authentic liturgical participation, though they may learn it in different ways than previous generations learned it. The old adage *Sacramenta sunt propter homines* (Sacraments are for humans) applies analogously in this case too: authentic liturgy is for people here and now; it is not a museum piece.

Authentic liturgy has become a *habit* when the act of participating in the liturgy emerges from a stable disposition to perform the liturgy authentically. Habits figure prominently in a long stream of thought about moral formation that can be traced back to Aristotle. Medieval Christian and Muslim philosophers like Thomas Aquinas and Abu Hamid Al-Ghazali redefine certain habits but retain their overall centrality in accounting for human actions.[30] Habits are the building blocks of character. They may be virtuous, if they incline people toward acts that fulfill the ends to which they have been set, or they

---

[29] As we will see in chapter 5, Yves Congar also compares authentic liturgy to fruitful sacraments in an important article first published in 1948. See Yves Congar, " 'Real' Liturgy, 'Real' Preaching," in *At the Heart of Christian Worship: Liturgical Essays of Yves Congar*, trans. Paul Philibert (Collegeville, MN: Liturgical Press, 2010), 1–12.

[30] Saba Mahmood, *Politics of Piety: The Islamic Revival and the Feminist Subject* (Princeton, NJ: Princeton University Press, 2005), 135–37.

may be vicious if they lead to acts that frustrate those ends.[31] In *all* of its activity—including the liturgy, but not limited to it—the church and its members have been set to the ends of divine glorification and human sanctification (SC 10). For Christians, authenticity is a virtuous habit (a *virtue*) if it inclines them to act in ways that bring greater glory to God and greater holiness to themselves.

Habits inform actions, and actions form habits. "We become just by doing just acts, temperate by doing temperate acts, brave by doing brave acts."[32] It would seem easy enough to add that we become authentic participants in the liturgy by performing the liturgical act authentically. But for modern people, *performing* the liturgical act authentically is precisely the problem that Guardini believes will require "a great deal of thought and experiment" to solve.[33] In its human aspect, the liturgical act is a type of ritualized performance—a "cult act," in Guardini's parlance, or a *ritual*, in the language of social scientists. This is the distinctly modern "problem" for authentic liturgy: the liturgical act is a ritual. And in the context of ritual action, it is disputed whether the modern proclivity to authenticity is a virtue or a vice.

## Ritual and the modern ethic of authenticity

Ritual and authenticity have a difficult relationship in modernity. Because it's a socially regulated performance, some modern people think that ritual is the opposite of authentic human action. This view emphasizes the performative meaning of authenticity and "criticizes ritual's acceptance of social convention as mere action (perhaps even acting) without intent, as performance without belief." Seeking to avoid mere external activity with no internal conviction, the modern "reaction against ritual" instead adopts "the sincere mode of behavior."[34] When the liturgical act is seen as opposed to a sincere way of doing things, Christians interested in liturgy are accused of lacking

---

[31] See the definition of *virtue* in Wawrykow, *Westminster Handbook to Thomas Aquinas*, 167.

[32] Aristotle, *The Basic Works of Aristotle*, ed. Richard McKeon (New York: Random House, 1941).

[33] Guardini, "Letter from Romano Guardini," 238.

[34] Adam B. Seligman et al., *Ritual and Its Consequences: An Essay on the Limits of Sincerity* (Oxford: Oxford University Press, 2008), 103.

"Christian sincerity."[35] The novelty in this criticism isn't the call to Christian sincerity, but the belief that collective ritual *can't* be authentic because the behavior proceeds from social convention and socialized habit, not from individual decision.

Christian Smith, a sociologist of religion, captures the sincere orientation to action in his pithy explanation of why many young evangelical Christians shop around for novel worship services outside the churches their parents attend: "If you don't choose it, it's not authentic for you."[36] While this sounds narcissistic, it would be a mistake to interpret criticism of inherited ritual as anti-social or anti-religious, especially as it becomes increasingly common for young Americans to attend no church. Among those who do practice, the search for new and alternative ways of worship is often accompanied by strong commitments to church congregations, outreach ministry, and social activism.[37]

Contemporary Christians can feel alienated from the ritual and routine of so-called liturgical churches, yet still desire worship that is authentic in the genealogical sense. Consider the comments of Rachel Held Evans, whose passing in 2019 at the age of thirty-seven was especially mourned by fellow millennials—a generation, she notes, "for whom the charge of 'inauthentic' is as cutting an insult as any":

> When I left church at age 29, full of doubt and disillusionment, I wasn't looking for a better-produced Christianity. I was looking for a truer Christianity, a more authentic Christianity: I didn't like how gay, lesbian, bisexual and transgender people were being treated by my evangelical faith community. I had questions about science and faith, biblical interpretation and theology. I felt lonely in my doubts. And, contrary to popular belief, the fog machines and light shows at those slick evangelical conferences didn't make things better for me. They made the whole endeavor feel shallow, forced and fake.[38]

[35] Guardini, "Letter from Romano Guardini," 237.
[36] Neela Banerjee, "Teenagers Mix Churches for Faith That Fits," *The New York Times*, December 30, 2005.
[37] See Jessica M. Barron and Rhys H. Williams, *The Urban Church Imagined: Religion, Race, and Authenticity in the City* (New York: New York University Press, 2017).
[38] Rachel Held Evans, "Want Millennials Back in the Pews? Stop Trying to Make Church 'Cool,'" *Washington Post*, April 30, 2015.

Her search for "more authentic Christianity" led Evans to the Episcopal Church, which had the "inclusivity" she was looking for, but also the "strange rituals and traditions Christians have been practicing for the past 2,000 years." The key to keeping millennials, she writes, is to "keep worship weird":

> Every week I find myself, at age 33, kneeling next to a gray-haired lady to my left and a gay couple to my right as I confess my sins and recite the Lord's Prayer. No one's trying to sell me anything. No one's desperately trying to make the Gospel hip or relevant or cool. They're just joining me in proclaiming the great mystery of the faith—that Christ has died, Christ has risen, and Christ will come again—which, in spite of my persistent doubts and knee-jerk cynicism, I still believe most days.[39]

In seeking a church whose worship feels "more authentic," modern Christians are hoping to unite their voices more fully with present companions *and* their ancient ancestors in the faith. Unfortunately, their quest for authentic liturgy is hindered by a deeply ingrained suspicion that worship—whether a "slick" show or a "weird" ritual—is inauthentic because it is a scripted performance of something that should be "from the heart."

For this reason, some believe that authenticity has become an individualist vice rather than a virtue and that the ability to ritualize collectively has atrophied as a result. According to one interdisciplinary team of authors, opposition to ritual has contributed not only to the decline of participation in organized religion, but also to the rise of fundamentalist movements. In both cases, "it is less God's work that is being realized in the world than one's own projection of selfhood. Too often this is the unfortunate result of a privileging of authenticity and choice as touchstones of religious action in today's world."[40] Because the modern demand for authenticity values interior conviction over external conformity, collective ritual ceases to provide a widely shared frame of reference for believers in different circumstances and with varying levels of commitment.

---

[39] Evans, "Want Millennials Back in the Pews?"
[40] Seligman et al., *Ritual and Its Consequences*, 10.

While I share these authors' concern about the privileging of individual choice, I don't agree that the modern ethic of authenticity prevents vigorous collective ritualization. I contend that authenticity is a virtue, and it *remains* a virtue in ritual action. Liturgy can and must be authentic while remaining a ritualized performance. It's important to understand, however, that authenticity and ritual have come to be seen as different and even opposite orientations to action. In the present era of late modernity, "the concept of authenticity permeates the whole of culture."[41] Lindholm offers examples of the contemporary interest in authenticity, which approaches obsession: "The quest for authenticity touches and transforms a vast range of human experience today—we speak of authentic art, authentic music, authentic food, authentic dance, authentic people, authentic roots, authentic meanings, authentic nations, authentic products. A desire for authenticity can lead people to extremes of self-sacrifice and risk; the loss of authenticity can be a source of grief and despair."[42] While authenticity is a part of the moral, intellectual, and religious landscape that most of us take for granted, Charles Taylor has argued in several influential books that "the ethic of authenticity is something relatively new and peculiar to modern culture."[43] In the past half-century, the idea has become so omnipresent in moral and political discourse that he has dubbed the present era "The Age of Authenticity."[44]

In the Age of Authenticity, collective ritual occupies a smaller part of religious activity than it ever did in the past. Evidence from history, archaeology, and cultural anthropology indicates that this is a great reversal. Taylor explains, "In early religion, we primarily relate to God as a society." The "primary agency of important religious action" belongs to "the social group as a whole, or some more specialized agency recognized as acting for the group." The usual expression of

---

[41] Brian J. Braman, *Meaning and Authenticity: Bernard Lonergan and Charles Taylor on the Drama of Authentic Human Existence* (Toronto; Buffalo: University of Toronto Press, 2008), 3.

[42] Lindholm, *Culture and Authenticity*, 1.

[43] Charles Taylor, *The Ethics of Authenticity* (Cambridge, MA: Harvard University Press, 1992), 25. See also Taylor, *Sources of the Self: The Making of the Modern Identity* (Cambridge, MA: Harvard University Press, 1989); Taylor, *Modern Social Imaginaries* (Durham, NC: Duke University Press, 2003); Taylor, *A Secular Age* (Cambridge, MA: Belknap Press of Harvard University Press, 2007).

[44] Taylor, *A Secular Age*, 473.

this *corporate* agency (to use Guardini's term) is "collective ritual action, where the principal agents are acting on behalf of a community, which also in its own way becomes involved in the action."[45] From the human side, the Christian liturgical act closely resembles the primary way of relating to God in early religion.

But Christianity is not and never was a pure example of "early religion," in the sense that Taylor means. His work aims to show that the modern understanding of the individual as the principal agent of moral, political, and religious action is already nascent in Christian teachings. The gospel of Jesus represents a revolutionary "break" from how earlier religious systems embedded the self in a social, cosmic, and moral order. The writings of the Hebrew prophets and the teachings of Socrates, Confucius, and the Buddha initiate a comparable break, but the influence of Christianity is decisive in the Western understanding of the self. The death and resurrection of Jesus "assert the unconditional benevolence of God towards humans," but the call to imitate Christ in his self-abandonment simultaneously redefines the ultimate good for humans. "The structures of society and the features of the cosmos through which [human] flourishing was supposedly achieved" are fallen and in need of redemption. Above all, Christians are called to "self-transformation."[46] For Christians, the primary way of worshipping God and pursuing their own good is no longer through the collective religious action of a nation, tribe, or family. Those who would follow Jesus must "hate father and mother" (Luke 14:26), distinguish the "commandment of God" from "human tradition" (Mark 7:8), and beware of practicing their piety before others (Matt 6:1). When modern Christians insist on discerning their own unique spiritual paths, different from the ones marked out for them by society, they are not far removed from Paul's exhortation: "Do not be conformed to this world, but be transformed by the renewing of your minds" (Rom 12:2).

The Christian gospel questions external conformity and demands interior conviction in ways that profoundly differentiate the Christian liturgical act from "early religion," despite their apparently similar reliance on collective ritual. An element of the modern critique of ritual is, therefore, perennial in Christianity. Like the Hebrew prophets

---

[45] Taylor, *A Secular Age*, 148.
[46] Taylor, *A Secular Age*, 151–53.

before him, Jesus questions the ritual acts performed collectively under the leadership of priests and teachers of the law, and he finds that these rituals lack authenticity. Of course, the early followers of Jesus do not simply abandon collective ritual altogether. The New Testament bears the marks of early Christian churches perpetuating the presence of their Lord through more or less ritualized acts of baptizing, sharing the "Lord's supper," and praying in common. Subsequent Christian history has repeatedly shown that "reform movements based on sincerity tend to be tamed over time with new creations of ritual."[47] Still, there is always a risk that "ritual may in practice render blunt the cutting blade of the gospel message." If that happens, warns Louis-Marie Chauvet, "the liturgy loses its Christian status."[48] Authentic liturgy is possible only when participants imitate Christ's persistent testing of the harmony between their minds and voices.

## Liturgy and the habits of authenticity

A major claim of this book is that the tuning adjustments for authentic liturgy proceed in two directions: from interior discernment to exterior performance (*inside-out*), and from exterior practice to interior transformation (*outside-in*). Moving from the inside out, the people and their leaders must adjust what they say with their voices and do with their bodies to better match their understanding of the liturgy. Most of the time, these adjustments are subtle and require no special authority: singing louder or extending a silence, emphasizing certain words in the text or making use of permission to compose different words, choosing alternative musical settings or writing new hymns. Only rarely are adjustments to the liturgy's external forms needed on such a scale that an ecumenical council must set them in motion. But Vatican II called for many large adjustments to external forms, to "adapt more closely to the needs of our age those institutions which are subject to change" (SC 1).

---

[47] Seligman et al., *Ritual and Its Consequences*, 104.

[48] Louis-Marie Chauvet, *Symbol and Sacrament: A Sacramental Reinterpretation of Christian Existence*, trans. Patrick Madigan (Collegeville, MN: Liturgical Press, 1995), 351.

*Sacrosanctum Concilium* also called for more than a one-time adjustment of the external forms of the Roman Rite. True, the council declared that no one "may add, remove, or change anything in the liturgy on their own authority," except for the pope and, within certain limits, bishops and territorial conferences of bishops (22). But the bishops at Vatican II, acting under and with the pope, exercised their own authority to define how external elements of the liturgy could and should continue to be adjusted, even after the revisions of the Missal and other liturgical books were completed. Some adjustments must be made at nearly every celebration of the liturgy: sermons, which are "part of the liturgical action," have to be prepared (35, 52); intercessions may be written for the prayer of the faithful (53–54); appropriate songs and musical settings should be chosen or composed (112–121); and churches must be fittingly furnished and ornamented (122–129). Beyond these routine adjustments, *Sacrosanctum Concilium* also declares the Roman Rite open to vernacular translations and to "legitimate variations and adaptations to different groups, regions, and peoples." These "adaptations" are adjustments to the texts, rubrics, and structure of the liturgy, permitted either through flexibility written into the "typical editions" of the liturgical books or through a process by which conferences of bishops seek Rome's consent for "even more radical adaptation of the liturgy" (37–40).

Radical or routine, formal or informal, subtle or sweeping, these adjustments share the same movement from interior discernment to exterior expression. A requirement of authentic liturgy is that individual participants, whole congregations, and even entire cultural and linguistic groups discern the movement of the Holy Spirit in their minds and hearts. Augustine advises those who seek the highest truth to transcend the limits of human reasoning, paradoxically, by turning inward. "Do not go outward; return within yourself. In the inward man dwells truth."[49] The individual soul is not the standard of truth, but each soul participates in the truth by the light of reason, planted by God in the inmost self. From interior discernment emerges authentic participation in God's creative activity. The human participants in liturgy do not create the truth it celebrates, but they do create poetry, music, images, and ritual actions that authentically express a

---

[49] Augustine, *De vera religione*, 39.72, quoted in Taylor, *Sources of the Self*, 129.

part of God's truth, beauty, and goodness. The liturgy is a gift from above, but it does not drop into our midst from the heavens. Its external forms do not mindlessly accumulate over the course of generations. Rather, each time the church celebrates the liturgy, those who "have the mind of Christ," by the gift of God's Spirit (1 Cor 2:9-16), actively receive and adjust what their bodies and voices have been given to do and say.

What I have been describing as *tuning adjustments* are essential not only to authentic liturgy, but also to the cultivation and practice of authenticity as a virtue. They are not the product of secondary theological reflection but are *theologia prima* itself. As Aidan Kavanagh says, "It is the *adjustment* which is theological," both in the "deep change in the very lives of those who participate in the liturgical act" and in the "gradual evolution of the liturgical rites themselves."[50] Whether they proceed from the interior to the exterior or from the exterior to the interior, these tuning adjustments are the activity most properly called liturgical theology. Since both kinds of adjustment contribute to the formation of authenticity as a virtuous *habit* that informs authentic action, we can appreciate practitioners who *inhabit* the liturgy with their own creativity, even as we affirm those who prefer to *habituate* themselves to inherited liturgical forms. "There are two ways of feeling at home," Tzvi Novick observes, "in all contemporary communities that purport to interpret a tradition." Like the practitioners of Judaism that Novick describes, most practicing Christians primarily adopt either the posture of an "author" or an "expert." But the authors who make themselves at home by refashioning the community's practices don't wish to "altogether reinvent" the tradition, and the experts who seek the "self-assurance" of extended residence in the tradition can't "forgo invention" entirely.[51]

Christian authenticity is a cultivated, dynamic habit, and authentic liturgy is the church's living, evolving habitat. Both habit and habitat—the virtue of authenticity and the authentic liturgical act—are subject to growth, decay, disease, and renewal. The strength of the habit and the health of the habitat go hand in hand, so that the attunement of

---

[50] Aidan Kavanagh, *On Liturgical Theology* (Collegeville, MN: Liturgical Press, 1992), 73–74. Emphasis in original.

[51] Tzvi Novick, "The Author and the Expert," *Commonweal* 146, no. 15 (October 2019): 74.

one participant's mind and voice is not just a matter of individual concern. Each member's authentic participation in the liturgy contributes to the authenticity of the whole assembly's corporate performance of an integrated liturgical act. As Martin Stuflesser observes, Vatican II "formulated a demanding goal" for the whole church when it called for "full participation" by "each and every member of the faithful" (see SC 14, 21, 41).[52] There are no "strangers or silent spectators" at authentic celebrations of the liturgy because *all* "should take part in the sacred action, actively, fully aware, and devoutly" (SC 48).

---

[52] Martin Stuflesser, "*Actuosa Participatio*: Between Hectic Actionism and New Interiority. Reflections on 'Active Participation' in the Worship of the Church as Both Right and Obligation of the Faithful," trans. Robert J. Daly, *Studia Liturgica* 41, no. 1 (2011): 104–5.

*Chapter Two*

# Authentic Worship in the Bible

"Let us stand to sing the psalms in such a way that our minds are in harmony with our voices" (RB 19). The Rule of Benedict's exhortation about the right way to sing the psalms at the Divine Office is a "commonplace," according to the editor of the Rule's modern critical edition.[1] St. Benedict is repeating advice handed down by generations of Christian and Jewish writers, all of whom appeal to similar texts in the Scriptures. This call to authentic public prayer is so ancient and ubiquitous that we can misinterpret the commonplace as a platitude. It would be a serious mistake, however, to underestimate the importance of this perennial injunction or to ignore the danger of inauthentic worship. The Scriptures equate false worship of God with the worship of false gods. Authentic worship is God's gift to those who put their trust in God alone. As the psalmist testifies, those who do not stray after illusory powers, but trust God to save them, will delight in their hearts even as they sing with their lips:

> Happy are those who make
>     the LORD their trust,
> who do not turn to the proud,
>     to those who go astray after false gods.
> You have multiplied, O LORD my God,
>     your wondrous deeds and your thoughts toward us;
>     none can compare with you.

---

[1] Adalbert de Vogüé, *La règle de saint Benoît*, vol. 2, Sources chrétiennes 182 (Paris: Éditions du Cerf, 1972), 536 n. 7. See Terrence G. Kardong, *Benedict's Rule: A Translation and Commentary* (Collegeville, MN: Liturgical Press, 1996), 206.

Were I to proclaim and tell of them,
　　they would be more than can be counted.
Sacrifice and offering you do not desire,
　　but you have given me an open ear.
Burnt offering and sin offering
　　you have not required.
Then I said, "Here I am;
　　in the scroll of the book it is written of me.
I delight to do your will, O my God;
　　your law is within my heart."
I have told the glad news of deliverance
　　in the great congregation;
see, I have not restrained my lips,
　　as you know, O LORD.
I have not hidden your saving help within my heart,
　　I have spoken of your faithfulness and your salvation;
I have not concealed your steadfast love and your faithfulness
　　from the great congregation. (Ps 40:4-10)

Authentic prayer in the "great congregation" of God's people has always been about faithfully returning God's steadfast love with single-minded devotion and perfect praise. Harmony of mind and voice in this offering of prayer isn't a private or peripheral issue; authenticity concerns the central acts of faith performed by the whole people of God. The congregation recounts the uncountable deeds of God by passing on the "glad news of deliverance" from generation to generation with genealogical authenticity. Yet this only happens if the psalmist's descendants also worship with performative authenticity. They must not conceal God's "saving help" within their hearts and substitute an empty outward offering that God doesn't desire. Rather, they must delight within and sing without, doing God's will with minds and voices in tune. Such harmony demands both open ears and unrestrained lips—the humility to listen and the magnanimity to sing a new song.

The central contention of this chapter is that the Bible consistently calls the people of God to integral worship. The Scriptures demand *authentic* worship in Guardini's sense of an "integrated liturgical act." This requirement means that exterior acts of worship—animals sacrificed, prayers spoken, hymns sung, fasts observed, festivals celebrated, alms donated, or communal meals shared—are acceptable to

's of understanding, obe-
dience, and love. Frequently, the Scriptures confront disharmony
between the exterior offering and the interior offering. In these situations, the call to reform often prioritizes interior transformation of
"hearts" or "minds," but the external forms of worship are neither
suppressed nor allowed to continue unchanged. Despite the great
variety in these biblical calls to reform worship, they all share a concern for what we called *performative authenticity* in the last chapter—
neither interiority nor exteriority alone, but the harmonious
integration of the internal and external activity of corporate prayer.
The Scriptures also share a common repertoire of metaphors, mainly
drawn from the human body, that are repeatedly used to call God's
people to more authentic worship.

## Worship with hearts and lips

St. Benedict's call to performative authenticity employs metaphors
that evoke human activities or faculties: "voice" (*vox*) stands for
exterior activity and "mind" (*mens*) stands for interior activity. "*Concordia*"—the desired correspondence between mind and voice—is
accurately translated with a musical metaphor: *in harmony* or *in tune*.
But *concordia* is built around the Latin word for the heart (*cor*), which
evokes a set of biblical metaphors that use parts of the human body
to represent interior and exterior activity. In the usage of multiple
ancient languages and both testaments, the heart (Greek *kardia*, Hebrew *lēb*) is "not especially confined to the feelings and moral acts in
distinction from the intellectual." Neither does the Bible define the
heart in radical contrast to the rest of the human body. Instead, the
heart "stands for the central part in general, the inside, and so for
*the interior man* as manifesting himself in all his various activities, in
his desires, affections, emotions, passions, purposes, his thoughts,
perceptions, imaginations, his wisdom, knowledge, skill, his beliefs
and his reasonings, his memory and his consciousness."[2]

---

[2] Daniel R. Goodwin, "On the Use of Lēb and Καρδία in the Old and New Testaments," *Journal of the Society of Biblical Literature and Exegesis* 1 (June 1881): 67. Emphasis in original.

As Daniel Goodwin pointed out more than a century ago, the modern tendency to sharply distinguish the heart from the mind can confuse our interpretation of Scripture. Most problematically, it can lead us to confine the act of faith to one part of the human psyche—either the emotive *or* the intellectual part—and to one type of exterior activity—usually a spoken profession of faith. When Paul describes the basic act of faith in terms drawn from Deuteronomy, modern readers can misunderstand his point:

> [I]f you confess with your lips that Jesus is Lord and believe in your heart that God raised him from the dead, you will be saved. For one believes with the heart and so is justified, and one confesses with the mouth and so is saved. (Rom 10:9-10, see Deut 30:14)

Goodwin cautions:

> Now here heart is not opposed to mind but to mouth, the *inward* to the *outward*; and "in the heart" adds no more to the believing than "with the mouth" adds to the confessing. It is merely said that one is an *internal* act, and the other an *external* act. . . . No doubt the apostle means a true, honest, lively faith, and a true, honest confession; and this he would equally mean, if "in the heart" and "with the mouth" were not there. Man believeth to righteousness, and confession is made unto salvation; he believeth with the *inner* man, and confesseth with the *outer* man.[3]

As Goodwin observes, believers can't confine a "true, honest, lively faith" to one part of their interior activity. Neither can worshippers make a "true, honest confession" with words bereft of deeds. Both Moses and Paul insist upon *integration* of the interior and exterior in a single act of faith that brings righteousness and salvation. Integrity of action is the point of Scripture's repeated assurances—or warnings—that God "searches minds and hearts" (Rev 2:23), and is not deceived by outward appearances.[4] The biblical injunction to purity of heart doesn't presume a complicated human psychology, with a bifurcated

---

[3] Goodwin, "On the Use of Lēb and Καρδία," 71–72. Emphasis added.
[4] E.g., 1 Sam 16:7; 1 Kgs 8:39; 1 Chr 28:9; 29:17; 2 Chr 6:30; Pss 7:9; 19:14; 26:2; 44:21; 139:23; Prov 15:11; 17:3; 21:2; 24:12; Jer 11:20; 12:3; 17:10; 20:12; Wis 1:6; Sir 42:18; Luke 16:15; Acts 1:24; 15:8; Rom 8:27; 1 Cor 4:5; 1 Thess 2:4; Heb 4:12; 1 John 3:20; Rev 2:23.

self capable of contradictory interior and exterior acts. It simply names and denounces the frequent human tendency to offer God incomplete love and partial obedience, usually as the result of willfulness and culpable ignorance of God.

The basic statement of the complete, integral worship owed to God is the *Shema*, recorded in Deuteronomy as Moses's instruction to the assembled people as they are about to enter the Promised Land:

> Hear, O Israel: The Lord is our God, the Lord alone. You shall love the Lord your God with all your heart, and with all your soul, and with all your might. Keep these words that I am commanding you today in your heart. Recite them to your children and talk about them when you are at home and when you are away, when you lie down and when you rise. Bind them as a sign on your hand, fix them as an emblem on your forehead, and write them on the doorposts of your house and on your gates. (Deut 6:4-9)

Obedience to God should flow from a total and unstinting love that cherishes God's words within the heart and honors them outwardly. As Jesus says, the first and greatest commandment is to keep God's commandments with complete love (Mark 12:28-30). The second commandment is "like" the first in that the love of one's neighbor must be integral to one's love of oneself (Matt 22:39). Such love of God and neighbor is authentic because it is total, embracing everything a person is and has, both within and without.

In Mark's gospel, the scribe who asks Jesus to name the greatest commandment makes one further observation about the *Shema*. Agreeing that the command to "love [God] with all your heart, with all your understanding, [and] with all your strength" is paired with the command to "love your neighbor as yourself," the scribe adds that keeping both commandments "is worth more than all burnt offerings and sacrifices" (12:33). As the climactic conclusion to a series of disputations with religious authorities in the Jewish temple, the scribe's admission casts the cult of public worship in an unflattering, but hardly unprecedented, light. Here and elsewhere, the New Testament takes up a recurrent theme of the Hebrew prophets: the most valuable cultic worship amounts to nothing in God's eyes, if the external offering of slaughtered animals and verbose prayers isn't accompanied by an offering of human hearts.

## Lip service

Psalm 40, as seen above, spurns empty cultic sacrifice while also affirming God's desire for *heartfelt* outward worship in the "great congregation." The first part of the book of Isaiah—associated by scholars with the ministry of the eighth-century prophet in Jerusalem—is more severe in its critique of the temple cult. The pretense of worship, coming from a people with injustice in their hearts, is not only uninvited, but offensive to the God of justice:

> What to me is the multitude of your sacrifices?
>> says the LORD;
> I have had enough of burnt offerings of rams
>> and the fat of fed beasts;
> I do not delight in the blood of bulls,
>> or of lambs, or of goats.
> When you come to appear before me,
>> who asked this from your hand?
>> Trample my courts no more;
> bringing offerings is futile;
>> incense is an abomination to me.
> New moon and sabbath and calling of convocation—
>> I cannot endure solemn assemblies with iniquity.
> Your new moons and your appointed festivals
>> my soul hates;
> they have become a burden to me,
>> I am weary of bearing them.
> When you stretch out your hands,
>> I will hide my eyes from you;
> even though you make many prayers,
>> I will not listen;
>> your hands are full of blood.
> Wash yourselves; make yourselves clean;
>> remove the evil of your doings
>> from before my eyes;
> cease to do evil,
>> learn to do good;
> seek justice,
>> rescue the oppressed,
> defend the orphan,
>> plead for the widow. (Isa 1:11-17)

The Israelites' outward acts of injustice belie their outward acts of worship, and this exterior incongruity reveals interior pollution. The "blood" that God sees on the hands of Judah's leaders isn't the blood of sacrificed animals, which anyone may view, but the hidden "blood guilt" that stains a person guilty of shedding human blood.[5]

In Isaiah's view, the integrity of the act of worship has been corrupted. The exterior appearance of approaching God to utter prayers and offer sacrifice is joined to an interior withdrawal from God to ignore the law and justify the unjustifiable. The bodily metaphor that the prophet uses to call out such incongruity will become commonplace in later critiques of inauthentic worship:

> The Lord said:
> Because these people draw near with their mouths
>     and honor me with their lips,
>     while their hearts are far from me,
> and their worship of me is a human commandment learned by rote;
> so I will again do
>     amazing things with this people,
>     shocking and amazing.
> The wisdom of their wise shall perish,
>     and the discernment of the discerning shall be hidden.
> Ha! You who hide a plan too deep for the Lord,
>     whose deeds are in the dark,
>     and who say, "Who sees us? Who knows us?"
> You turn things upside down!
>     Shall the potter be regarded as the clay?
> Shall the thing made say of its maker,
>     "He did not make me";
> or the thing formed say of the one who formed it,
>     "He has no understanding"? (Isa 29:13-16)

This ominous oracle, which Jesus quotes to the religious leaders of his day (Mark 7:6-8; Matt 15:8-9), is among the Hebrew Bible's most direct condemnations of false worship offered not to foreign gods but to the God of Israel. It is therefore important to precisely define the offense that provokes God's ire and to see how the punishment foretold by the prophet fits the crime.

---

[5] J. J. M. Roberts, *First Isaiah: A Commentary*, Hermeneia—A Critical and Historical Commentary on the Bible (Minneapolis: Fortress, 2015), 23.

It doesn't appear that in the face of foreign threats, the kingdom of Judah has abandoned its traditional religious rituals. Although God is unsatisfied by the performance of a "human commandment learned by rote," Isaiah never specifies which merely human rule of worship Judah's leaders have been blindly following. Citing the oracle in Isaiah 1:10-20, J. J. M. Roberts suggests that Isaiah may not have in mind any single practice, but is instead criticizing his opponents for being "punctilious in carrying out the prescribed religious rituals, while not allowing the deeper significance of those rituals to shape or affect their personal and political decisions." Although Judah's prophets were under pressure to support the royal policy of preferring alliance with Egypt to reliance on God, the court was "not overtly hostile to Judah's religious traditions." The nation's leaders "maintained the appearance of honoring Yahweh and cultivating piety toward God. The outward expressions of piety remained, though the inner commitment of their heart had grown distant from God. A contemporary may have had difficulty seeing Isaiah as more religious or more devoted to God than his opponents."[6]

Yet Isaiah doesn't claim that his opponents have plotted to deceive anyone about the motives behind their public displays of piety. He doesn't say, for example, that Judah's human leaders have invented a sophistic interpretation of God's law to minimize its demands, as Jesus will accuse the scribes and Pharisees of doing.[7] Instead, as Roberts puts it, Isaiah paints a picture of "record breaking attendance and offerings" that would delight "even the most rabid proponents of church growth." And although Isaiah dismisses their scrupulous and opulent public piety as so much lip service, he never suggests that Judah's worship lacks sentiment or fervor. "What links Isaiah's critique of the cult in Isa. 1.10-17 and 29.13-14," Roberts concludes, "is not a concern about the absence of feeling, spirit or emotion in Israel's worship."[8]

[6] Roberts, *First Isaiah*, 369.

[7] See Mark 7:1-23 and the discussion of this passage, below.

[8] J. J. M. Roberts, "Contemporary Worship in the Light of Isaiah's Ancient Critique," in *Worship and the Hebrew Bible: Essays in Honor of John T. Willis*, ed. M. Patrick Graham, Richard R. Mars, and Steven L. McKenzie, Journal for the Study of the Old Testament Supplement Series 284 (Sheffield, UK: Sheffield Academic Press, 1999), 272.

Nor is the problem simply that Judah's leaders and their followers offer good worship but make bad ethical and political decisions. The cult is more than a convenient target for Isaiah's political attacks; it is broken despite every appearance to the contrary. Inauthentic worship is intensely painful to a man who has seen the heavenly worship of the Lord of Hosts (Isa 6:1-13). The prophet's negation of the temple cult is, as Abraham J. Heschel argues, based on a deep affirmation of authentic worship. "The prophets disparaged the cult when it became a substitute for righteousness. It is precisely the implied recognition of the value of the cult that lends force to their insistence that there is something far more precious than sacrifice."[9] That which is more valuable than the sacrifice of animals includes action to reverse social injustice, but God desires even more than that. Citing Isaiah 29:13, Heschel continues, "It is not only action that God demands, it is not only disobedience to the law that the prophet decries. . . . The fault is in the hearts, not alone in the deeds."[10] Authentic worship wouldn't replace ritual words and gestures with practical work for social justice. Rather, it would root both kinds of outward offering in an interior offering of hearts.

In Isaiah's view, Judah's worship lacks something integral to the act of prayer itself, but the deficiency is neither a failure to respect the traditional rituals nor a dearth of emotional content. The missing ingredient is *true knowledge of God*, and the absence of *understanding* is what causes the prophet to declare that the hearts of these worshippers remain far from God despite the prayers that proceed almost continually from their lips. In the indictment that opens the book of Isaiah, God charges his rebellious "children," whom God has raised into a great nation, with willful ignorance: "The ox knows its owner, and the donkey its master's crib; but Israel does not know, my people do not understand" (1:3). Isaiah later laments that his people "go into exile without knowledge" because they "do not regard the deed of the LORD, or see the work of his hands" (5:12-13). The prophet Hosea also says that God's people "are destroyed for lack of knowledge"

---

[9] Abraham Joshua Heschel, *The Prophets* (New York: Harper & Row, 1962), 250.

[10] Heschel, *The Prophets*, 266. Heschel cites additional examples of God's desire for the people's hearts: "They do not cry to Me from the heart" (Hos 7:14); "Their heart is false; now they must bear their guilt" (Hos 10:2); "Thou art near in their mouth, and far from their heart" (Jer 12:2).

(Hos 4:6), but as Roberts explains, ignorance manifested itself in different ways. "Hosea's northern audience falsely attributed their blessings to the pagan deity Baal," but the idolatry of Isaiah's southern audience was of another kind. "A socially oppressive materialism rather than simple idolatry was the source of their willful ignorance (Isa 30:9-11)." Jerusalem's elite refuses to see that God's gifts are intended not for their own amusement, but for the care of the oppressed, the widow, and the orphan.[11]

Judah's willful ignorance is especially troubling because it coincides with the outward appearance of wisdom, knowledge, and fear of the Lord, at least in cultic matters. "Israel's problem was not religious ignorance in the sense that they failed to acknowledge God with the confession of their lips."[12] Isaiah doesn't say that his people are perishing for lack of religious expertise. And if rote learning has accomplished nothing else, it has accurately transmitted the intellectual content of the Mosaic covenant that God told the Israelites to recite to their children (see Deut 6:7). "A saving knowledge of God, however, involves more than just a passing and passive intellectual assent to traditional formulations of the faith. It means actively interpreting the world, evaluating the events around oneself and ordering one's life in accordance with what the tradition claims about God."[13] Despite an elaborate liturgical *anamnesis* that purports to remember how God has rescued Israel from oppression, the worshippers "do not regard" what God is doing *now*, when the cry of the poor has again reached God's ears (Isa 5:7). Their refusal to read the signs of their own times is fatal to the authenticity of Judah's worship.

It may seem that no change in Judah's *worship* is needed, if the problem is with their ethical and political behavior *outside* the temple. Isaiah is determined, however, to show Judah's leaders that such divided thinking, which isolates the affairs of God from human affairs, has led the nation to the brink of destruction. Were their hearts not divided, it would be inconceivable for Judah to go on trampling God's courts even as they "trust in chariots" to defend them and "trust in oppression and deceit" to build the armies and alliances they believe will be their salvation (Isa 31:1; 30:12). Were the leaders to be of "steadfast mind" and trust in God alone (26:3), their foreign

11 Roberts, *First Isaiah*, 21.
12 Roberts, *First Isaiah*, 20.
13 Roberts, "Contemporary Worship," 273.

policy *and* their public piety would both look very different. Seeing in the dire events unfolding around them the vanity of trusting to arms and alliances, they would *know* that "the Lord God of hosts called [them] to weeping and mourning, to baldness and putting on sackcloth" (22:12). But the copious prayers of Judah apparently include no outward signs of repentance.

Isaiah foretells a frighteningly appropriate consequence of continuing to offer inauthentic worship to God in willful ignorance of the wholehearted, single-minded love that God desires. Judah's leaders think they can honor the God of their ancestors while scoffing at God's plans for them now (5:19). They offer external sacrifices to the Holy One of Israel, but they carry out a plan of their own making (29:15; 30:1-11). They have become stubborn in their blindness, like the Egyptians with whom they seek an alliance once were. Therefore, God will do "shocking and amazing" things, as God once did to free Israel from Egypt. This time, however, the plague will be upon Israel, and it will ultimately lead them into exile and slavery. Because they honor God with their lips while in their hearts they trust to their own wisdom and hidden plans, "the wisdom of their wise shall perish, and the discernment of the discerning shall be hidden" (29:14). God will allow the self-inflicted deafness and blindness of Judah's leaders to become complete.[14] The nature of the punishment indicates that Judah's crime is not the *invention* of a man-made substitute for traditional worship, but the *evacuation* of divine wisdom and discernment from divine worship, leaving behind an artificial husk of ritual.

## A clean heart and open lips

God's threat of punishment is tempered with mercy, for Isaiah and other prophets are sent to warn the people and call for a renewal of trust in God. Ideally, worship should contribute to such renewal. "One praises God or approaches God in prayer because one knows and believes the tradition of what God has done in the past. But worship itself can, in the best of circumstances, give the worshipper a clearer knowledge of this God, which in turn gives the worshipper a clearer understanding of him- or herself and a clearer vision of what God demands of the worshipper."[15] Hearing "the glad news of

---

[14] Compare Isa 29:9-14 to the prophet's commission in Isa 6:10.
[15] Roberts, "Contemporary Worship," 274.

deliverance in the great congregation" can edify hearts inclined to
understand what God is telling them through the "unrestrained lips"
of those who have trusted God in the past (Ps 40:9).

Yet as Roberts emphasizes, worshipping God with true understanding is not necessarily comforting. In Isaiah's case, the liturgical
experience that launched his prophetic career was terrifying, causing
him to exclaim, "Woe is me! I am lost, for I am a man of unclean lips,
and I live among a people of unclean lips; yet my eyes have seen the
King, the Lord of hosts!" (6:5). Granted a sudden, inward vision of
the living God who was the supposed object of the elaborate external
ritual going on around him, Isaiah understood only too well what it
all meant. "If Isaiah's vision occurred during communal worship in
the temple as we have suggested, both the future prophet and his
people were involved in an outward display of devotion to Yahweh,
but Isaiah's vision enabled him to see that display for what it really
was. . . . Public worship that does not lead on to a transformed life
and the everyday pursuit of God's will for justice is an abomination
to God (Isa 1:10-17) and leaves one with lips stained unclean by hypocrisy (Isa 6:5)."[16] Isaiah's inward vision evokes a critique in which
the prophet "seems to square off against the priest" as leader of the
cult. In reality, David Fagerberg argues, such passages from the Hebrew prophets and from the Psalms oppose only the hypocrisy of
priests and other participants, not their practice of cultic religion itself. "The prophet does not mind someone going into the temple—he
is only bothered if a person does not take the temple with him when
he comes back out! The prophet is not criticizing the practice of cultic
religion, though he is criticizing the fact that what has been tilled in
the sacred cult (cultivated) does not produce seed that takes root in
the daily world."[17]

Like Fagerberg and Heschel, Roberts argues that Isaiah does not
desire the eradication of the sacrificial cult, but hopes that after a
period of purification, Israel's public worship will be reformed and
renewed.[18] One convincing proof of Isaiah's high regard for an *au-*

---

[16] Roberts, *First Isaiah*, 99.

[17] David W. Fagerberg, *Consecrating the World: On Mundane Liturgical Theology* (Kettering, OH: Angelico Press, 2016), 105.

[18] Roberts similarly argues that Hosea's rejection of the northern kingdom's sacrificial cult is not total but is aimed at purifying it from idolatrous and selfish elements.
See J. J. M. Roberts, "Hosea and the Sacrificial Cultus," *Restoration Quarterly* 15, no. 1 (1972): 15–26.

*thentic* cult of public worship is that his own lips are purified for his prophetic mission with a live coal carried from the altar of sacrifice by a seraph (Isa 6:6-7). "If Isaiah linked the purification of his own unclean lips to the altar, it is hard to believe that he denied any role to the altar in the purification of the people's unclean lips."[19] Still, for Isaiah and the other prophets of the Hebrew Bible, the first role of public worship is usually to intensify the discomfort of drawing close to God externally while trying to keep God far away from one's heart. The prophet's gift is to have an ear for dissonance between voices and minds, and the prophet's intention in critiquing the cult is to amplify the dissonance until the stubbornness of the people becomes painfully obvious to all. Hence the strangely negative task that God gives Isaiah: "Make the mind of this people dull, and stop their ears, and shut their eyes, so that they may not look with their eyes, and listen with their ears, and comprehend with their minds, and turn and be healed" (6:10). Isaiah wants to know "how long" his people will remain under this judgment of incurable intransigence (6:11), but its term is set by their own willful incomprehension. As long as they ignore the dissonance of their minds and voices, they will remain unrepentant and unhealed.

Isaiah's commitment to the cult he criticizes reveals that external worship can lose much of its authenticity without losing all purpose. There is a role even for deeply flawed liturgy, in which voices and minds clash as the words and gestures of prayer belie the rebellious thoughts that outward participants harbor in their hearts. Inauthentic ritual may sometimes anesthetize worshippers, but it can also occasion a distressing awareness that God is not pleased with what they are offering. It is a lesson in divine negation that the worshipper in Psalm 51 has learned, perhaps through the painful failure of merely external ritual:

> You desire truth in the inward being;
>     therefore teach me wisdom in my secret heart. . . .
> Create in me a clean heart, O God,
>     and put a new and right spirit within me. . . .
> Deliver me from bloodshed, O God,
>         O God of my salvation,
>     and my tongue will sing aloud of your deliverance.

---

[19] Roberts, *First Isaiah*, 100.

> O Lord, open my lips,
>> and my mouth will declare your praise.
> For you have no delight in sacrifice;
>> if I were to give a burnt offering, you would not be pleased.
> The sacrifice acceptable to God is a broken spirit;
>> a broken and contrite heart, O God, you will not despise.
> Do good to Zion in your good pleasure;
>> rebuild the walls of Jerusalem,
> then you will delight in right sacrifices,
>> in burnt offerings and whole burnt offerings;
>> then bulls will be offered on your altar. (Ps 51:6, 10, 14-19)

Acknowledgment of God's displeasure with merely external worship is a crucial first step toward the "truth in the inward being" that God desires. Having learned humility, the psalmist asks for a "clean heart," but also for God to take new delight in the outward offerings of the tongue, the lips, and the altar. Although the acceptable sacrifice is "a broken and contrite heart," receipt of such a heart is not imagined as the inward spirit's liberation from rites performed externally with the body. Instead, salvation is deliverance from inauthentic worship to authentic worship.

## The tradition of the elders

Isaiah's critique of Judah's worship is important not because it's unique, but because it's typical:

> Isaiah's contemporaries had allowed their attention to traditional ritual detail—Isaiah's "commandment of men" (29:13)—to block their vision of God and his central demands. This was a major concern in the OT prophets (e.g., Amos 4:4-5; 5:21-24; Jer 7:1-15), and as both Jesus (Mt 15:1-11; Mk 7:1-13) and Paul (Col 2:20-23) in the New Testament point out, the danger is a recurring one. God's people must constantly strive for a renewed vision of God to prevent custom from stifling obedience.[20]

Like the Hebrew Bible, the New Testament associates true knowledge of God less with external sacrifice and more with "truth in the

---

[20] Roberts, *First Isaiah*, 99.

inward being" (Ps 51:6). In Matthew's version of the Beatitudes, Jesus declares, "Blessed are the pure in heart, for they will see God" (5:8). Nowhere, however, does Jesus or Paul advocate a religion purely of the heart that banishes exterior acts of public worship altogether.

The choice in the New Testament, as in the Old, is not between interior prayer and exterior ritual, but between authentic worship and inauthentic worship. To express the ideal of performative authenticity, the New Testament uses the same bodily metaphors of "hearts" (or "minds") and "lips" (or "voices"), and occasionally it quotes the Hebrew Scriptures directly. The Gospels of Mark and Matthew, for example, depict Jesus quoting Isaiah 29:13 against the Pharisees and scribes who ask why his disciples "eat with defiled hands." Jesus does not dispute the charge that his disciples don't "live according to the tradition of the elders" (Mark 7:5; cf. Matt 15:2). Instead, he attacks the Pharisees for betraying the "commandment of God" with their human "tradition" (*paradosis*), which ironically has the alternative meaning of "betrayal" in Greek:[21]

> He said to them, "Isaiah prophesied rightly about you hypocrites, as it is written,
>
> > 'This people honors me with their lips,
> >     but their hearts are far from me;
> > in vain do they worship me,
> >     teaching human precepts as doctrines.'
>
> You abandon the commandment of God and hold to human tradition." (Mark 7:6-8; cf. Matt 15:6-9; Isa 29:13)

Jesus backs up his charge with an example, accusing the Pharisees of subverting God's commandment to honor one's father and mother by inventing a tradition whereby children may withhold the means of their parents' sustenance. Again, the irony is thick. By pledging their parents' sustenance as an "offering" (*korban*) to God, children can avoid fulfilling the *commandment* of God—without necessarily delivering the promised sacrifice (Mark 9-13; cf. Matt 15:3-6).[22]

---

[21] Joel Marcus, *Mark 1–8: A New Translation with Introduction and Commentary*, The Anchor Bible, vol. 27 (New York: Doubleday, 2000), 452.

[22] Marcus, *Mark 1–8*, 444–46, 451–52.

Like the important quote from Isaiah that Mark and Matthew include in this story,[23] Jesus's dispute with the Pharisees over "tradition" and "defilement" exemplifies the overlap of performative authenticity and genealogical authenticity. The surest way to lose continuity with the authentic tradition that transmits the commandment of God intact is for the people to continue honoring God with their "lips" while allowing their "hearts" to stray. As it was in Isaiah's Jerusalem, the fall of Jesus's contemporaries into inauthenticity is essentially a failure of *understanding*—a tragic yet willful ignorance of God's true will for his people. Joel Marcus comments on this failure, which earns Jesus's opponents the name "hypocrite" in the Synoptic Gospels:

> This "hypocrisy" is not conscious dissimulation but the reflection of a deep malady that results in a tragic split between claim and reality. The heart has strayed from God, and the people have fallen under the sway of a human tradition that has emptied the divine word of its force and blinded its possessors to God's true will (cf. [Mark] 4:11-12); therefore when Jesus' disciples show signs of a similar tendency, he will say to them, "Are you also *without understanding*?" ([Mark] 7:18).[24]

How would Jesus have his disciples understand the "tradition of the elders"? How may they *fulfill* God's commandment by following the tradition, instead of setting human tradition in *opposition* to God's commandment? Jesus turns from the Pharisees to the crowd to drive his message home: "Listen to me, all of you, and understand: there is nothing outside a person that by going in can defile, but the things

---

[23] Marcus comments on the importance of Isa 29:13 in Jewish apocalyptic literature composed around the same time as the New Testament. These texts "prophesy an end-time apostasy in which many Jews will prefer the commandments of human beings to the divine, Mosaic laws and will thereby make themselves impure like the heathen." It's possible that Isaiah's critique was first deployed *against* early Christians by Pharisaic Jews who accused Jesus's disciples of abandoning the divine commandments handed down from Moses in order to follow the new teachings of a mere human being. If this was a charge leveled against early Christians, then Mark's quotation of Isa 29:13 may represent an attempt to turn the tables on the Pharisees and scribes of his time by casting doubt on their claim to be the true inheritors and interpreters of the Mosaic tradition. Marcus, *Mark 1–8*, 449–51.

[24] Marcus, *Mark 1–8*, 450–51. Italics in original.

that come out are what defile" (Mark 7:14-15, cf. Matt 15:10-11). In making this bold declaration, Jesus's "original message may not have been so different from the prophets, who railed against their fellow Israelites' preoccupation with external ritual rather than justice, and even proclaimed that God despised their sacrifices and festivals— without thereby intending to abolish those ceremonies (e.g., Amos 5:21-57; Hos 6:6; Isa 1:11-17)."[25] But when his own disciples "also fail to understand" his point, the Jesus of Mark's gospel redoubles his criticism of traditional notions of ritual purity by "declaring all foods clean" and locating the source of impurity in the heart itself: "For it is from within, from the human heart, that evil intentions come: fornication, theft, murder, adultery, avarice, wickedness, deceit, licentiousness, envy, slander, pride, folly. All these evil things come from within, and they defile a person" (Mark 7:17-23; cf. Matt 15:15-20).[26] According to Jesus, the "tradition of the elders" that insists upon exterior ritual purity is not itself the source of defilement. But the tradition becomes a source of misunderstanding and ignorance of God when its followers believe that the external rituals can purify people who continue to harbor "evil intentions" in their hearts. When such inauthentic religion persists, the "internal corruption . . . chokes the life out of tradition, turns it into an enemy of God, contorts it into a way of excusing injustice, and blinds those afflicted by it to their own culpability for the evils that trouble the world."[27]

Although Jesus's teaching on purity and defilement takes a pessimistic view of the intentions that proceed from the human heart, the very next episode in Mark's gospel shows that faith and obedience can also "come from within" and purify a person who, from the outside, appears to be a source of defilement. The Syrophoenician woman who approaches Jesus to ask him to cast an "unclean spirit" out of her daughter threatens his ritual purity and that of his male disciples, for she is both a woman and a Gentile. She shamelessly

---

[25] Marcus, *Mark 1–8*, 453.

[26] Marcus notes that the Jesus of Matthew's gospel is less radical in his rejection of Jewish traditions of ritual purity. Matthew omits, for instance, the assertion that Jesus's comments amount to "declaring all foods clean." Instead, he depicts Jesus granting much more limited permission to eat with unwashed hands. "This toning down may reflect Matthew's Law-observant, Christian Jewish perspective." Marcus, *Mark 1–8*, 446–47.

[27] Marcus, *Mark 1–8*, 461.

ignores the widespread ancient expectation that honorable women don't approach strange men, and she violates the sanctity of a Jewish home. His initial response, which strikes us as cruel, dramatically demonstrates the ability of these traditional expectations about external behavior to shape even Jesus's impression of a person. He insultingly compares the foreign woman to an unclean animal: "It is not fair to take the children's food and throw it to the dogs" (Mark 7:27; cf. Matt 15:26). The next words that come out of the woman's mouth, however, convince Jesus that he has misjudged her, for she rejects his cultural and religious expectations with a marvelous display of humility and creative wit: "Sir, even the dogs under the table eat the children's crumbs" (Mark 7:28; cf. Matt 15:27). Jesus grants the woman's request "for saying that" (Mark 7:29), when she might have been expected to retreat in silence from his insult. It is the only instance in the New Testament of someone's words persuading Jesus to change his mind. Matthew's version of the same story (which describes the woman as a "Canaanite") specifies what is within the woman's heart that Jesus hears in the words her lips utter: "Woman, great is your faith!" (Matt 15:28). The contrast with the Pharisees and even with Jesus's own disciples could hardly be more powerful. Those men claim to know a lot about the exterior piety and purity demanded by the "tradition of the elders," but only this Gentile woman knows how to approach and speak to Jesus with true understanding.

### Praying in secret

While these episodes broadly and forcefully challenge Jewish traditions of ritual purity, they don't directly question the rites of the temple cult or the public prayers of the synagogue. Public rituals could be occasions for hypocrisy, but Jesus doesn't single them out as targets for his critique of inauthentic devotion. In Matthew's gospel, however, a passage from the Sermon on the Mount appears to deprecate external ritual as such:

> And whenever you pray, do not be like the hypocrites; for they love to stand and pray in the synagogues and at the street corners, so that they may be seen by others. Truly I tell you, they have received their reward. But whenever you pray, go into your

room and shut the door and pray to your Father who is in secret; and your Father who sees in secret will reward you.

When you are praying, do not heap up empty phrases as the Gentiles do; for they think that they will be heard because of their many words. Do not be like them, for your Father knows what you need before you ask him. (Matt 6:5-8)

Probing the ancient roots of modern critiques, Ramie Targoff calls this passage a "forceful injunction against externalized devotion," in which "Christ explicitly connects the public practice of prayer with hypocrisy." She adds, "What renders public prayer hypocritical, Christ seems to suggest, lies specifically in its performative nature: the worshipper caters to a visible and earthly rather than an invisible and divine audience. According to this logic, sincere devotion depends upon 'shutting' off the public world and turning 'in secret' toward the internal realm that is viewed only by God."[28]

Targoff's interpretation—however well it may represent *modern* (especially early modern) readings of the Sermon on the Mount—contrasts with how most biblical scholars believe Matthew's earliest audiences would have understood Jesus's injunction. These disciples were not being asked to avoid the unavoidably performative practices of public prayer. "This passage is not intended to prohibit audible prayer in public as such." Such a prohibition, R. T. France observes, would be inconsistent with Matthew's portrayal of Jesus, who prays aloud in front of others (Matt 11:25; 14:19; 26:39, 42), despite often seeking solitude. Also, immediately after the injunction to shun prayers with "empty phrases" and "many words" (6:7), Jesus supplies words in which his disciples *are* to pray. The Lord's Prayer (Matt 6:9-13) "is worded in the plural, as a corporate rather than a private prayer, and gatherings for prayer together were a regular feature of the life of Jesus' disciples from the beginning."[29]

It is "anachronistic and ethnocentric" to think that the earliest disciples could have found much of the *personal* privacy that modern Westerners take for granted. When Jesus tells his listeners to "shut the door" of the "room" in which they pray (Matt 6:6), "we should

---

[28] Ramie Targoff, *Common Prayer: The Language of Public Devotion in Early Modern England* (Chicago: University of Chicago Press, 2001), 7.

[29] R. T. France, *The Gospel of Matthew* (Grand Rapids, MI: Eerdmans, 2007), 239.

not envision a modern house of many rooms where an individual might find personal privacy," Jerome Neyrey cautions.[30] Jesus employs "humorous hyperbole" by sending worshippers to the tiny "storeroom" (*tameion*) of a peasant house—a closet useful for hiding grain from would-be thieves, but not a place that ancient Jews would have used for prayer.[31] The imagery emphasizes *secrecy* rather than individual *privacy* in the modern sense. The location of prayer is not the primary issue. Instead, the question is whether the secrecy that Jesus requires of worshippers can be maintained in the performance of public prayer.

Although it is doubtful that Christ himself viewed "external devotion as at best an opaque, at worst a misdirected or fraudulent performance," Targoff is right to conclude that Jesus is exhorting worshippers to perform *not* for the visible audience of other humans, but for the invisible divine audience.[32] According to Jesus, God not only "sees in secret," but "is in secret" (*en tō kryptō*) (Matt 6:6). This "remarkable" description of God, France notes, is also used in Paul's Letter to the Romans to describe the authentic Jew in contrast with one who makes a merely outward profession of fidelity to the law: "For a person is not a Jew who is one outwardly, nor is true circumcision something external and physical. Rather, a person is a Jew who is one inwardly [*en tō kryptō*], and real circumcision is a matter of the heart—it is spiritual and not literal. Such a person receives praise not from others but from God" (Rom 2:28-29). The point of praying *en tō kryptō* ("in secret" or "inwardly"), then, is "not so much concealment as such but rather the genuineness of that which is inward and unseen as opposed to what is put on for others. God himself is the model of that essential genuineness which he requires in his people."[33]

So, in this important passage from the Sermon on the Mount, containing Christ's most explicit teaching on the performance of prayer, Jesus is not asking his disciples to shun exterior prayer in favor of interior prayer or to prefer individual prayer to communal prayer.

[30] Jerome H. Neyrey, *Honor and Shame in the Gospel of Matthew* (Louisville, KY: Westminster John Knox, 1998), 220–21.

[31] Craig S. Keener, *A Commentary on the Gospel of Matthew* (Grand Rapids, MI: Eerdmans, 1999), 211; Neyrey, *Honor and Shame*, 220.

[32] Ramie Targoff, "The Performance of Prayer: Sincerity and Theatricality in Early Modern England," *Representations*, no. 60 (Autumn 1997): 7.

[33] France, *Gospel of Matthew*, 239 n. 43.

Instead, whether one prays alone or in the assembly, the external words and actions of prayer must be in harmony with the interior act of prayer that God sees "in secret." "The issue," Ulrich Luz summarizes, is "*how* one should pray both for oneself and *mutatis mutandis* in the gathered community as well." Alone or with others, the worshipper's purpose should be to address God and not any other audience. "With images and hyperboles the saying is designed to emphasize the right attitude for prayer, saying that even prayer can become a means of self-promotion. It intends to make people aware of this danger and then to teach them to pray the right way."[34] France agrees: "The issue here is not the prayer but the motive."[35]

Still, we must ask whether the inward motive of the one who prays can change radically without major changes to the outward forms of prayer. The interior change demanded by Christ is radical: worshippers who formerly aimed to please a human audience with their piety must instead *avoid* the "reward" of humans to receive the "reward" of their "Father who sees in secret" (Matt 6:5-6). To perform the other two pillars of piety—almsgiving and fasting—with the right internal motive, Jesus advises some playacting to obscure what one is doing from external observers: "When you give alms, do not let your left hand know what your right hand is doing, so that your alms may be done in secret. . . . When you fast, put oil on your head and wash your face, so that your fasting may not be seen by others but by your Father who is in secret" (Matt 6:3-4, 17-18). But with prayers traditionally performed in public, how does Jesus expect his disciples to externally manifest their conversion from a human audience to a divine audience? Sensing the hyperbole in his call to prefer one's "storeroom" over "synagogues" and "street corners," some commentators assume that the practical message of Jesus's injunction is simply that his disciples should avoid external ostentation when praying in public.[36] If this were all that Jesus wished to say, it would add little to Jewish and Hellenistic texts from the same period, which

[34] Ulrich Luz, *Matthew 1–7: A Commentary*, ed. Helmut Koester, trans. James E. Crouch (Minneapolis: Fortress, 2007), 302.

[35] France, *Gospel of Matthew*, 239. See also Keener, *Commentary on the Gospel of Matthew*, 212.

[36] Thus Keener, *Commentary on the Gospel of Matthew*; France, *Gospel of Matthew*; Luz, *Matthew 1–7*.

criticize wealthy citizens who ostentatiously perform *leitourgia*—civic and religious "contributions for the public good"—only to win praise for themselves.[37]

Neyrey uncovers further implications, however, by contextualizing the Sermon on the Mount in an ancient Mediterranean culture of honor and shame. To gain honor and avoid shame, male contemporaries of Jesus and Matthew were *expected* to be seen performing acts of piety in public. For Jewish males, this included visible participation in the public prayers of synagogues and the public rites of the temple.[38] Females, as we saw with the Syrophoenician/Canaanite woman, were evaluated by a different code of honor and shame based on the expectation that they would remain *out* of public view and perform their acts of piety within their households. Viewed through the lens of his society's gender expectations, Jesus's instructions on prayer appear much more culturally subversive than a mere call to avoid ostentation would be. As Neyrey puts it, Jesus "commands his disciples to vacate the traditional playing field" upon which males won honor for themselves:

> Jesus requires of his male disciples nothing less than a radical break with the public world and an espousal of the household as the locus of piety. Thus we interpret the phrase "in secret" to mean the household, the private world of females. Jesus' demands will cost the disciples dearly in the court of public opinion for avoiding male but frequenting female space.[39]

It is a mistake to overly psychologize the command to pray "in secret" in the "storeroom" of one's house. Jesus's demands, though hyperbolic and aimed at purifying the motives of worshippers, require costly external changes in social behavior. While the overtly ostentatious *leitourgia* of the rich obviously runs afoul of the Sermon on the Mount, the "ordinary members of the church" who constituted the bulk of Matthew's first readership do not escape its demands.[40]

---

[37] Luz, *Matthew 1–7*, 300–301.

[38] See, for example, Deut 16:16.

[39] Neyrey, *Honor and Shame*, 220.

[40] Luz, *Matthew 1–7*, 16. Luz shares Neyrey's assumption that the "readers presupposed by the text" of Matthew's gospel are "male." Even so, Jesus's command to pray "in secret" also implied significant social consequences for female members of the Matthean church.

A first-century Jewish male of small means still desired honor. His social peers and his social betters would reward him with honor simply for participating visibly and regularly in the customary piety of his fellow Jewish males. Ostentation in prayer, fasting, or alms-giving wasn't necessary for honor, and it could make a poor man appear to be reaching beyond his rank. But by forbidding even the ordinary performance of prayer in the ordinary meeting places of males—the "streets" and "synagogues"—Jesus ensures that his disciples will *not* have already "received their reward" of honor from the social group that previously formed the basis of their identity.

Despite advising secrecy and even dissimulation in performing works of piety, Jesus does not intend his disciples to acquire an odious reputation by doing evil or antisocial works in public instead. He tells his followers, "Let your light shine before others, so that they may see your good works and give glory to your Father in heaven" (Matt 5:16). Here, however, Jesus envisions the honor for performing virtuous acts in public redounding to God, insofar as the "Father" is the head of the new household formed by his Son's disciples. The apparent discrepancy in Jesus's instructions about public behavior is explained by the difference between "generic virtuous actions" and "'piety,' which is expressed in almsgiving, prayer, and fasting, very specific actions pertaining to ethnic identity and self-definition."[41] The social shame incurred by Christians who refuse to participate in traditional acts of Jewish piety cannot simply be offset by performing other good deeds. Nor could Christians or Jews expect their good deeds to excuse their refusal to show public piety to the Roman emperor and pagan gods. As the First Letter of Peter indicates, the "honorable deeds" of believers will win them no honor from their unbelieving neighbors. But the same good deeds will testify, at the final judgment, to the glory of God and the ignorance of all who had accused them of impiety: "Conduct yourself honorably among the Gentiles, so that, though they malign you as evildoers, they may see your honorable deeds and glorify God when he comes to judge" (1 Pet 2:12). Remarkably, by refusing to seek honor through expected public displays of piety, believers deflect *all* human honor for virtuous behavior from themselves and direct it toward God.

---

[41] Neyrey, *Honor and Shame*, 216.

Are we to understand that Jesus forbids public prayer in common, even with fellow Christians? Certainly not. Instead, Jesus replaces one "public" with another in which the source of honor and the rules for winning it are radically different. The new "public" is the nascent church, as Neyrey explains: "Let us not exclude by Matthew's time the very 'church' which had formed and preserved Jesus' words: it too served as a court of public opinion." This court of "public" opinion is different, however, because Jesus conceives the church as a "private" household in which men and women do not receive honor from their neighbors but directly from God, who is "Father" and head of the household.[42] This household will appear shameful in the eyes of one's neighbors, for it disregards the traditional boundaries that define separate playing fields within which men win honor from other males, women from other females, and Jews from fellow Jews.

Paul's letters claim even more explicitly that the household established by Christ has room for Gentiles and no room for some of the most basic traditional social distinctions. Though he was "far more zealous" than many of his fellow Jews for the "traditions of [his] ancestors" (Gal 1:14), Paul insists, "There is no longer Jew or Greek, there is no longer slave or free, there is no longer male and female; for all of you are one in Christ Jesus" (3:28). Paul's point is not that these distinct identities have disappeared, but that they "no longer" determine one's membership and status in the household of God. Anyone who is "in Christ Jesus" should not turn to one of these old sources of social identity for approval or censure. God alone is the source of honor, justification, and reward. God's Son alone won the only honor that "counts for anything" (5:6) in the household of God when he "gave himself" for those he loves (1:4; 2:20). Christians need not earn this honor for themselves, for they inherit it as adopted "children of God through faith" (3:26). "Because you are children," Paul tells the Galatian Gentiles, "God has sent the Spirit of his Son into your hearts, crying, 'Abba! Father!'" (4:6). Paul writes similarly to the Romans, "When we cry, 'Abba! Father!' it is that very Spirit bearing witness with our spirit that we are children of God, and if children, then heirs, heirs of God and joint heirs with Christ" (Rom 8:15-17). Thus, when Paul claims in the same letter that the "real circumcision" is "spiritual" and a "matter of the heart," he is chal-

[42] Neyrey, *Honor and Shame*, 221.

lenging Christians to reimagine the *community* of worship more than the *psychology* of worship. The only public that worshippers who are "in the Spirit" should refer to for identity, approval, and correction is the assembly of all who have become God's people *en tō kryptō* ("in secret" or "inwardly"). The "real" heirs of God's chosen people respect the "requirements of the law"; they only disdain the enforcers of "external and physical" circumcision, who offer human praise for "literal" observance of the law's requirement that Jews and Greeks remain separate despite having become one in Christ (Rom 2:28-29).

### Praying with the spirit and with the mind

Insofar as the household of God functions as a court of opinion that evaluates the public prayers of its own members, what are the church's criteria for acknowledging honorable or shameful displays of piety? Can the community identify with confidence certain exterior manifestations of interior prayer that the Father "who sees in secret" will reward? The community must be careful not to usurp the place of God, who alone "searches the heart" (Rom 8:27).[43] They must resist the inclination to draw conclusions about the quality of another worshipper's relationship with God from external appearances.

This is the main lesson of the parable of the Pharisee and the tax collector who go up to the temple to pray (Luke 18:9-14). The tax collector's humble words—"God, be merciful to me, a sinner"—quickly became a favorite Christian prayer. But Luke does not have Jesus prescribing a prayer formula so much as issuing a warning to some of his own disciples, "who trusted in themselves that they were righteous and regarded others with contempt" (18:9). The Pharisee's prayer is perhaps ostentatious, but the real cause of his disgrace is his contempt for the "other people" that he is "not like," including one "other" who is praying nearby. Although he is not the only worshipper in the temple, the Pharisee is "praying by himself" or even "praying to himself," depending on how one reads the words of Jesus (18:11).[44] This suggestive description implies that physical distance

---

[43] See the additional references to God searching hearts and minds in note 4 above.

[44] See François Bovon, *Luke 2: A Commentary on the Gospel of Luke 9:51–19:27*, ed. Helmut Koester, trans. Donald S. Deer, Hermeneia—A Critical and Historical Commentary on the Bible (Augsburg Fortress, 2013), 546–47.

is a negligible obstacle to authentic common prayer, as compared with the barrier erected within human hearts when some worshippers presume their own righteousness and deny it of others. So, the first rule that the church derives from Jesus for evaluating the prayer of other members of the community is clear: "Do not judge, so that you may not be judged" (Matt 7:1).

Still, the New Testament *does* contain instructions on how members of the household of Christ should comport themselves outwardly when they come together for worship. First Corinthians, for example, prescribes veils for women at prayer and forbids men from covering their heads, though the reasons for this instruction are obscure, and its attribution to Paul is debatable (11:2 16).[45] More often, Paul's point is not how a worshipper should appear in the eyes of others, but with which others a worshipper should appear before God. Paul's rhetoric in First Corinthians is mainly directed against the "divisions" between members of the community that are manifest when they "come together as a church" (11:18). Paul particularly criticizes the way the Corinthians enact "the Lord's supper," saying that divisions within the community have made the meal inauthentic:

> When you come together, it is not really to eat the Lord's supper. For when the time comes to eat, each of you goes ahead with your own supper, and one goes hungry and another becomes drunk. What! Do you not have homes to eat and drink in? Or do you show contempt for the church of God and humiliate those who have nothing? What should I say to you? Should I commend you? In this matter I do not commend you! (1 Cor 11:20-22)

Historians are quick to point out that we know few details about this "Lord's supper" that is mentioned in First Corinthians and nowhere else in the New Testament. It is "obviously a substantial meal" involving more food than the symbolic portions of bread and wine that would come to characterize the Christian Eucharist. "Scholars have long disputed whether the Eucharist proper took place before, after or during the meal at Corinth," Paul Bradshaw notes. And although Paul quotes a "received" narrative of the Last Supper (11:23-25), he

---

[45] See Richard B. Hays, *First Corinthians*, Interpretation: A Bible Commentary for Teaching and Preaching (Louisville, KY: John Knox Press, 1997), 182–90.

does so "not to remind the Corinthians of a ritual sequence that they are neglecting but rather to underscore a meaning of the meal of which they have lost sight."[46] Yet that meaning *is* enacted ritually, insofar as Christians are supposed to eat the Lord's Supper differently than their other meals, precisely to make a hidden reality visible. The Corinthians cannot authentically claim to see and enact the hidden, inner reality of their unity in Christ if, in their "contempt" for one another, they refuse to outwardly participate in one meal, shared between those who "have" food and those who "have nothing."

It might be objected that Paul's instructions regarding the Lord's Supper are about communal dining, not communal worship. Richard Hays cautions against assimilating the Corinthian "Lord's supper" to later examples of eucharistic liturgies. Paul "is not talking about a liturgical ritual celebrated in a church building." The first Christians had no public houses of worship, so Paul is discussing "an actual meal eaten by the community in a private home."[47] Regardless, the whole point of Paul's argument is to remind the Corinthian Christians that when they "come together" to eat the Lord's Supper—even if they assemble in a private home—they are participating in the *public* worship of God. This would not be very surprising to the Corinthians because they would be familiar with formal Graeco-Roman and Jewish meals, such as the *symposium* and the *eranos*, in which prayers and ritual offerings were part of an extended gathering at the home of one of the community's wealthier members. The host of such a meal would be expected to make distinctions among the guests, providing better food and better places to the higher-status members of the community.[48] Though held in a "private" home, the meal offered a public display of the community's social hierarchy and reinforced it through religious ritual.

---

[46] Paul F. Bradshaw, *Eucharistic Origins* (Oxford: Oxford University Press, 2004), 44–45.

[47] Hays, *First Corinthians*, 193.

[48] See Bradshaw, *Eucharistic Origins*, 43–45; Hays, *First Corinthians*, 196–97. But cf. Joseph A. Fitzmyer, *First Corinthians: A New Translation with Introduction and Commentary*, The Anchor Yale Bible, 32 (New Haven, CT: Yale University Press, 2008), 428–29, 434–35, for caution about determining with too much precision the social and economic contours of the Corinthian church or the nature of the Corinthians' "misdemeanor." Fitzmyer agrees, however, that the "divisions" Paul criticizes here are apparently between Christians of unequal social and economic status.

We learn from another part of Paul's letter that the Corinthians did perform a ritual of shared food and drink that, in his view, should have reinforced a very different understanding of the community:

> The cup of blessing that we bless, is it not a sharing in the blood of Christ? The bread that we break, is it not a sharing in the body of Christ? Because there is one bread, we who are many are one body, for we all partake of the one bread. (1 Cor 10:16-17)

Most commentators warn against inferring the ritual sequence of the Corinthians' worship from Paul's rhetoric, since this part of the letter is not dispensing liturgical instructions, but making an argument against eating food sacrificed to idols.[49] Bradshaw, however, plausibly hypothesizes a Corinthian "eucharistic practice" that resembles "the general sort of pattern that we encounter later in *Didache* 9," in which a thanksgiving over the cup *precedes* a thanksgiving over the bread and a concluding prayer for unity.[50] Even though such a "cup-bread" pattern would seem to contradict the "bread-cup" pattern of the institution narrative that Paul quotes in 11:23-25, there is no evidence that the New Testament institution narratives were used liturgically "until several centuries later, when they appear to be innovations in eucharistic prayers rather than the continuation of an ancient tradition."[51]

Whatever the sequence of blessing and sharing the cup and bread may have been, the Corinthians were familiar with the ritual expressions and gestures to which Paul appeals. They could go through the motions, but apparently they did not take to heart the unity that the external rite was supposed to symbolize. Maybe they didn't understand because the meaning of the rite wasn't clear. "If Paul had instructed the Corinthian church at that time when he originally founded it that the cup they drank was a participation in Christ's blood and the bread that they shared was Christ's body, that lesson had obviously not been reinforced by the words that they said week

---

[49] See, for example, Hays, *First Corinthians*, 167.

[50] Bradshaw, *Eucharistic Origins*, 45–48. Bradshaw largely follows the argument of Enrico Mazza, *The Origins of the Eucharistic Prayer* (Collegeville, MN: Liturgical Press, 1995), 76–90. Bradshaw does not agree, however, with Mazza's conclusion that the eucharistic prayer in *Didache* 9 predates Paul's First Letter to the Corinthians.

[51] Bradshaw, *Eucharistic Origins*, 11.

by week."[52] Perhaps the words or other exterior elements of the ritual needed adjustment to be more effective at instilling habits of unity such as considering the conscience of others (1 Cor 10:28-29), seeking the advantage of the many (10:33), and waiting for one another (11:33). Although Paul's letter aims to remind the Corinthians of these *interior* dispositions, his words in chapters 10 and 11 eventually assumed a prominent role in the *exterior* eucharistic rites of churches far beyond Corinth.

Proof that the meaning of the cup-and-bread ritual had not taken root in the hearts of the Corinthians comes not only in chapter 10, where Paul is talking about food sacrificed to idols, but also in chapter 11, where he is directly addressing the Lord's Supper. We have no evidence that the cup-and-bread ritual cited by Paul in chapter 10 took place *during* the Lord's Supper described in chapter 11. But the Lord's Supper was another ritual meal at which it became evident that some who eat the bread and drink the cup of the Lord do so "in an unworthy manner" that leaves them "answerable for the body and blood of the Lord" (1 Cor 11:27). The Corinthians would not have been surprised by Paul's assumption that a meal is a ritual enactment of a community's faith, but they might have been taken aback by his fierce insistence that *this* community's faith is incompatible with the divided and unequal way its communal meal was ritually staged. If the church's fellowship had been merely human, then the customs of the *symposium* or *eranos* might have been acceptable. But, as Paul emphasizes, the church's communion is in the body and blood of the Lord. And at the *Lord's* Supper, special honor cannot be shown to the household of one of the community's leading men without showing "contempt" for the household of God. The Lord's household takes precedence whenever the church assembles, even if they come together in a private home. If the members of God's household will not "wait for one another" and share one common meal, so that no one is humiliated and everyone is equally at home, then they do not authentically eat the Lord's Supper. Whatever else they might do or say, their display of contempt puts the lie to any claim to recall what was done by "the Lord Jesus on the night when he was betrayed" (1 Cor 11:23). Paul sarcastically tells the "hungry" offenders it would be better for them to satiate themselves with their own food in their

[52] Bradshaw, *Eucharistic Origins*, 47.

own homes. He knows that pride, not hunger, is to blame for this betrayal of the Lord, which has brought "condemnation" upon some members of the community (11:33-34).

Repeatedly throughout the Bible, we have seen inauthentic worship described as worship without understanding. Paul attributes this culpable ignorance of God to a failure of *discernment*, especially by the self-important Christians who would rather not be seen eating with fellow believers at the opposite end of the social hierarchy. All those who prefer to "go ahead" as they usually do, eating their "own supper" with peers, have blinded their minds and hearts to the spiritual reality of the Lord's Supper through their outward display of contempt. In Paul's famous words, they "eat and drink without discerning the body" of the Lord whose supper they claim to share (1 Cor 11:29). While "discerning the body" has a long and contentious history of interpretation, Paul's ultimate goal in these instructions is for the Corinthians to see and understand their unity in the "body of Christ" (10:16; 12:27), whose "mind" they also share, by the gift of God's spirit:

> What human being knows what is truly human except the human spirit that is within? So also no one comprehends what is truly God's except the Spirit of God. Now we have received not the spirit of the world, but the Spirit that is from God, so that we may understand the gifts bestowed on us by God. And we speak of these things in words not taught by human wisdom but taught by the Spirit, interpreting spiritual things to those who are spiritual.
>
> Those who are unspiritual do not receive the gifts of God's Spirit, for they are foolishness to them, and they are unable to understand them because they are spiritually discerned. Those who are spiritual discern all things, and they are themselves subject to no one else's scrutiny.
>
> > "For who has known the mind of the Lord
> > so as to instruct him?"
>
> But we have the mind of Christ. (1 Cor 2:11-16)

Those who can "discern the body" in the bread and wine they take into themselves from outside are those who have within themselves the "Spirit of God" and the "mind of Christ" that allow them to "understand" and "discern all things." Those whose exterior words and actions show contempt for the body of Christ are "unspiritual" within themselves and "do not receive the gifts of God's Spirit."

In Paul's rhetoric linking the Lord's mind, the Lord's body, and the Lord's Supper, the call to participate with discernment and understanding aims to harmonize interior worship that is *spiritual* with *corporate* ritual that is both collective and composed of external, bodily actions. The exterior ritual that the church performs when its members come together is only authentic when accompanied by an act of discernment involving the "spirit that is within." When this happens, the ecclesial body "comprehends" the worship that is "truly God's," for the individual members all discern the body they share through the "Spirit that is from God," which they also share. The bodily metaphors in Paul's rhetoric simultaneously refer to individuals and to the whole society of the church. The *interior* of the metaphorical body points not only to the hearts and minds of individual believers, but to the spirit that unites and animates the church. To exercise discernment, the church and its individual members need the "Spirit that is from God." Similarly, the *exterior* act of eating the bread and drinking the cup is not defined by the behavior of any individual member alone, but by how the ritual symbolically orders the whole body. If the supper ritually divides members who "go ahead" from those who "wait," elevates those who "have homes" above those who "have nothing," and honors some by "humiliating" others, then it is not really the *Lord's* Supper.

Paul summarizes his ideal of authentic worship in another famous passage cited by author after author, from Cyprian to Benedict to Bunyan. The context is an instruction regarding glossolalia and prophecy in the assembled congregation of the church. Paul emphasizes the corporate character of worship, discernment, and understanding:

> One who speaks in a tongue should pray for the power to interpret. For if I pray in a tongue, my spirit prays but my mind is unproductive. What should I do then? I will pray with the spirit (*tō pneumati*), but I will pray with the mind (*tō noi*) also; I will sing praise with the spirit, but I will sing praise with the mind also. Otherwise, if you say a blessing with the spirit, how can anyone in the position of an outsider say the "Amen" to your

thanksgiving, since the outsider does not know what you are saying? For you may give thanks well enough, but the other person is not built up. I thank God that I speak in tongues more than all of you; nevertheless, in church I would rather speak five words with my mind, in order to instruct others also, than ten thousand words in a tongue. (1 Cor 14:13-19)

Paul's determination to "pray with the spirit" but also "with the mind" (14:15)—which will become a slogan for later authors—is made more difficult to interpret because Paul often draws a contrast between interior spirit (*pneuma*) and exterior flesh (*sarx*). Here, however, the mind (*nous*) represents the interior understanding from which an intelligible (*eusēmon*) word emerges (14:9).[53] In this context, *nous* stands in contrast to *pneuma*, which is the "breath" that externalizes the word through utterance and carries its meaning into the mind of another.[54]

While a glossolalic prayer, song, or blessing might still be said to originate internally, proceeding from the movement of the spirit within the speaker, it cannot be internalized by anyone listening unless someone else interprets. If no one has the gift of interpreting tongues, then the speaker of tongues "will be speaking into the air" (1 Cor 14:9). The unintelligible utterance remains external to the other members of the assembly and cannot become an integrated act of the whole body. Especially "in church," Paul prefers five words addressed to the minds of those assembled than ten thousand words spoken into the air. The listening members of the assembly should be able to understand what they hear. Whether or not the speakers of tongues should understand their own words is left unsaid, but in the early church, Paul's injunction to pray with the mind "was usually taken in a personal sense as referring to the understanding of the worshipper" who is speaking.[55]

---

[53] For this reason, English translations and citations of 1 Cor 14:15 often render *nous* as "understanding," as in the title of John Bunyan's polemical tract, *I Will Pray with the Spirit, and I will Pray with the Understanding also: Or, A Discourse Touching Prayer, From I Cor. 14.15* (London: Printed for the Author, 1663). See below, p. 136.

[54] Giles Constable, "The Concern for Sincerity and Understanding in Liturgical Prayer, Especially in the Twelfth Century," in *Classica Et Mediaevalia: Studies in Honor of Joseph Szövérffy*, ed. Helmut Buschhausen and Irene Vaslef (Leyden: Brill, 1986), 17–30, at 17.

[55] Constable, "Concern for Sincerity," 27 n. 1.

In the last analysis, the understanding of the speaker and the understanding of the listener go together. At issue is not the idiosyncratic understanding of any member in isolation from the others but the shared understanding of all members of the body, who together "have the mind of Christ" (1 Cor 2:16). Every prayer and every song must be "spiritually discerned" (2:14)—even if it is a tongue ecstatically uttered "with the spirit." Those who speak and those who listen share the responsibility of searching everything with "the Spirit that is from God" so they "may understand the gifts" bestowed by God on the whole assembly (2:12).

## Worship with one heart and soul

What could justify stringing together the preceding examples from Scripture and calling them a coherent and sustained biblical account of authentic worship? Their historical, cultural, literary, and rhetorical contexts are disparate. Centuries separate Isaiah from Jesus and Paul. Even within the first century, Jerusalem, Galilee, and Corinth had very different ethnic and religious cultures. And a prophetic oracle differs from a gospel sermon or an epistle. Nevertheless, we find these passages addressing questions of authentic worship with a common set of metaphors drawn from the human body. Isaiah contrasts the Judeans' worshipful "lips" with their distant "hearts." Jesus says that the evil intentions that come out "from the human heart" defile, but that which "goes into the mouth" cannot defile a person. Paul claims that "true circumcision" is "of the heart," not "external and physical." We can speak, therefore, of a coherent biblical phenomenology of worship because the distinction between hearts and lips, interior and exterior, intention and behavior is consistently articulated across the diverse texts of the Hebrew Bible and the New Testament. The question of authentic worship repeatedly turns on integrating the two terms in acts of devotion that conform to the commandment of God *and* proceed from true understanding.

Although this biblical account of authentic worship may appear to elevate interior devotion above exterior, the case is not so simple. While Paul criticizes mere external conformity to the law, he also excoriates those who believe that their superior understanding of the law permits them to eat food ritually offered to idols. Their claim to "possess knowledge" inwardly does not excuse the "sin against Christ" that they incur when their outward behavior defiles the "weak" conscience of fellow believers (1 Cor 8:11-13). Jesus similarly warns his followers to put no confidence in the purity of their hearts unless they also guard what comes out of their mouths:

> For out of the abundance of the heart the mouth speaks. The good person brings good things out of a good treasure, and the evil person brings evil things out of an evil treasure. I tell you, on the day of judgment you will have to give an account for every careless word you utter; for by your words you will be justified, and by your words you will be condemned. (Matt 12:34-37; cf. Luke 6:45)

Jesus echoes the prophets, who condemn the "careless words" that lead others astray, even as they denounce false intentions:

> For from the least to the greatest of them,
>     everyone is greedy for unjust gain;
>     And from prophet to priest,
>     everyone deals falsely.
> They have treated the wound of my people carelessly,
>     saying, "Peace, peace,"
>     when there is no peace. (Jer 6:13-14)

Adducing a botanical metaphor, Jesus says there is no inward understanding of God that doesn't manifest itself in outward conformity to God's commandment: "Either make the tree good, and its fruit good; or make the tree bad, and its fruit bad; for the tree is known by its fruit" (Matt 12:33; cf. Luke 6:43-44).

The point is not to *prefer* devotion from the heart to worship from the lips, but to *harmonize* the interior and exterior in an integral act of obedience and true knowledge of God. Psalm 19 expresses the biblical ideal of authentic worship well: "Let the words of my mouth and the meditation of my heart be acceptable to you, O Lord, my rock and my redeemer" (Ps 19:14). Crucially, the Scriptures consistently depict interior worship as taking place *within* the body, not apart from it. Heart, mind, and soul are all distinguished from the body, but never extracted from it. Even Paul, who tells Christians to "put to death the deeds of the body" and "make no provision for the flesh" (Rom 8:13; 13:14), also teaches them to glorify God in their bodies (1 Cor 6:20). The goal is not *disembodied* worship, but *total* worship. Thomas Aquinas cites yet another example from the psalms: "My heart and my flesh sing for joy to the living God" (Ps 84:2).[56] The acceptable offering of prayer is an act of the whole person, which fulfills the Great Commandment: "You shall love the LORD your God with all your heart, and with all your soul, and with all your might" (Deut 6:5). Such total worship is what Guardini means by "an integrated liturgical act," and it is characterized by the correspondence of interior and exterior action that we have been calling performative authenticity. The Scriptures demand integral worship: the lips and hearts of each individual worshipper should be in tune, and a similar harmony should characterize the corporate prayer of the whole congregation.

If the body at worship is an image of the church, then *hearts* and *lips*—interior and exterior—have a social meaning and an individual meaning. When the psalms and the prophets speak of worshipping God with lips, hands, and flesh, they do not isolate specific liturgical words or bodily rituals for criticism or approval. These external parts of the body evoke the people's entire cult of ritual worship. Similarly, God's repeated promise is to restore the whole people's interior worship: "The LORD your God will circumcise your heart and the heart of your descendants, so that you will love the LORD your God with all your heart and with all your soul, in order that you may live" (Deut 30:6).[57] Such promises allow Paul to insist that "real circumcision is a matter of the heart" and claim that the promises have been fulfilled in the Gentiles who "show that what the law requires is written on their hearts" (Rom 2:15, 29).

In Colossians, Paul claims that Christ enables his "toil and struggle" on behalf of the Gentiles by "all the energy that he powerfully inspires within" his apostle (Col 1:29). Still, it isn't the personal privilege of Paul or of any individual Christian alone to know the "mystery that has been hidden throughout the ages and generations but has now been revealed to his saints." Everyone who accepts the gospel has a share in "the riches of the glory of this mystery." The mystery, Paul says, is nothing less than "Christ in you," for the same Christ dwells in each member of "his body, that is the church" (Col 1:24-27). Once

---

[56] Aquinas cites this as Psalm 83, according to the Vulgate: *"Cor meum et caro mea exultaverunt in Deum vivum."* ST I-II q. 101 a. 2 co.

[57] See also Deut 10:16; Jer 4:4; 31:33; Ezek 11:19; 18:31; 36:26.

"estranged and hostile in mind," Christ has now reconciled the Gentiles "in his fleshly body through death," so that they have become a "holy and blameless and irreproachable" offering to God (1:21-22). Thus given a new mind and heart, the whole body is becoming "mature in Christ," growing together in "wisdom" and mutual affection (1:28). The interior heart and mind of the church's worship is precisely this *communion* of "the saints and brothers and sisters in Christ" (1:2).

This dynamic, active love within the church is also depicted with a bodily metaphor in the Acts of the Apostles, in its description of the apostolic church in Jerusalem: "Now the whole group of those who believed were of one heart and soul" (Acts 4:32). Early Christian writers would frequently cite this ecclesial ideal. A similar text, Geoffrey Wainwright notes, "runs as a golden thread through ecumenical endeavors in the twentieth century" because it insists that " 'right worship' can only occur when Christians are united in faith and life." That recurring text is Paul's exhortation to "have the same mind among you according to Christ Jesus, that you may with one heart and one mouth glorify God the Father of our Lord Jesus Christ" (Rom 15:5-6).[58]

This communion of the social body cannot, from the viewpoint of the Scriptures, be reduced to a static description, characteristic, or structural feature of the church as a social group. Communion isn't a state of affairs, a social structure, or even a shared experience. Communion is the name given to an *activity* of the body: the *cooperation* of its members. When the interior communion and the exterior cult are in harmony, this cooperative activity is an *offering*. Just as the individual members obey the command to love God with everything they have and everything they are, so the whole body offers itself completely in prayer, praise, supplication, thanksgiving, and sacrifice to God. In Paul's view, the self-offering of the ecclesial body is complete only when it is made in cooperation with Christ as head of his body.

How does Scripture suggest that the mind of the church and the voice of the church may be brought into tune? The consistent theme is that the authenticity of worship is a collective responsibility of the

---

[58] Geoffrey Wainwright, *Worship with One Accord: Where Liturgy and Ecumenism Embrace* (New York: Oxford University Press, 1997), 1. The translation of Rom 15:5-6 is Wainwright's.

whole people, even though it involves the innermost part of each individual worshipper. It is for the whole assembly to discern the tuning adjustments they must make as a social body. As we just saw, Paul's call to "discern the body" is more than an instruction about individual faith and piety. Discernment is only possible by the Spirit and "mind of Christ" that all members of the church share. What each member should discern is the whole ecclesial body's unity in Christ. Paul reinforces the sense of corporate responsibility for discernment by concluding his exhortation in the first-person plural: "If we judged ourselves [with discernment], we would not be judged" (1 Cor 11:31).[59] Since Paul also repeatedly uses the verb for discernment (*diakrinein*) to "describe the community's activity of judging and regulating prophecy in their midst,"[60] Hays suggests that "we should perhaps understand 11:31 not just as a summons to individual self-judgment but rather as a call for the *community* to exercise self-regulatory judgment to bring greater order to the Lord's Supper by disciplining those who treat it as their own private dinner party."[61] In any such disciplining of individuals, however, the community does not *enforce* long-established regulations so much as it *adjusts* once-traditional expectations of external social ritual to correspond to the new internal spirit of communion that unites the members of the Lord's body.

According to the Scriptures, worship with minds and voices in tune is also the only public ritual prayer that possesses genealogical authenticity. The metaphorical words of Isaiah, cited by Jesus in Mark and Matthew, exemplify the connection between the two meanings of authenticity. It is only when "lips" and "hearts" are both close to God that "human tradition" avoids setting itself in opposition to "the commandment of God" (Isa 29:13; Mark 7:6-8; Matt 15:6-9). The law that God commands the chosen people to recite to their children must also be kept in their hearts (Deut 6:6-7). Isaiah doesn't accuse his

---

[59] A more literal translation of this verse might be, "If we discerned ourselves, we would not be judged." The NRSV tries to capture Paul's play on *diakrinein* (to discern) and *krinein* (to judge). See Fitzmyer, *First Corinthians*, 446–47; Hans Conzelmann, *1 Corinthians: A Commentary on the First Epistle to the Corinthians*, ed. George W. MacRae, trans. James W. Leitch, Hermeneia—A Critical and Historical Commentary on the Bible (Philadelphia: Fortress, 1975), 202–3.

[60] See also 1 Cor 6:5; 14:29.

[61] Hays, *First Corinthians*, 202.

opponents of failing to hand on what they have "learned by rote" (Isa 29:13). Paul doesn't deny that the Jews alone "have the written code and the circumcision" (Rom 2:27). And Jesus doesn't dispute that the Pharisees have kept the "tradition of the elders" that they were taught. A tradition that hands on the letter of the law without handing on its spirit remains a tradition, but a tradition that lacks an authentic genealogical connection to its origin in the commandment of God. As we have seen, Jesus rebuts the accusation of dishonoring the tradition of the elders by citing the commandment to honor one's father and mother. He tells the Pharisees, "[Y]ou no longer permit doing anything for a father or mother, thus making void the word of God through your tradition that you have handed on" (Mark 7:12-13; cf. Matt 15:6). While hyperbolic, Jesus's countercharge is precisely chosen to demonstrate the absurdity of honoring the elders' tradition while dishonoring the elders themselves. In the Bible, the genealogical and performative meanings of authenticity are coordinated: worship can be neither traditional nor integral if it is not both.

Harmony among all who offer God worship—and harmony among worshippers past, present, and future—requires each member of the assembly to seek harmony between exterior and interior worship. Worshippers seek to honor God with lips *and* with hearts, with voices *and* with minds, with the spirit *and* with the understanding that comes from the Spirit. *Each one* seeks this harmony so that *all* who believe may be "of one heart and soul" (Acts 4:32). In no way does this make liturgy a mere tool of social harmony, much less an instrument of historical preservation. What is ultimately at stake in the unity of worshippers is the integrity of worship, the fulfillment of the command to "love the LORD your God with all your heart, and with all your soul, and with all your might" (Deut 6:5).

*Chapter Three*

# Harmony and Authentic Prayer

If Romano Guardini is right to say that a fully integrated liturgical act is "a forgotten way of doing things,"[1] then a look to history is a necessary first step toward relearning it. It quickly becomes clear, however, that the call to relearn authentic liturgy is itself a recurring theme in Christian history. The modern case that Guardini raises is special only because modern accounts and practices of authenticity have drifted away from a focus on *harmonizing* interior and exterior activity to an emphasis on *liberating* the activity of the individual from that of society. While the radical character of such modern individualism is novel, the need to break free of the structures and strictures of an "old" society to make way for the birth of a "new" society is essential to the Christian gospel. The New Testament understands this new society, the church, as a "body" whose internal, mystical communion is the dwelling place of the same Holy Spirit who inhabits the minds and hearts of each individual member.[2] When the ecclesial body's mystical communion in Christ animates each member's participation in liturgical prayer, then the external corporate

---

[1] Romano Guardini, "A Letter from Romano Guardini," *Herder Correspondence* 1, no. 8 (August 1964): 238.

[2] The New Testament contains, of course, many images of the church in addition to that of the body. The Johannine images of "flock" and "vine and branches," for instance, are discussed below, in chapter 6. In one way or another, however, all of these images depict the church as a new society whose unity is a communion in Christ. See, for example, John 10:14-16; 15:1-17.

ritual of the whole society will harmonize with the external ethical behavior of each member.

History supports Guardini's assertion that liturgical prayer is *corporate* prayer and that "the prayer of a corporate body must be sustained by thought."[3] But precisely because the exterior ritual of the church is sustained by interior thought, *authentic* Christian liturgy "begins as ritual practice but ends as ethical performance," as Nathan Mitchell claims.[4] To determine whether the interior thought that sustains corporate prayer is of the Spirit, it's not enough to attend to the exterior *ritual* performance alone. Neither does an exterior *ethical* performance alone determine the internal quality of prayer. Instead, when the minds of worshippers are in tune with their voices, then ritual performance and ethical performance will also harmonize, being sustained by the same interior communion.

We find Christians in every period of history turning to ethics to verify the authenticity of liturgy. While this isn't a new observation, modern authors (including Guardini) often mistakenly assume that the turn to ethics is motivated by a desire to demystify the liturgy and liberate "Christian sincerity" from hidebound ritual.[5] This chapter aims to show, however, that the turn to ethics aims to serve the harmonization of minds and voices, so that worshippers can perform an integrated liturgical act that is interior *and* exterior. During the first five centuries of Christianity, which we examine here, teaching on prayer posits a close alliance between harmony of mind and voice and harmony among members of the church. The earliest Christian treatises on prayer are replete with ethical imperatives because their concern is to make prayer a pure and complete sacrifice of praise that incorporates the whole person and the whole people of God. This is another way of saying that the commandment to love the neighbor serves the commandment to love God with all that one has and all that one is.

[3] Romano Guardini, *The Spirit of the Liturgy*, trans. Ada Lane, Milestones in Catholic Theology (New York: Crossroad, 1998), 2.

[4] Nathan D. Mitchell, *Meeting Mystery: Liturgy, Worship, Sacraments* (Maryknoll, NY: Orbis, 2006), 38.

[5] See Guardini, "Letter from Romano Guardini," 237.

## A pure sacrifice: James, the Didache, and Tertullian

For at least the first three centuries of Christianity, says Allan Bouley, "traditions, values and beliefs got their vitality from those who lived by them and expressed them chiefly by the spoken word." Christian liturgy—like Jewish synagogue worship of the same period—wasn't transmitted primarily in fixed words or written texts. This doesn't mean that early liturgy lacked any recognizable exterior order; it simply means that particular performances of liturgical prayer weren't expected to conform to scripted formulas. Even for celebrations of the Eucharist, "there was no common awareness that fixed or written prayer texts for the use of leaders might or might not be a good thing."[6] The gradual displacement of extemporaneous prayer by written texts in the fourth and fifth centuries made it possible to ask whether a particular celebration was enacted using specified words and actions. But from the beginning, Christians had been asking whether the outward offering of prayer was accompanied by a corresponding interior offering. Concern for authentic liturgy was concern for the integrity and harmony of this offering of prayer.

In the early church, the ideal of authentic prayer often appears in discussions of the relationship between worship and ethics. Maxwell Johnson argues that the New Testament's "concern for the connection between what happens in worship and what the implications of worship are for ethics, or how ethics 'authenticates' or 'verifies' worship, is clearly reflected in various places in the first five centuries of the church's history."[7] The early church's concern for the connection between liturgical celebration and ethical praxis is of a piece with its concern for the authenticity of the liturgical act itself. This concern is typically expressed in terms of *purity*. The roots of this concern for purity are biblical, as we have seen. Johnson draws our attention to a clear example from the Letter of James, in which "pure worship" (*thrēskeia kathara*, usually translated as "religion that is pure") is verified by the just treatment of widows, orphans, and the poor. But the letter, which appears to be addressed "precisely to a liturgical

---

[6] Allan Bouley, *From Freedom to Formula: The Evolution of the Eucharistic Prayer from Oral Improvisation to Written Texts* (Washington, DC: Catholic University of America Press, 1981), 153.

[7] Maxwell E. Johnson, *Praying and Believing in Early Christianity: The Interplay between Christian Worship and Doctrine* (Collegeville, MN: Liturgical Press, 2013), 110–11.

assembly,"[8] is also clear that the point of examining an assembly's outward ethical behavior is to confirm that the worshippers' "tongues" and "hearts" are in accord. Only such Christians have reason to consider themselves authentically "worshipful" or "religious" (*thrēskos*):

> If any think they are religious (*thrēskos*), and do not bridle their tongues but deceive their hearts, their religion (*thrēskeia*) is worthless. Religion that is pure (*thrēskeia kathara*) and undefiled before God, the Father, is this: to care for orphans and widows in their distress, and to keep oneself unstained by the world.
>
> My brothers and sisters, do you with your acts of favoritism really believe in our glorious Lord Jesus Christ? For if a person with gold rings and in fine clothes comes into your assembly, and if a poor person in dirty clothes also comes in, and if you take notice of the one wearing the fine clothes and say, "Have a seat here, please," while to the one who is poor you say, "Stand there," or, "Sit at my feet," have you not made distinctions among yourselves, and become judges with evil thoughts? (Jas 1:26–2:4)

In "offering what can certainly be called a 'liturgical' theology," James doesn't promote "works" over "faith," but instead describes an ethical perspective "grounded firmly in baptism and so rooted actually in God, the giver of all good gifts (1:22)."[9] The ethical conduct that James promotes is not an end in itself, but an exterior means to purifying the people's worship of all interior partiality, duplicitousness, and self-deception. To "show partiality" in following the command to love one's neighbor is to give evidence that one's worship of God is also culpably partial—ignorant of the "whole law" of love and therefore "accountable for all of it" (2:9-10). Early Christian writers unanimously concur: outward contempt for one's neighbor reveals a division in the interior communion of love among members of the assembly. The resulting disharmony of minds and voices defiles the church's pure sacrifice of praise.

---

[8] Johnson, *Praying and Believing in Early Christianity*, 103. Johnson attributes the insight about translating *thrēskeia* as "worship" to Reginald H. Fuller and Daniel Westberg, *Preaching the Lectionary: The Word of God for the Church of Today*, 3rd ed. (Collegeville, MN: Liturgical Press, 2006), 349.

[9] Johnson, *Praying and Believing*, 105.

The early Christians' description of their liturgical offering of praise as a "pure," "reasonable," or "unbloody" sacrifice apparently aimed to cast a contrast with the animal sacrifices of pagans. The absence of animal blood, however, was a necessary but insufficient condition for the purity of the Christian sacrifice. The essential qualification for offering a "pure sacrifice" outwardly was having a "pure heart" within. Christians had inherited from the Hebrew Scriptures the conviction that God takes "no delight in sacrifice" of any kind if the offerer lacks "truth in the inward being" (Ps 51). The New Testament cemented the idea that the sacrificial offering that had to be kept "undefiled" and "unstained" was one's own life, in its totality, both inward and outward. "Coupled with sacrifice as prayer and praise is the continuation of the New Testament understanding that the very life of Christians is itself the sacrifice Christians are to offer God in Christ (see Rom 12:1-3)."[10]

To offer themselves wholeheartedly and single-mindedly to God *in Christ*, however, Christians had to do more than keep themselves *individually* "unstained by the world." They had to be of one mind and one heart in Christ (see Acts 4:32). The *Didache*, usually dated to the first or second century, makes such unity a prerequisite for communal worship: "Assembling on every Sunday of the Lord, break bread and give thanks, confessing your faults beforehand, so that your sacrifice may be pure. Let no one engaged in a dispute with his comrade join you until they have been reconciled lest your sacrifice be profaned."[11] The *Didache* offers an early example of Christians applying to their own sacrifice of prayer and praise the advice that Jesus gives to his fellow Jews about how to purify their temple offerings from hidden anger and discord: "When you are offering your gift at the altar, if you remember that your brother or sister has something against you, leave your gift there before the altar and go; first be reconciled to your brother or sister, and then come and offer your gift" (Matt 5:23-24).

The earliest surviving treatise on Christian prayer, penned by Tertullian of Carthage around the end of the second century, similarly

---

[10] Johnson, *Praying and Believing*, 121.

[11] *Didache* 14.1–3, ed. Kurt Niederwimmer, *The Didache: A Commentary*, trans. Linda M. Maloney, Hermeneia—A Critical and Historical Commentary on the Bible (Minneapolis: Fortress, 1998), 194.

takes Jesus's words to mean that a pure sacrifice requires concord among Christian brothers and sisters. Tertullian urges Christians to be "mindful" of their Lord's instructions about prayer:

> And the chief of them is that we should not go up to the altar of God before resolving whatever there might be of offense or discord contracted with the brothers. For how can one approach the peace of God without peace, how seek the remission of debts whilst retaining them?[12]

While Tertullian is concerned about the restoration of peace among members of the Christian community, the primary reason he gives for seeking social harmony is to preserve the harmony of interior and exterior activity at prayer:

> The intent of prayer should be free not from anger alone, but from all manner of perturbation of the soul, as it should be sent forth from the same sort of spirit to which it is sent. For a polluted spirit cannot be known by a holy spirit, any more than a saddened spirit may be known by a gladdened spirit, nor a shackled spirit by one that is free. . . .
>
>   Moreover what reason is there for going to prayer with hands which are washed but a spirit which is filthy, when the hands themselves are in need of spiritual cleanliness so that they may be lifted up pure of fraud, murder, violence, sorcery, idolatry, and the other stains which originate in the spirit but which are put into effect through the hands?[13]

Tertullian opposes the Jewish ritual of washing one's hands before prayer, unless the hands are outwardly dirty. His objection isn't to ritual washing, for he holds that the external washing of baptism has power to cleanse body and spirit together.[14] It is rather the false display of external cleanliness to conceal internal corruption that Tertullian compares to Pilate washing his hands before handing Christ over for crucifixion (Matt 27:24):

---

[12] Tertullian, *De oratione* 11, in Tertullian, Cyprian, and Origen, *On the Lord's Prayer*, trans. Alistair Stewart-Sykes (Crestwood, NY: St. Vladimir's Seminary Press, 2004).

[13] Tertullian, *De oratione* 12–13.

[14] See also Tertullian, *De baptismo* 2.1; 4.5.

> We venerate the Lord, we do not betray him. It is better that we should not wash hands and so to show ourselves to be the reverse of this pattern, unless we should need to wash, being aware of impurity caused by human circumstances. Otherwise, the hands that, along with the whole body, have been washed in Christ once for all, are clean enough.[15]

Tertullian similarly declares Gentile customs of dress and posture—removing coats and sitting down "when the prayer is sealed," for example—to be "vanity" unworthy of Christian public prayer. "Things of this nature are to be considered not true religion but superstition, they are affected and forced, are not reasonable service but fussiness, and should surely be suppressed."[16]

Yet Tertullian doesn't simply criticize the "empty expression" of Jews and Gentiles; he also identifies authentic displays of external piety for Christians. It's "irreligious" if Christians fail to stand upright when worshipping "in the sight of the living God." Tertullian reproaches those who sit: "Are we protesting to God that prayer has tired us out?"[17] But no one should stand all the time, since "no prayer is to be observed without kneeling and the remaining postures of humility," except on "the Lord's day of the resurrection" and during "the period of the Pentecost."[18] At all times, "we shall commend our prayers to God if we worship with restraint and humility, not even raising our hands too high, but lifting them up temperately and soberly, not presumptuously lifting up our countenance."[19] When Christians raise their hands with understanding, Tertullian explains, it's no empty gesture, for "we do not simply lift them up but spread them out in imitation of the passion of the Lord, so confessing Christ as we pray."[20] The exterior posture does not merely express an interior belief; it makes the act of confessing Christ complete. For the same reason, those fasting should not decline to exchange the kiss of peace with other members of the assembly. "How can prayer be complete when it is divorced from the holy kiss? . . . What sort of sacrifice is

[15] Tertullian, *De oratione* 13.
[16] Tertullian, *De oratione* 15–16.
[17] Tertullian, *De oratione* 16.
[18] Tertullian, *De oratione* 23.
[19] Tertullian, *De oratione* 16–17.
[20] Tertullian, *De oratione* 14.

that from which one departs without making peace?"[21] In these and many other positive stipulations about Christian public prayer, Tertullian displays as much concern for exterior ritual as for exterior ethics—neither for its own sake, but for performing worship with a pure heart, since "God is a listener not to the voice but to the heart."[22]

Tertullian also offers us a glimpse of how early Christians discerned authentic external forms of prayer. Besides appealing to the instructions of Jesus, the evidence of Scripture, and even such authorities as the *Shepherd* of Hermas,[23] early Christian communities settled disputes about ritual practice through discussion and debate, relying on God to inspire their collective discernment with grace. Tertullian notes, for example, that there is "a variety of observance in the matter of bending the knee, for a few will not kneel on the Sabbath," apparently in obedience to a Jewish custom of the time. He favors kneeling, as we just saw, but admits the matter is not settled: "As this debate is even now putting its case to the churches, the Lord will give his grace so that they shall either desist or should have their opinion sustained without giving cause for offense to others."[24] The basic criterion for discerning the correct ritual practice here is identical to that in Paul's First Letter to the Corinthians: unity throughout the whole body of Christ without giving offense to any of Christ's "weaker" members.[25] Tertullian also assumes a variety of customs about women's dress, though here he is even less willing to concede that his own opinion might not be universally accepted. According to him, the prescription that unmarried women should cover their heads in public "is a matter of general observation throughout the churches." This is likely an exaggeration, given that Tertullian devotes an outsized portion of his treatise on prayer to arguing his case "as though it were undecided."[26] Whatever the status of such questions may have been in Tertullian's day, prescriptions about ritual order and propriety could not be made without ecclesial discernment. Such discernment relied on the grace of the Holy Spirit, recognized a variety of customs, and sought concord among the members of Christ's body.

---

[21] Tertullian, *De oratione* 18.

[22] Tertullian, *De oratione* 17. See Heb 4:12.

[23] Tertullian, *De oratione* 16.

[24] Tertullian, *De oratione* 23.

[25] See especially 1 Cor 8:1-13; 10:23-33; 12:12-27.

[26] Tertullian, *De oratione* 20–22. See also Tertullian, *De virginibus velandis*.

Tertullian's treatise identifies the *concordia* that should prevail throughout the praying assembly with the harmony of mind and voice that God requires of each Christian who wishes to offer a pure sacrifice of praise. All who wish to pray authentically, with pure hearts, must seek reconciliation, justice, and peace in the exteriority of ethics *and* the exteriority of ritual. Performative authenticity—minds and voices in tune—can't be found without corporate harmony.

## A fruitful prayer: Cyprian

This close connection between authentic worship and communal unity is even more striking in the instructions on prayer given by Tertullian's admirer Cyprian some fifty years later:

> The Lord instructs you, therefore, to be peaceable and agreeable and of one mind in his house. He wishes that we should remain as we are when we are reborn in our second birth, that those who are children of God should remain in the peace of God, and that those who are in possession of one spirit should also possess one mind and one heart. Thus God does not accept the sacrifice of one who is in disrepute, and sends him back from the altar, ordering him first to be reconciled to his brother, so that he may pacify God by praying as a peacemaker. The greater sacrifice to God is our peace and brotherly agreement, as a people unified in the unity of the Father and the Son and the Holy Spirit.[27]

The bishop of Carthage views the pursuit of social harmony and communion as the path that must be trod by those who dare to address God as "our Father" in prayer. In giving his disciples this form of words for their prayer, "the teacher of peace and master of unity" shows he desires harmony (*concordia*) "before all else":

> We should not make our prayer individually and alone, as whoever prays by himself prays only for himself. We do not say: "My father, who are in the heavens," nor "Give me my bread this day." Nor does anybody request that his debt be pardoned for himself alone, nor ask that he alone be not led into temptation and delivered from the evil one. Our prayer is common and collective, and when we pray we pray not for one but for all people,

---

[27] Cyprian, *De dominica oratione* 23, trans. Stewart-Sykes, *On the Lord's Prayer*.

because we are all one people together. The God of peace and master of concord, who taught us that we should be united, wanted one to pray in this manner for all, as he himself bore all in one.[28]

Being the model of prayer authorized by Christ himself, the Lord's Prayer establishes an essential rule for all authentic Christian prayer: harmony of mind and voice should prevail among all whenever anyone prays. It's likely that the occasion for Cyprian's discourse is the *traditio orationis*—the handing over of the Lord's Prayer to the catechumens who will soon be "reborn" through the exterior washing of baptism.[29] By the prayer that Jesus "authorized" them to say, Christians enjoy the unparalleled privilege of being "considered sons of God, as Christ is the son of God." But they must also be children of God inwardly: "Let us act as temples of God, so that it may appear that God dwells in us. Let our conduct not fall away from the spirit; rather, we, who have begun to be spiritual and heavenly, should think and perform spiritual and heavenly things."[30] Above all, Christians must imitate the "master of concord" by performing their prayers for all and in unity with all.

Like Tertullian, Cyprian declares God a "hearer not of the voice but of the heart." This doesn't mean, however, that one's exterior conduct is unimportant. It's *because* God is "an examiner of the kidney and heart" (Rev 2:23) that reverent worshippers should aim to harmonize thought, speech, and posture in an act of spiritual and reasonable sacrifice. "We should be mindful of reverence and order, not forever tossing ill-judged phrases into the air, nor seeking to commend our requests by bombarding God with a tumultuous verbosity." Instead, by addressing God in the words that Christ taught them, Christians should adopt "a friendly and familiar manner of praying" that not only pleases the Father, but reveals his Son dwelling within them. "When we make our prayer, let the Father recognize the words of his own Son. May he who lives inside our heart be also in our voice."[31] By remaining mindful of their external appearance and

---

28 Cyprian, *De dominica oratione* 8.
29 See Stewart-Sykes, *On the Lord's Prayer*, 22–26.
30 Cyprian, *De dominica oratione* 11.
31 Cyprian, *De dominica oratione* 3–4.

activity, Christians can fulfill the Son's command to pray to the Father "in secret" even when they "gather together to celebrate the divine sacrifices with the priest of God." Cyprian perceives that Jesus's words in Matthew have more to do with the audience of prayer than with its location:

> Let us call to mind that we are standing before the face of God. Both the posture of our body and the modulation of our voice should be pleasing to the divine eyes. For whereas the shameless groan and cry out, by contrast it is fitting that the reverent man should pray reserved prayers; for the Lord in his pronouncement commands each of us to pray in secret, in hidden and private places, in our inner rooms.[32]

For Cyprian, the interiority of authentic prayer—the desire to perform only for the "Father who sees in secret" (Matt 6:6)—calls for more attention, not less, to exterior signs of reverence. It is why Hannah "pleaded with God by crying her petition not out loud but quietly and modestly within her inner heart. She was speaking a secret prayer and made her faith manifest as she spoke, not with her voice but with her heart, since she knew that God would so hear her."[33]

Cyprian expects new Christians to make many exterior adjustments of voice and posture to their habits of public prayer. Knowing they are seen by the "divine eyes," Christians stand upright but do not "brazenly raise" their eyes or "insolently raise" their hands.[34] Believing that God hears in the silence of their hearts, they carefully modulate their voices. Still, Christians make these external adjustments not for God's sake, but for their own. To harmonize the exterior ritual behavior with the internal activity of prayer is to be "mindful" of what one is doing. Cyprian asks rhetorically, "Do you want God to have you in mind when you are making prayer when you are not even mindful of yourself?" Christians begin their liturgical prayer by adjusting their outward behavior and speech to match their inner awareness of being in God's presence. The attention they give to the external ritual of worship reciprocally helps them adjust and perfect

---

[32] Cyprian, *De dominica oratione* 4.
[33] Cyprian, *De dominica oratione* 5. See 1 Kgs 1:13.
[34] Cyprian, *De dominica oratione* 6.

their interior offering of their own hearts to God. For Cyprian, such correspondence of minds and voices qualifies as prayer with pure hearts and "sincere intent":

> Now when we stand to pray, dearest brothers, we should be watchful and apply ourselves to our prayers with our whole heart. Every fleshly and worldly thought should depart, nor should any mind dwell on anything other than the prayer that it is offering. Therefore, before the prayer, the priest prepares the minds of the brothers by first uttering a preface as he says: "Hearts on high!" And as the people reply: "We have them to the Lord,"[35] so they are warned that they should think of nothing other than the Lord. The heart is closed against the enemy and lies open to God alone, so that the foe of God might not enter at a time of prayer. For he creeps around constantly and insinuates himself with subtlety, deceitfully calling away our prayers from God, so that we have one thing in our hearts and another on our lips. It is not the sound of our voice but the mind and the heart which should pray to God with sincere intent (*intentione sincera*).[36]

In this liturgical scenario, those who participate without "sincere intent" are less the *perpetrators* of deception than the *victims* of the "deceiver of the whole world" (Rev 12:9). They are guilty nonetheless of letting down their guard and allowing their interior participation in the offering to be incomplete. Cyprian doesn't appear to expect perfect mindfulness at every moment of prayer. Yet he warns the catechumens not to give into "lethargy," lest the deceiver draw their hearts far away even as they draw near to God with their lips.[37]

Cyprian's warning echoes the words of Isaiah that Jesus quoted to rebuke the Pharisees (Isa 29:13; Mark 7:6; Matt 15:8). Isaiah and Jesus, however, each criticize an incongruity between exterior ritual worship and the exterior practice of justice. Their immediate demand

---

[35] Stewart-Sykes notes there is reason to believe that this is a reference to the opening dialogue of the eucharistic prayer. With "the absence of a call to thanksgiving," however, it is possible that Cyprian has the beginning of some other liturgical prayer in mind. Stewart-Sykes, *On the Lord's Prayer*, 88 n. 22.

[36] Cyprian, *De dominica oratione*, 31. The end of this passage appears to be a reference to 1 Cor 14:15, "I will pray with the spirit, but I will pray with the mind also; I will sing praise with the spirit, but I will sing praise with the mind also."

[37] Cyprian, *De dominica oratione* 31.

isn't for worshippers to eliminate stray worldly concerns from their thoughts, but to rid their ethical behavior of injustice. Has Cyprian abandoned the "verification" of authentic worship "through the *exteriority* of ethical action"[38] to call Christians to a strictly *interior* self-examination when they participate in liturgy? This he has not done, for after telling the catechumens to banish worldly thoughts from their offering of prayer, he next instructs them to fill the same offering with the "fruit" of almsgiving and good deeds:

> Those who pray should not come to God with unfruitful or barren prayers. A request is futile when a sterile prayer is made to God. For just as every tree that does not bear fruit is cut down and thrown into the fire (Matt 7:19), so an utterance that has no fruit cannot be well-pleasing to God because it does not supply any works. And so the divine Scripture instructs us when it says: "A prayer with fasting and almsgiving is good" (Tob 12:8). For he who, in the day of judgment, shall return a reward for works and almsgiving is a kindly listener today to the prayer of one who comes to him in prayer associated with good deeds.[39]

Neither the liturgical "utterance" nor the ethical "fruit" alone pleases God. Instead, God is pleased by the wholehearted act of faith and love that animates both the utterance of prayer and the good deeds. For Cyprian, the good deed is part of the exterior offering of prayer, just as Tobit's proverb suggests. The gift of alms, as Gary Anderson puts it, is "a means for the religious believer to enact what he professes, putting his money where his mouth is." Charity is "not just a good deed" because it enacts "*a declaration of belief about the world and the God who created it.*"[40] The ethical act of charity perfects not just the exterior "utterance" of prayer, but also the interior act of freeing one's heart from selfish love in order to make a complete offering of oneself to God. As evidence of this, Cyprian quotes God's promise to answer the prayers of those whose way of fasting is "to loose the bonds of injustice, to undo the thongs of the yoke, to let the

---

[38] Mitchell, *Meeting Mystery*, 38. Italics in original.

[39] Cyprian, *De dominica oratione* 32.

[40] Gary A. Anderson, *Charity: The Place of the Poor in the Biblical Tradition* (New Haven: Yale University Press, 2013), 4. Italics in original. See also 172–73 for an analysis of Cyprian's *Works and Almsgiving*.

oppressed go free, and to break every yoke" (Isa 58:6). "[God] promises that he will be present and says that he hears and protects those *who loosen the knots of unrighteousness from their hearts*, and give alms to the servants of God, and act in accordance with his directions."[41] By acting in accordance with God's justice and showing mercy to God's servants, worshippers show that they utter their prayers not only with their voices, but "with the mind also" (1 Cor 14:15). Their good deeds don't in themselves "merit a hearing from God" so much as they exemplify the integrity of action, internal and external, with which they offer their sacrifices of prayer and praise. Their prayers "ascend quickly to God" because when they pray outwardly, they also inwardly "hear what God demands should be done," and they do it in faith, holding nothing back in their hearts. Such praying with understanding is, for Cyprian, the polar opposite of "sterile," "barren," and "unfruitful" prayer.[42]

## A harmonious and integrated prayer: Origen

Origen of Alexandria, Cyprian's approximate contemporary, also tackles the subject of authentic prayer in a treatise composed in Caesarea sometime between 233 and 234. More than twice as long as either of the North African treatises on prayer, Origen's text seems less likely to have originated in instructions delivered to catechumens.[43] Supporting his points with citations from all over the Scriptures, Origen unfolds the meaning of each petition in the Our Father. But his exegesis of the Lord's Prayer comes with lengthy discourses about how prayer should be performed. Despite the additional sophistication, Origen shares with Tertullian and Cyprian the central conviction that the pure, reasonable, and true sacrifice by which Christians please God is an offering of prayer made with understanding and concord. Like Tertullian and the *Didache*, Origen reminds Christians that Jesus instructed worshippers to seek reconciliation with one another before approaching God's "altar" (Matt 5:23-24).

---

[41] Cyprian, *De dominica oratione* 33. Emphasis added.

[42] Cyprian, *De dominica oratione* 32–33.

[43] See the introduction to Origen's treatise in Stewart-Sykes, *On the Lord's Prayer*, 95–109. See also John Anthony McGuckin, ed., *The Westminster Handbook to Origen* (Louisville, KY: Westminster John Knox, 2004), 38–39.

The command especially applies to a Christian's unbloody offering, Origen argues, "for what greater gift for God from a rational creature can there be than the sending up of fragrant speech in prayer, offered from a conscience devoid of the taint of sin?"[44]

Origen introduces additional precision, however, by identifying the main source of discord that would disrupt the reasonable and harmonious offering of prayer. *Passion* (*pathē*), which Origen associates with failure to exercise rational control over the emotions and desires of the flesh, undermines authentic prayer. Disordered thoughts and emotions upset the harmony of interior and exterior worship. The hypocritical, sterile, or careless prayer of individuals ruptures the concord between members of the praying community and generates more disordered thoughts. Harmony (*symphōnia*) "dissipates the discord of passion."[45] The dispassion (*apatheia*) necessary for true prayer is not an evacuation of emotion and desire from prayer, but rather the harnessing of the internal activity of the mind to the external words, postures, and motions of prayer:

> None might obtain particular things except by praying in this way: with a particular disposition, believing in a certain way, having lived in a certain way prior to prayer. So we are not to babble (Matt 6:7), nor ask after petty things, nor are we to plead for earthly things, nor come to prayer in anger and with our thoughts confused. Without purity it is not possible to consider giving oneself over to prayer, nor is it possible to obtain forgiveness of sins in prayer unless one has forgiven from the heart one's brother who has trespassed and has asked to receive pardon.[46]

Because "the highest of virtues, according to the divine word, is love toward one's neighbor,"[47] the most important thing that Christians must do to obtain the right disposition for prayer is to forgive one another from the heart. Such reconciliation is part of the act of prayer

---

[44] Origen, *Peri euchēs* 2.2, trans. Stewart-Sykes, *On the Lord's Prayer*. Greek words appearing below are supplied from the text on which Stewart-Sykes's translation is based, in *Origenes Werke*, ed. Paul Koetschau, Griechische Christlichen Schriftsteller (Leipzig: J. C. Hinrichs'sche Buchhandlung, 1899), 2.295–403.

[45] Origen, *Peri euchēs* 2.2.

[46] Origen, *Peri euchēs* 8.1.

[47] Origen, *Peri euchēs* 11.2.

itself. It completes the external gesture of piety, making it into a true and holy offering of prayer:

> The one who prays should lift up holy hands by forgiving anyone who has done him wrong, banishing the passion of anger from his soul, bearing antagonism to no one. And, so that his mind is not disturbed by extraneous thoughts, at the time of prayer he should forget everything apart from prayer. Is this not a state of supreme blessedness! So Paul teaches in the first letter to Timothy, when he says: "I desire therefore that men should pray in every place, lifting up holy hands free of anger and dissent" (1 Tim 2:8).[48]

God's commandment to pray is always a command to overcome passion and attain harmony. This is a threefold harmony, encompassing agreement among brothers and sisters, correspondence of interior and exterior activity, and conformity of human desires to the will of God. Altogether, such harmony of minds and voices constitutes praying with *understanding*, and the power of such prayer participates "in the very power of God." The psalmist who says, "Let us exalt his name together" (Ps 34:3), "enjoins us to attain the true and exalted understanding of the particular quality of God with harmony (*symphōnias*), being of one mind and of one knowledge."[49] Such prayer finds its fulfillment in deification (*theōsis*), a participation in the knowledge, love, and power of God. To attain such authentic prayer is to gain everything. "If nothing else should accrue to us in praying, we have nonetheless received the best of gains by praying with understanding of the manner in which we should pray and keeping to this."[50]

On their own, however, humans are powerless to free themselves from passion and offer authentic prayers. "So much is lacking with regard to knowledge of the manner in which we ought to pray," Origen admits, following Paul's observation that "we do not know the manner in which we should pray for things for which we ought to pray." The Holy Spirit must intercede on behalf of those who wish to pray (Rom 8:26-27). Origen closely links Paul's assurance of the

---

[48] Origen, *Peri euchēs* 9.1.
[49] Origen, *Peri euchēs* 24.4.
[50] Origen, *Peri euchēs* 10.1.

Spirit's intercession to the apostle's instruction to pray not in unintelligible tongues, but with the Spirit and mind working together in harmony:

> Akin to the passage concerning what we should pray, "We do not know the manner in which we should pray but the Spirit intercedes with God with unutterable groanings," is "I will pray in the Spirit, and I will pray in the mind also. I will sing out in the Spirit and I will sing out in the mind also" (1 Cor 14:15). For our mind cannot pray unless the Spirit pray first, as it were within earshot, just as it cannot sing out with rhythm and melody and tempo and harmony (*symphōnōs*), hymning the Father in Christ, unless the Spirit which searches all things, even the depths of God, first gives praise and hymns him whose depths he has searched out and, as he is able, comprehended.[51]

In this passage, the musical metaphor for authentic prayer stands out clearly. When Christians "sing out in the Spirit," sound and meaning—voices and minds—come together in harmony. For Origen, this is because the Spirit is both the "breath" that gives outward voice to prayer and the divine person that comes to dwell within the hearts of believers.[52] The association of the Holy Spirit with both the voice of prayer and the mind of God allows Origen to make sense of Paul's claim that "the one who searches out the hearts knows what the *mind of the Spirit* is, because his intercession with God on behalf of the saints is in accordance with God" (Rom 8:27).[53] When Christians pray "within earshot" of the Holy Spirit, the exterior sounds of their worship correspond to the "unutterable groanings" of the Spirit in the depths of their own hearts. Their interior activity—thinking, desiring, willing—is no longer directed by the passions, for "the Spirit prays in the hearts of the saints." The same breath of life, whose mind God

---

[51] Origen, *Peri euchēs* 2.4.

[52] Although Origen argues at length that Christians should pray "only to God the Father of all" (15.1–16.1), he acknowledges the divinity of Christ and of the Holy Spirit, holding that "glory should be ascribed to God according to one's ability, through Christ *who is glorified with him*, and in the Holy Spirit *who is to be hymned with him*" (33.1, emphasis added). For an overview of Origen's pneumatology, see Peter Martens, "Holy Spirit," in McGuckin, *Westminster Handbook to Origen*, 125–28.

[53] Origen, *Peri euchēs* 2.3. Emphasis added.

already knows, also inspires the voice that utters prayer. Origen himself prays for the Spirit's intercession at the beginning of his treatise, for "the discussion of prayer is such a task that the illumination of the Father is needed, as well as the teaching of the firstborn Word and the *inner working of the Spirit*, so that it is possible *to think and to speak* worthily on such a topic."[54] If the inner working of the Holy Spirit is required to speak worthily of prayer, the same inspiration is necessary for worthy prayer itself, in which minds and voices sing out together, "with rhythm and melody and tempo and harmony."

To cooperate with the inner working of the Spirit, one who prays must first abandon "the love of glory as a passion that leads to destruction." For Origen, this explains Christ's instructions about praying "in secret," unobserved by others (Matt 6:5-9). The Savior's commandment concerns the audience of prayer rather than its location. "For it is hypocrisy to desire human admiration for one's piety, rather than to seek communion."[55] The passion of glory-seeking corrupts prayer as surely as the passion of anger or the passion of lust. "Even should an act be considered honorable and praiseworthy, it is corrupted when performed so that we might receive human glory or so that we might be seen by people." This seems to leave Christians in a bind, for how can they avoid being seen by people while praying together in church? And Origen is clear that male Christians, at least, are bound to "appear before the Lord God" by praying "in the churches," fulfilling "the commandment that states: 'Three times each year should every male appear before the Lord God'" (Deut 16:16).[56]

Origen's articulation of the dilemma is remarkable for its application of a theatrical metaphor to prayer. The analogy is inspired by the Synoptic Gospels' word for people who are not what they appear to be, "hypocrites" (*hypokritai*), which is also the generic word for actors in a drama:

---

[54] Origen, *Peri euchēs* 2.5–6. Emphasis added.

[55] Origen, *Peri euchēs* 19.2. Stewart-Sykes follows an emendation made by Anglus in the seventeenth century: "For it is hypocrisy to desire human admiration for one's piety rather than to seek communion *with God*" (emendation in italics). It could be argued, however, that Origen means to contrast not only a *human* audience versus a *divine* audience, but also desiring *admiration* versus desiring *communion* with God and with the (human) saints.

[56] Origen, *Peri euchēs* 19.2.

We should pay careful attention to the term "appear" (*phanōsin*), for nothing that is merely apparent (*phainomenon*) is worthy, since it seems to exist but does not actually do so, deceiving sense-perception (*phantasian planōn*) and not giving a true or accurate representation. For just as actors (*hypokritai*) playing in the theater are not what they say they are, nor is their appearance like that of the character masks which they wear, so all those who put on an outward show (*phantasian*) of goodness to be observed are not righteous, but are acting the part (*hypokritai*) of righteousness, and are acting in a theater of their own, namely the synagogues and the street corners.[57]

While some worshippers may only be "acting the part," Origen does not urge Christians to abandon the churches that have become for the hypocrites like the "synagogues and street corners" that Jesus taught his disciples to shun (Matt 6:2, 5). Instead, the way to "appear" for public prayer without making one's prayer "merely apparent" is to build another kind of "theater" within oneself:

Whoever is not an actor (*hypokritēs*), but has put off all that is alien, who rehearses to make himself pleasing in a theater vastly superior to any that has been mentioned, goes to his own room, where his riches are stored, and locks his treasury of wisdom and knowledge behind him. He does not recognize the outside world, he pays no attention to anything outside, but shuts up every door of the senses, so that the world of the senses should not distract, nor his mind receive any impression from sense-perception, praying to the Father who neither shuns nor deserts such a secret place but dwells there together with the only-begotten one.[58]

Still, in what practical way would a Christian follow Origen's radical advice to shut "every door of the senses" while also fulfilling the command to appear before God in the church's public worship? Origen can hardly recommend literal blockage of the sensory organs, as if distraction and hypocrisy during prayer could be prevented by earplugs and a blindfold. Rather, the intended remedy is spiritual

[57] Origen, *Peri euchēs* 20.2.
[58] Origen, *Peri euchēs* 20.2.

purification of the mind's power of perception and imagination, so it does not focus on the superficially apparent sensory impression (*phainomenon*). Paying no attention to anything outside (*ta exō*) means concentrating instead on the inner essences or principles (*logoi*) that true representations give.[59] In attending to prayer, as in reading the Scriptures, Christians are to "train" themselves to "listen to the spiritual law with spiritual ears," preferring what is "presented by analogy" (*analōgēs*) over the "surface meaning" (*lexin*) of words written on the page or spoken by the voice.[60]

The main component of this training and purification of the mind is persistence in prayer. The Holy Spirit ultimately overcomes passion and hypocrisy, but worshippers must cooperate by making a continuous effort to harmonize their interior and exterior activity. Persistence includes regular participation in spoken prayer, which "should not be performed less than three times each day." Beyond spoken prayer, however, training in authentic worship requires the integration (*synaptōn*) of liturgy and life. "Since works of virtue and the keeping of the commandments have a part in prayer," the worshipper who isn't just acting the part "integrates (*synaptōn*) prayer with good works and noble actions with prayer." Good works don't supplement the exterior words of prayer so much as they reveal the interior disposition with which the words are uttered. The saints integrate prayer with good works "in order that they should not say 'Our Father' half-heartedly." The important thing is that "the heart, which is the font and origin of good works, believes 'for righteousness' alongside their works, and the mouth confesses salvation in harmony with them (Rom 10:10)."[61] The goal is to "pray ceaselessly" (1 Thess 5:17), which is "realistic if we say that the whole life of the saint is one, mighty, integrated (*synaptomenēn*) prayer."[62]

Like Cyprian, Origen describes integral prayer as fruitful prayer. Those who pray ceaselessly don't utter hollow sounds or make empty gestures, for the Holy Spirit fills their prayers with true understand-

---

[59] Stewart-Sykes notes that Origen maintains "the fundamental Platonic division between that which truly is, and is perceived by the mind, and those things that are impermanent and apparent which is the world perceived by the senses." *On the Lord's Prayer*, 157 n. 47.

[60] Origen, *Peri euchēs* 13.4.

[61] Origen, *Peri euchēs* 22.3.

[62] Origen, *Peri euchēs* 12.2.

ing. "The words of the saints are full of power, especially when, in their prayer, they are praying 'in the Spirit and with the understanding' (1 Cor 14:15), by the light, so to speak, which arises from the mind of the one who prays and goes forth from his mouth to dissolve, by the power of God, the spiritual poison which is injected by the enemy powers into the mind of any who neglect prayer."[63]

Despite his emphasis on training the mind away from passion, Origen doesn't advocate replacing exterior prayer with interior prayer. Instead, he cites example after example from the Scriptures in which people of great faith persist in praying outwardly even when God is the only audience who could hear and help them. Hannah, though silent, still moves her lips (1 Sam 1:12-13). Judith speaks a prayer from within the tent of Holofernes (Jdt 13:4-8). Hananiah, Azariah, and Mishael sing praises inside the furnace (Dan 3:24-90). God hears and answers all of these prayers, just as he hears and answers Daniel from within the lions' den and Jonah from inside the whale's belly (Dan 6:22; Jonah 2:1-10). From such evidence, Origen concludes that prayers repeated with the persistence of true faith cannot fail to bear fruit in due season. "Souls that had long been barren have realized the sterility of their own motivation and the barrenness of their own minds, and have become pregnant from the Holy Spirit through constancy in prayer, and have given birth to words of salvation filled with the perception of truth."[64]

## Dispassion and harmony: The Stoics

To attain the *symphōnia* of mind and voice that gives birth to fruit-ful prayer, Origen accords a central role to overcoming the tyranny of passion and aspiring to *apatheia* of the soul. This emphasis brings his thought into close contact with the Stoic philosophical tradition and shows the influence of the latter on Christian spiritual theology. The Stoics built a detailed analysis of the interior life and sought to perfect it by consistently distinguishing external actions and events from internal movements of the emotions, intellect, and will. In Stoic thought, *apatheia* is "the healthy state of the human soul" attained when disordered emotion, or "passion" (*pathē*), is eradicated "through

---

[63] Origen, *Peri euchēs* 12.1–2.
[64] Origen, *Peri euchēs* 13.3.

an educational process that leads to correct judgment and mental attitude toward external reality."[65] While Christian writers greatly modified the definition of *apatheia*, they readily assimilated the Stoic distinction between external and internal movements. These teachers and ascetics were steeped in Scriptures that distinguish lip service from worship of the heart, praying in a tongue from praying with understanding, and things that "go in" from things that "come out."

The potential for biblical exegesis and Stoic philosophy to become intertwined in reflections on moral and spiritual perfection is already evident in the Jewish philosopher Philo of Alexandria. Although there isn't a single, straightforward line of Stoic influence to trace through Christian thought, its presence is unmistakable among the most important authors in the early church. Those with some connection to Origen and the catechetical school of Alexandria include his teacher, Clement, his student, Didymus, his translator, Rufinus, and his fierce opponent, Jerome. Among the Cappadocians, the concept of *apatheia*, filtered through Origen, appears in the writings of Basil (320–79), Gregory of Nyssa (332–95), and Gregory of Nazianzus (329–89). Regarding authentic prayer, however, the most significant Christian interlocutors with Stoicism are Evagrius of Pontus (346–99), John Cassian (c. 360–430), and Augustine of Hippo (354–430).[66] All three wrote texts that would become foundational in Eastern and Western monasticism and leave a lasting mark on Christian theology.

Before examining these Christian theologians, however, we should consider the Stoic tradition of seeking harmony of mind and voice in prayer—an ideal that precedes Stoicism's interaction with Jewish and Christian thought. The Stoic contribution is distinct enough that Winfrid Cramer sets it alongside the biblical tradition in importance. "For the correct interpretation of the sources" of the Rule of Benedict and other monastic rules that call for minds in tune with voices, "one must clearly distinguish two streams of tradition of different origins."[67]

---

[65] Joseph H. Nguyen, *Apatheia in the Christian Tradition: An Ancient Spirituality and Its Contemporary Relevance* (Eugene, OR: Cascade Books, 2018), 1–3.

[66] Richard Sorabji, *Emotion and Peace of Mind: From Stoic Agitation to Christian Temptation* (Oxford: Oxford University Press, 2000), 345–417.

[67] Winfrid Cramer, "*Mens Concordet Voci*: Zum Fortleben Einer Stoischen Gebetsmaxime in Der Regula Benedicti," in *Pietas: Festschrift Für Bernhard Kötting*, ed. Ernst Dassmann and K. Suso Frank, Jahrbuch Für Antike Und Christentum Ergänzungband 8 (Münster: Aschendorff, 1980), 449. My translation.

An important example of the Stoic stream can be seen in Cicero's *On the Nature of the Gods* (45 BCE). In book 2 of the treatise, Cicero sets out the Stoic view of true religion, repudiating the stories of the Greek and Roman gods as "nonsense and absurdity." It still remains "our duty to revere and worship these gods under the names which custom has bestowed on them." Avoidance of superstition is no excuse for failing to worship the gods outwardly, using their traditional names. "But the best and also the purest, holiest and most pious way of worshipping the gods is ever to venerate them with purity, sincerity and innocence both of thought and of speech (*et mente et voce*)."[68] The juxtaposition of mind (*mens*) and voice (*vox*) bears a striking resemblance to the formula in the Rule of Benedict (19), as does the use of the verb *concordare* in a separate Stoic maxim from one of Seneca's letters: "Let us speak what we feel, let us feel what we speak: speech should be in agreement with life (*concordat sermo cum vita*)."[69] While the Stoic doctrine of harmony between interior and exterior action is similar to the biblical tradition in many respects, Cramer argues that it contributes a distinct vocabulary to later Christian formulations of the injunction, including those in the Rule of Benedict and the closely related Rule of the Master.[70]

More important than any possible textual relationship between later Stoic writings and early monastic rules, however, are the concept of *apatheia* and the methods of attaining it. Central to Stoic thought is "the belief that human beings are endowed with reason and intellectual will suitable for a life in pursuit of knowledge and virtue." But the passions obstruct knowledge and virtue, for they are "unnatural movements of the soul caused by ignorance and lack of self-discipline." The goal of training in virtue and reason is "the state of 'spiritual peace,' or the 'well-being' of the human soul wherein excessive and negative emotions, such as lust, excessive desire for food and drink, anger, envy, resentment, self-love, and pride are replaced by reasonable desires, love, and humility." Joseph Nguyen rightly adds that this state is poorly described as "apathy" or "indifference."

[68] Cicero, *De natura deorum* 2.70–71, in *On the Nature of the Gods*, trans. H. Rackham, Loeb Classical Library 268 (London: Heinemann, 1933).

[69] Seneca, *Epistulae morales ad Lucilium* 75.4, trans. in Giles Constable, "The Concern for Sincerity and Understanding in Liturgical Prayer, Especially in the Twelfth Century," in *Classica Et Mediaevalia: Studies in Honor of Joseph Szövérffy*, ed. Helmut Buschhausen and Irene Vaslef (Leyden: Brill, 1986), 17.

[70] Cramer, "*Mens Concordet Voci*," 450–54.

Even "dispassion" is a misleading translation, for "the Stoic *apatheia* really is the state of spiritual joy and the most natural state of the human consciousness."[71] "Purity of heart" (*puritas cordis*)—John Cassian's translation of *apatheia* for the Christian West—resonates with biblical metaphors and comes close to the mark, so long as we do not take "purity" to mean the eradication of sensation, emotion, or desire. Still, even in Stoic thought, *apatheia* is more fullness than emptiness. "Harmony" comes closest to describing *apatheia*, which implies the full agreement of a person's interior and exterior faculties. *Apatheia* as interior and exterior *harmony* is well expressed in the Rule of Benedict (19), which calls not simply for *puritas cordis* but for *concordia*.

## Ascending to true prayer: Evagrius and John Cassian

Since early Christian ascetics believed that human nature had been created by God but wounded by the Fall, they sought *apatheia* not only as the most natural state of the human soul but also as the restoration of creation's order and goodness. Like the Stoics, they undertook training (*askesis*) in self-discipline, reason, and virtue. "Through experimentation on their souls," however, these Christian monks discovered that "*apatheia* is the restoration of purified love"—the restoration of the *agape* that humans are commanded to offer God with all their heart, all their understanding, and all their strength. The powerful but finite human faculties of reasoning, feeling, and desiring are not curses but gifts given by God along with the freedom to use them rightly or wrongly. Turning these faculties from self-love to love of God and neighbor requires dying to oneself, but the result of the monk's self-mortification is a return to the original human vocation of offering God a pure sacrifice, as David Fagerberg writes:

> Our faculties were well made, and they were made good, and should have opened us up to return God's love, as a flower is opened by the sun. . . . Our faculties should operate as God intended them, but if they are displaced from their proper orientation, then they need curing. Curing, or overcoming, or containing, or correcting, or purifying these passions is the aim of *askesis*. It will bring one into a state of "dispassion," which does not mean

[71] Nguyen, *Apatheia in the Christian Tradition*, 1–6.

being listless or disinterested, but standing aright: having our faculties operate in accordance with human nature as God intended human nature to operate.[72]

In systematizing and teaching the ascetical path to Christian *apatheia*, Evagrius of Pontus coins his well-known maxim, "If you are a theologian, you will pray truly; and if you pray truly, you will be a theologian."[73] For Evagrius, "theology" (*theologia*) corresponds to the third and most advanced stage of training in *apatheia* and *agape*, in which the "theologian" enjoys immediate knowledge of God by way of spiritual communion. To reach *theologia*, one must first learn the virtues of the "practical life" (*praktike*) and then those of "natural contemplation" (*physike*), which aims to know the Creator through created things. Prayer is the constant work of the monk, but perfect prayer—pure, authentic, "true" prayer—is only received at the end of this journey of *askesis*. "We pursue the virtues for the sake of the reasons (*logoi*) of created beings, and these we pursue for the sake of the Word (*Logos*) who gave them being, and he usually manifests himself in the state of prayer. The state of prayer is an impassible habit (*hexis apathēs*), which by means of a supreme love carries off to the intelligible height the spiritual mind beloved of wisdom."[74] Prayer is both "the ascent of the mind (*nous*) towards God" and the exalted destination of that ascent. It's the activity for which God created humans, for "prayer is an activity befitting the dignity of the mind, or, indeed, the superior and pure activity and use of the mind."[75]

Evagrius wrote extensively on the practical asceticism needed to combat specific passions and cultivate the opposing virtues. In his

---

[72] David Fagerberg, "A Theologian Is One Who Prays," *Word & World* 35, no. 1 (2015): 59–60. For a thorough examination of the early Christian monastic way of articulating the "malady" of *pathē*, the "cure" of *askesis*, and the "joy" of *apatheia*, see David W. Fagerberg, *On Liturgical Asceticism* (Washington, DC: Catholic University of America Press, 2013).

[73] Evagrius of Pontus, *Peri proseuchēs* 60, in *Evagrius of Pontus: The Greek Ascetic Corpus*, trans. Robert E. Sinkewicz (Oxford: Oxford University Press, 2006), 191–209. All translations are from this edition, and all citations refer to the paragraph numbers contained therein. Greek words, however, have been supplied from Évagre le Pontique, *Chapitres sur la prière*, ed. Paul Géhin, Sources chrétiennes 589 (Paris: Éditions du Cerf, 2017).

[74] Evagrius, *Peri proseuchēs* 51–52.

[75] Evagrius, *Peri proseuchēs* 35, 84.

153 *Chapters on Prayer*, however, he focuses on guiding monks in purifying and perfecting their prayer. The aim of this purification is revealed in the adverbs that accompany the verb "to pray." Most often, Evagrius echoes John 4:23-24 and speaks of praying "truly" (*alēthōs*). He also urges monks to pray "without distraction," "without trouble," "soundly," "with love for the truth," "with purity," and "without passion" (*apathōs*).[76] For Evagrius, only authentic prayer attains the heights of *theologia*, and authentic prayer is only possible when the mind is undivided and undistracted by false appearances that assail the monk from without and rebellious passions that attack from within. Paul Géhin writes, "The way of prayer is long and fraught with difficulties; the obstacles come from exterior and interior disorder and from the hostility of demonic powers. . . . This disorder affects the human being at every level: body, soul, intellect."[77] True prayer requires the restoration of harmony, with the lower faculties subordinated to the higher.

The *Chapters on Prayer* mainly treat the interior parts of the human person: the soul (*psyche*), which is the seat of emotion and desire, and the mind (*nous*), which is the rational intellect and highest faculty of a human. In many places, Evagrius almost seems to urge monks to slough off the bodily senses and leave behind contemplation of creaturely goodness as they progress through "practical" and "natural" *askesis* toward the "theological" stage of "pure prayer." He declares, "Blessed is the mind which becomes immaterial and free from all things during the time of prayer. Blessed is the mind which during the time of prayer has acquired perfect detachment from the senses." Evagrius's whole program for progress in prayer is summarized, Géhin observes, in his advice to "keep your eyes fixed downward during your prayer and, denying the flesh (*sarx*) and the soul (*psyche*), live according to the mind (*nous*)."[78] Such statements support Nguyen's critical conclusion that "Evagrius's prayer method in three stages seems to devalue the created world and the bodily senses."[79]

Still, Evagrius's method is no simple flight from the body, the emotions, and the world of sense perception. While "the main idea

---

[76] Paul Géhin, "Introduction," in Évagre le Pontique, *Chapitres sur la prière*, 20. Géhin lists the adverbs in Greek; the English translations are those of Sinkewicz.

[77] Géhin, "Introduction," 28. My translation.

[78] Evagrius, *Peri proseuchēs* 110. See Géhin, "Introduction," 29.

[79] Nguyen, *Apatheia in the Christian Tradition*, 18.

of the treatise is that prayer principally concerns the superior part of man, that is to say, his intellect, and in a subsidiary way the soul,"[80] the *Chapters on Prayer* show that the body is indispensable to the ascent of the mind. Evagrius adheres to the established wisdom of the desert ascetics who hold that shedding bodily tears is the first essential step toward pure prayer.[81] His opening imperative could never appeal to a Stoic, but only to a Christian: "Pray first to receive tears, so that through compunction (*penthous*) you may be able to mollify the wildness that is in your soul, and, having confessed against yourself your transgression to the Lord, you may obtain forgiveness from him."[82] Although tears are shed outwardly, they quench the unruly passions within—so long as the one pouring forth "fountains of tears" entertains "absolutely no exaltation within" over a gift that other worshippers have not received. That would "turn the remedy for passions into a passion," and, having "forgotten the purpose of tears," the weeping person would summon God's "greater anger" instead of God's forgiveness. Evagrius therefore prescribes not just any tears, but authentic weeping accompanied by the inward act of self-accusation called *penthōs* in the Eastern monastic tradition and *compunctio* in the West.[83]

The relationship between visible tears and invisible compunction is, as John Climacus (ca. 579–ca. 649) later said, "an obscure matter and hard to analyze."[84] Evagrius and his disciple John Cassian reached different conclusions about the ability of the outward act of weeping to soften a heart resistant to the interior act of self-accusation. In approaching compunction from the outside in, both monks saw the

---

[80] Géhin, "Introduction," 29.

[81] See Myrrha Lot-Borodine, "Le Mystère Du 'don Des Larmes' Dans l'Orient Chretien," in *La Douloureuse Joie: Aperçus Sur La Prière Personnelle de l'Orient Chrétien*, ed. Olivier-Maurice Clément, *Spritualité Orientale* 14 (Bégrolles: Abbaye de Bellefontaine, 1974), 131–95; Kallistos Ware, "'An Obscure Matter': The Mystery of Tears in Orthodox Spirituality," in *Holy Tears: Weeping in the Religious Imagination*, ed. Kimberley Christine Patton and John Stratton Hawley (Princeton, NJ: Princeton University Press, 2005), 242–54.

[82] Evagrius, *Peri proseuchēs* 5.

[83] See Irénée Hausherr, *Penthos: The Doctrine of Compunction in the Christian East*, trans. Anselm Hufstader (Kalamazoo, MI: Cistercian Publications, 1982).

[84] John Climacus, *The Ladder of Divine Ascent*, 7, quoted in Ware, "'An Obscure Matter,'" 242.

potential for spiritual growth but also the risk of inauthenticity, as Kallistos Ware explains:

> The early monks were well aware of the difficulties that arise from an exaggerated weeping, artificially induced by willful straining and self-conscious exertion. Tears should not be forced but should flow spontaneously. It is true that Evagrios writes, "At the beginning of prayer force yourself to shed tears and to feel compunction, so that all your prayer may become fruitful." But his disciple St. John Cassian (ca. 360–ca. 435), who in general faithfully follows the teaching of his master, at this point diverges from it. In the case of beginners, Cassian concedes, tears "which are squeezed by a hardened heart from dry eyes" may be "not utterly fruitless"; but in the case of the more experienced "an outpouring of tears should never be forced in this way." Tears "should not be laboriously striven for" but should be "spontaneous."[85]

Still, monks could hardly insist on spontaneous weeping "expressed in an outward and bodily manner" if not all who desire this *charisma* are granted the gift of tears. Summarizing Nilus of Ancyra (ca. 430), Ware writes, "If God does not grant us the grace of outward tears, then we may weep inwardly in our thoughts, and this will suffice to cleanse us from our sins. It is enough truly and sincerely to want to shed tears; this proves that we do indeed feel contrition."[86] In this "obscure matter" of tears, analysis cannot prove that interior weeping always induces exterior weeping or vice versa. But the monastic understanding of tears "has an immediate relevance for the Christian understanding of the human person." Because the authentic charism is always a harmony of interior and exterior weeping, tears "emphasize the integral unity of the human person and show how the body is redeemed and sanctified along with the soul."[87]

---

[85] Ware, "'An Obscure Matter,'" 244. Ware cites Evagrios, *Parainetikos*, ed. W. Frankenberg, Abhandlungen der Königlichen Gesellschaft der Wissenschaften zu Göttingen, Phil.–hist. Klasse, Neue Folge, Bd. XII, 2 (Berlin, 1912), 560; Cassian, *Conferences* 9:30, ed. M. Petschenig, *Corpus Scriptorium Ecclesiasticorum Latinorum* 13 (Vienna: Geroldi, 1886), 276.

[86] Ware, "'An Obscure Matter,'" 246. Ware cites Neilos, *Letters* 3:257 (*PG* 79:512A–513B).

[87] Ware, "'An Obscure Matter,'" 245.

Returning to the *Chapters on Prayer* with this integral understanding of the human person, one finds that Evagrius doesn't devalue the body, its senses, and its outward acts so much as he insists on their integration and harmonization with the soul and the mind. Monks should weep tears, lower their eyes, raise their hands, and "let the virtues of the body serve . . . as the basis for those of the soul, and those of the soul for those of the spirit; and these latter for the attainment of immaterial and substantial knowledge."[88] Use of the body is required to obtain the very detachment from the body that Evagrius frequently counsels. The body is an avenue of attack for demons who come "like wild beasts" upon the monk trying to pray, but the body is also the instrument for cultivating heroic endurance in prayer. Evagrius's emphasis on interior prayer doesn't keep him from handing on the legendary story of the saint who kept his hands raised in prayer while a lion clawed his thighs, the monk who "remained immovably fixed in communion with God" while a demon chewed his flesh, or the abbot who calmly arched his feet over attacking vipers without interrupting the spiritual conference he was giving. More commonly, being "bitten by a flea, a louse, a mosquito or a fly" reveals to a monk whether or not he has "set aside the needs of the body during the practice of prayer."[89] The body itself, however, cannot be set aside. The only way to overcome the flesh as an *obstacle* to prayer is to enlist it as an *aid* to prayer.

The impossibility of leaving the body behind while the mind ascends to pure prayer also implies the unavoidability of corporate prayer. Only once does Evagrius explicitly address prayers said in common, but the passage reveals considerable thought about what can go wrong when monks pray together:

> Watch to see if you have truly (*alēthōs*) stood before God in your prayer, or are overcome by human praise and are motivated to chase after this, using a show of prayer as a cover. Whether you are praying with the brothers or by yourself, struggle to practise prayer not by habit but with perception. Prayer with perception involves the engagement of the mind accompanied by reverence, compunction, and suffering of soul, along with confession of

---

[88] Evagrius, *Peri proseuchēs* 5–8, 78, 109, 132.
[89] Evagrius, *Peri proseuchēs* 105–12.

failings with unspoken groanings. If your mind still wanders at the time of prayer, it has not yet realized that it is a monk who prays, whereas it is still a secular, adorning the outer tent.[90]

The distinction between monk and secular, Géhin notes, does not mean that perfect prayer is attainable only by monks. The essential thing is the "interiorization of the monastic state," which is neither automatic for monks nor impossible for secular Christians.[91] Elsewhere, Evagrius warns that it is not enough to be a "monastic man" who avoids sin in outward deeds alone; one hopes to stand before God as a "monastic intellect . . . who has departed from the sin that arises from the thoughts that are in our intellect and who at the time of prayer sees the light of the Holy Trinity."[92] This interiorization of prayer cannot happen while a monk or a secular Christian remains preoccupied with external activity—"adorning the outer tent" (cf. 2 Cor 5:1-4) but not engaging the mind.

In the passage above, Evagrius warns of two ways the mind can wander while the body goes through the motions of public prayer. On the one hand, participation in prayer can become a mere "show"— an exterior "cover" for honor-seeking. This inauthenticity happens when worshippers mistake their true audience. Forgetting that they are standing before the Father "who sees in secret," they pray "so that they may be seen by others" (see Matt 6:5-6). On the other hand, the external ritual can become an empty routine, performed by force of "habit" alone. Habitual prayer can be just as inauthentic and forgetful of God as ostentatious prayer is. The force of this "habit" (*ethos*) differs greatly from the "impassible habit" (*hexis apathēs*) that Evagrius identifies as the "state of prayer" itself.[93] True, both *hexis* and *ethos* can be translated as "habit" in the very basic sense of something that a person "has" internally.[94] But *hexis* denotes an *active* state in which

<hr/>

[90] Evagrius, *Peri proseuchēs* 40–43.

[91] Évagre le Pontique, *Chapitres sur la prière*, 257 n. 44. My translation.

[92] Evagrius, *Antirrheticus*, Prologue, trans. in *Talking Back: A Monastic Handbook for Combating Demons*, trans. David Brakke, Cistercian Studies Series 229 (Collegeville, MN: Liturgical Press, 2009), 58.

[93] Evagrius, *Peri proseuchēs* 52.

[94] Because it is derived from the verb *echein* ("to have"), *hexis* is more accurately translated as "having" than is *ethos*, which is derived from the verb *ethein* ("to be accustomed"). This is reflected in the Latin word *habitus*, which translates *hexis* but not *ethos*. Augustine and Aquinas both begin discussions of habit with the observation

the higher, rational movements of the mind regulate all other movements of the soul and body. Far from being a passive or indifferent "habit," the *hexis apathēs* is our way of doing things when freed from the tyranny of the passions to act authentically. *Ethos*, by contrast, is better described as doing things in the way we have become accustomed to doing them through repetition.

Habituation through repetition is essential, nonetheless, to Evagrius's method of ascending to *apatheia*. Sinners accustomed to acting out of passion must first render themselves receptive to a different way of doing things by repeatedly doing different things. Before they can engage their minds rightly in prayer, they must disengage their outward deeds from the disordered thoughts enslaving them. The outward rituals of corporate prayer, faithfully practiced, can aid this pacification and liberation of the soul. But Evagrius saw as clearly as any modern observer that common prayer can also become a merely external routine—a "habit" in the sense usually meant by contemporary speakers of English. To avoid leaving an opening for the passions to reassert their dominion after monks have become accustomed to the routines of corporate prayer, there must be an ongoing "struggle to practice prayer not by habit (*ethos*) but with perception." One must "pay attention with mindfulness" while praying, heedless of distracting sensory impressions left by the world outside, but in no way ignorant of the created world itself.[95]

Above all, the monk in search of pure prayer must pay mindful attention to fellow monks, even while remaining insensitive to human praise and honor. "If He who wants for nothing and remains impartial did not receive the man who approached the altar with his gift until he had been reconciled with the neighbor who held a grievance against him (Matt 5:23-24), consider how great a watchfulness and discernment is required for us to offer at the intelligible altar incense acceptable to God."[96] The search for prayer, though it proceeds by way of *apatheia*, does not lead away from the neighbor, but to the neighbor with discernment and loving attention. In this crucial point, Evagrius's understanding of authentic prayer is in harmony with the other Christian theologians we've encountered so far.

---

that the noun *habitus* is derived from the verb *habere* ("to have"). See ST I-II, q. 49 a. 1; Augustine, *De diversis quaestionibus LXXXIII*, 73.1.

[95] Evagrius, *Peri proseuchēs* 41, 137.

[96] Evagrius, *Peri proseuchēs* 147.

## "The highest harmony": Augustine

Augustine, though formed in Latin philosophical and rhetorical traditions, was influenced by Stoic thought in ways similar to Origen, Evagrius, and other theologians of the Greek-speaking East. The most distinctive feature of Augustine's mystical theology, however, is also the most relevant to the question of authentic prayer. Andrew Louth identifies this characteristic precisely: "The most immediately obvious contrast between Augustine and the Greek Fathers is one of *feeling*. . . . His *Confessions* are unparalleled in the ancient world for introspective self-scrutiny. A whole new dimension is opened up of introversion and a searching, psychological self-probing." This "very seductive" feature of Augustine's thought deeply influenced Western theology and spirituality,[97] so that interior emotion would eventually come to play an outsized role in modern articulations of authentic prayer. A modern reader of Origen, Evagrius, or Cassian could be forgiven for misunderstanding their pursuit of *apatheia* as a struggle to eradicate emotion from prayer. Augustine's pursuit of a heart that rests in God could never be mistaken for a fight against feeling.

Augustine's approach to God is more and different, however, than an affirmation of emotion and desire. Like the Stoics, he seeks freedom from the passions, and like his Christian predecessors, he hopes to transform self-love into love of God. But where Evagrius aims at knowledge of God by contemplating the essences of things *outside* himself, Augustine hopes to reach the heights of *theologia* by a journey *inward* toward a deeper understanding of himself. Ultimately, these two paths must lead to the same place, since the creator of the universe is also the creator of the human soul. Even so, it is difficult to overestimate the significance of the shift that Augustine introduces into the act of knowing. According to Charles Taylor, "It is hardly an exaggeration to say that it was Augustine who introduced the inwardness of radical reflexivity and bequeathed it to the Western tradition of thought." By "radical reflexivity" Taylor means "adopting the first-person standpoint" in which we "become aware of our awareness, try to experience our experiencing, focus on the way the world

---

[97] Andrew Louth, *The Origins of the Christian Mystical Tradition from Plato to Denys* (Oxford: Oxford University Press, 1981), 133.

is *for* us."[98] While this sounds solipsistic to modern ears, for Augustine, "the inner true self is not yet the bounded, self-encapsulated self of modernity." Augustine learns through self-examination that the world is radically *for him* only because he is radically *for God.* "That this is so," Charles Guignon writes, "is evident from the opening words of the *Confessions,* where Augustine says to God, 'You have made us toward You' (the expression is equally odd in Latin: *fecisti nos ad te*), where this suggests that the self in its very being is initially, essentially and inextricably bound to God."[99] Augustine does not prize interiority for its own sake, but for harmony, both individual and corporate, with the will of God. The way of introspection carries Augustine beyond himself, first to the community of knowers and finally to the God by whom all things are known. In this way, what began as self-reflection leads to worship.[100]

"Do not go outward; return within yourself. In the inward man dwells truth." This famous line from *On True Religion* can stand for many similar injunctions found throughout Augustine's works, says Taylor.[101] Yet this introspection doesn't withhold love from oneself or from one's neighbor. The opposite is true, for the human soul exceeds all other creatures in its capacity to bear the image of the undivided triune God. Looking inward, Augustine perceives that he is most truly himself when his memory, intelligence, and will (*memoria, intelligentia, et voluntas*) act in harmony with one another, for then his mind, knowledge, and love (*mens, notitia, et amor*) form an integrated whole. "Man shows himself most clearly as the image of God in his inner self-presence and self-love. It is a kind of knowledge where knower and known are one, coupled with love, which reflects most fully God in our lives. And indeed, the image of the Trinity in us is the process whereby we strive to complete and perfect this self-presence and self-affirmation."[102] This introspective process of perfecting (not eliminating) self-love is therefore identical with perfecting prayer.

[98] Charles Taylor, *Sources of the Self: The Making of the Modern Identity* (Cambridge, MA: Harvard University Press, 1989), 130–31. Emphasis in original.

[99] Charles B. Guignon, *On Being Authentic* (London: Routledge, 2004), 15.

[100] Taylor, *Sources of the Self,* 134.

[101] Augustine, *De vera religione,* 39.72, quoted in Taylor, *Sources of the Self,* 129.

[102] Taylor, *Sources of the Self,* 136–37.

There remains the danger that the human soul will only become more closed in on itself in its inward pursuit of self-knowledge and self-love. Ideally, the introspective soul finds that the innermost self is the dwelling place of the most other, the God who is the light of true knowledge and the source of authentic love. But the journey inward and upward can be halted well short of its goal if reflection does not remain open to the indwelling of God in creatures other than oneself. Since what dwells *in interiore homine* is the "truth" that can be no one's exclusive possession, it is impossible to fully possess oneself without having communion with all who possess the truth. "For what you gain from that communion does not become your own private property; it remains intact for me. When you breathe it in, I need not wait for you to give it back so that I can breathe it too. No part of it ever becomes the private property of any one person; it is always wholly present to everyone."[103] Everyone chosen by God partakes of truth, and truth is not depleted.

Augustine compares communion in the truth to a word "heard simultaneously and in its entirety by everyone who hears it" or a form "seen equally by every eye that sees it." External things seen or heard by all "bear only a very distant resemblance to the truth,"[104] yet the similarity helps explain why corporate prayer plays an essential role in preventing the collapse of self-knowledge into narcissism. Communal prayer is not only analogous to communal truth; it is its effective external sign. Augustine thinks of liturgical prayer in a deeply sacramental way that has a lasting and decisive influence on Western theology. For although the truth dwells within, it is most clearly manifest not when it is individually grasped, but when it is communally offered. Therefore, when Augustine speaks of offering a "true sacrifice" of prayer and praise, he emphasizes the unity of Christians in the Body of Christ:

> The true sacrifice, then, is every act done in order that we might cling to God in holy fellowship. . . . Therefore, since true sacrifices are works of mercy, whether shown to ourselves or shown to our neighbors, which are directed to God; and since works of mercy are performed with no other object than that we might be

[103] Augustine, *De libero arbitrio*, 2.14.37, in *On Free Choice of the Will*, trans. Thomas Williams (Indianapolis, IN: Hackett, 1993), 57.

[104] Augustine, *De libero arbitrio*, 2.14.37.

delivered from misery and so become blessed . . . it obviously
follows that the whole redeemed city, that is, the congregation
and fellowship of the saints is offered to God as a universal
sacrifice through the great priest who, in his passion, offered
himself for us in the form of a servant, to the end that we might
be the body of such a great head. . . . This is the sacrifice of
Christians: *although many, one body in Christ* (Rom 12:5). And this
is the sacrifice that the Church continually celebrates in the sacrament of the altar (which is well known to the faithful), where it
is made plain to her that, in the offering she makes, she herself
is offered.[105]

Like the sacrifices offered by the patriarchs of Israel, the eucharistic
sacrifice of Christians "is the visible sacrament of an invisible sacrifice."[106] It is "where it is made plain" to the church that all the members of Christ's body participate in his act of authentic worship,
inwardly in communion of love and outwardly in celebration of the
liturgy. Crucially, however, the members must make their participation in the visible sacrament "true" if it is to deliver them from misery
and into blessedness. Augustine's famous sermon to newly baptized
Christians at Pentecost is therefore much more than a clarification of
eucharistic doctrine. It is an instruction in how to participate in the
sacrament authentically, with "understanding":

The reason these things, brothers and sisters, are called sacraments is that in them one thing is seen, another is to be understood. What can be seen has a bodily appearance, what is to be
understood provides spiritual fruit. So if you want to understand
the body of Christ, listen to the apostle telling the faithful, *You,
though, are the body of Christ and its members* (1 Cor 12:27). So if
it's you that are the body of Christ and its members, it's the
mystery meaning you that has been placed on the Lord's table;
what you receive is the mystery that means you. It is to what
you are that you reply *Amen*, and by so replying you express
your assent. What you hear, you see, is *The body of Christ*, and
you answer, *Amen*. So be a member of the body of Christ, in order
to make that *Amen* true.

---

[105] Augustine, *De civitate Dei*, 10.6, trans. William Babcock, The Works of Saint
Augustine, pt. 1, vol. 6 (Hyde Park, NY: New City Press, 2012), 310–12.
[106] Augustine, *De civitate Dei* 10.5.

Making their *Amen* true, Augustine goes on to say, requires the baptized to "understand and rejoice" at what they are becoming, "as though what holy scripture says about the faithful were happening: *They had one soul and one heart in God* (Acts 4:32)."[107] They are becoming what they receive: the *totus Christus* in which all his members are united with their head in love.[108] That "mystery meaning you" must be received with full interior agreement and exterior thanksgiving:

> That too is how the Lord Christ signified us, how he wished us to belong to him, how he consecrated the sacrament of our peace and unity on his table. Any who receive the sacrament of unity, and do not hold the bond of peace, do not receive the sacrament for their benefit, but a testimony against themselves.
>
> Turning to the Lord, God the Father almighty, with pure hearts let us give him sincere and abundant thanks, as much as we can in our littleness; beseeching him in his singular kindness with our whole soul, graciously to hearken to our prayers in his good pleasure; also by his power to drive out the enemy from our actions and thoughts, to increase our faith, to guide our minds, to grant us spiritual thoughts, and to lead us finally to his bliss; through Jesus Christ his Son. Amen.[109]

The duty to preserve the "bond of peace" between Christians applies during the celebration of the liturgy. In corporate worship, inwardly holding to unity requires accommodating oneself outwardly to different ways of praying. Augustine describes the Eucharist as the most communal of all acts of worship, but for that reason it embraces the widest range of individual piety: "That sacrament by which the world is conquered has a different taste in the heart of each Christian. For one person does not dare to receive every day out of respect, and another does not dare to skip any day out of respect. This food only refuses to tolerate contempt."[110] Augustine's view is that the *members* of Christ's body can hardly be less tolerant than the body

---

[107] Augustine, *Sermo* 272, trans. Edmund Hill, The Works of Saint Augustine, pt. 3, vol. 7 (Hyde Park, NY: New City Press, 1993), 300–301.

[108] See Kimberly F. Baker, "Augustine's Doctrine of the *Totus Christus*: Reflecting on the Church as Sacrament of Unity," *Horizons* 37, no. 1 (March 2010): 7–24.

[109] Augustine, *Sermo* 272.

[110] Augustine, *Epistula* 54.4, trans. Roland Teske, The Works of Saint Augustine, pt. 2, vol. 1 (Hyde Park, NY: New City Press, 2001), 212.

itself, which they receive as sacramental food and become by un-merited grace. "Our Lord Jesus Christ, as he himself says in the gospel, has made us subject to his gentle yoke and light burden. For this reason he bound together the society of the new people by sacraments very few in number, very easy in their observance, and most excellent in what they signify." Because Christian worship is corporate and sacramental, exterior elements of the liturgy that are "neither contrary to the faith nor contrary to good morals should be regarded as indifferent and should be observed in accord with the society of those with whom one is living."[111] Authenticity in corporate worship requires seeing, hearing, and responding to the other members of the body so that the whole church may worship with one accord.

The introspection so characteristic of Augustine's thought is never an end in itself, but always a means to greater harmony. His call to "return within" is joined to a deeply communitarian vision, rooted in the doctrine of the *totus Christus* and the model of the nascent church. Acts 4:32 is cited frequently in the monastic rule attributed to Augustine, forming "the basis for his monastic theology."[112] The *Praeceptum*, often known as the *Rule for Men*, opens with it: "In the first place—and this is the very reason for your being gathered together in one—you should live in the *house in unity of spirit* (Ps 67:7 [68:6]) and you should have *one soul and one heart* (Acts 4:32) centered on God."[113] Such mutuality joined to individual flexibility would cause Augustine to be "regarded in the middle ages in Western Europe as a monastic legislator second only to Benedict of Nursia," according to Gerald Bonner. Although some or all of the documents described as Augustine's "Rule" might be the work of other authors in his circle, the "emphasis on mutual sharing within the community" is "convincingly Augustinian" and constitutes the heart of Augustine's monastic teaching. "Augustine sums up his teaching about life in community in section 1.8 [of the *Praeceptum*]: 'Therefore you should all live *united in mind and heart* (Acts 4:32) and should in one another

---

[111] Augustine, *Epistula* 54.1–2.

[112] Gerald Bonner, "The Spirit of the Rule," in Augustine, *The Monastic Rules*, trans. Agatha Mary and Gerald Bonner (Hyde Park, NY: New City Press, 2004), 64.

[113] Augustine, *Praeceptum* 1.2, trans. in Augustine, *The Monastic Rules*, trans. Agatha Mary and Gerald Bonner (Hyde Park, NY: New City Press, 2004), 110.

honor God (Rom 15:6), whose temples you have become (2 Cor 6:16).' "[114]

Growing in mutual love so that the monks can honor God in one another "is—or should be—a progress, and a continuing one."[115] Harmony of minds and hearts is not preestablished in a monastery any more than it is in any other assembly of Christians. Progress toward "unity of spirit" requires coming together in external activity, above all in prayer. The monks must *persevere faithfully in prayers* (Col 4:2) at the appointed hours and times." Augustine says very little about the contents of the daily Office—only the barest outline for psalmody in the *Ordo Monasterii* and nothing in the *Praeceptum*. But he offers firm instruction in the right manner of saying and singing the appointed prayers: "When you pray to God in *psalms and hymns* (Col 3:16), meditate in the heart on what is expressed with the voice."[116] Besides anticipating the formula of Benedict's Rule (19), the injunction shows how strongly Augustine associates harmony *between* worshippers with the integrity of *each* individual's offering of interior and exterior prayer.

Beyond the monastic rules attributed to Augustine, many other works undoubtedly written by him link social harmony to purity of heart—*concordia* with the *cor unum*. Analyzing dozens of passages that cite parts of Acts 4:32-35, Luc Verheijen finds that Augustine probably noticed the individual meaning of having "one soul and one heart" before the communal meaning.[117] In one sermon, Augustine contrasts the single-heartedness of the first Christians with the duplicity described in Psalm 11 [12]: "They utter lies to each other; with flattering lips and a double heart they speak."[118] A letter from Paulinus of Nola might have directed Augustine's attention to the collective sense in which "the whole group of those who believed" actually *shared* one heart among themselves.[119] In any case, Augustine's understanding of the whole church at peace is not limited to

---

[114] Bonner, "The Spirit of the Rule," 63.

[115] Bonner, "The Spirit of the Rule," 63.

[116] Augustine, *Praeceptum* 2.1, 2.3.

[117] Luc Verheijen, *Saint Augustine's Monasticism in the Light of Acts 4.32–35* (Villanova, PA: Villanova University Press, 1979), 6–16.

[118] See Augustine, *Sermo Denis* 11.7 [*Sermon* 308/A].

[119] The letter from Paulinus is preserved in the correspondence of Augustine as *Epistula* 30. See *Epistula* 30.3 for Paulinus's reference to Acts 4:32.

individual sincerity or even to social harmony. His idea of harmony is a vision of eschatological worship:

> In the monastery and out, one must be part of the one soul of the Church which is called to the peace and unity of the heavenly City. When Saint Augustine quotes Acts 4.32a ("The whole group of believers had but one soul and one heart . . .") generally he adds "tending to God," *in deum*. Saint Augustine's spirituality is a synthesizing, theocentric, Christogonic dynamism, ascending to the heavenly and eternal life of the "total Christ." Bede has conserved an unfortunately very brief fragment, where Saint Augustine gives, instead of the usual *in deum*, the following interesting variation: *in laudes dei* [in praise of God], a fine precision, which stresses the eschatological character of Saint Augustine's ideal.[120]

The same eschatological goal of joining the *totus Christus* to offer perfect worship *in laudes Dei* underlies Augustine's characteristic emphasis on participating in corporate prayer with integrity and sincerity. In a sermon in which he again counsels his listeners to "return inwards," Augustine stirs up their desire to offer authentic worship by imagining the heavenly liturgy in which discord no longer troubles either the individual or the community. A foretaste of that authentic liturgy may be had here and now, Augustine says, if we harmonize our voices and our hearts until perfect charity governs both the words of our worship and the ways of our conscience:

> Since it has pleased the Lord our God that we, here present with you in person, and one with you in charity, should sing the Alleluia, which in Latin means, "Praise the Lord"—then let us give praise to the Lord, brethren, by our lives and by our speech (*vita et lingua*), by our hearts and by our voices (*corde et ore*), by our words and by our ways (*vocibus et moribus*). For the Lord wants us to sing Alleluia to him in such a way that there may be no discord (*discordia*) [lit., doubleness of heart] in him who gives praise. First, therefore, let our speech agree with our lives, our voice with our conscience (*Concordent ergo prius in nobis ipsis*

---

[120] Verheijen, *Saint Augustine's Monasticism*, 93. The fragment preserved by Bede is found in *Quaest. Ev. Apud Bedam* Lc. 4 (*Corpus Christianorum* 120, p. 293, lines 2494–95).

*lingua cum vita, os cum conscientia*). Let our words, I say, agree with our ways, lest fair words bear witness against false ways. O happy Alleluia on high, where the Angels are the temple of God! For the highest harmony (*concordia*) of those giving praise will be found there on high where the joy of those who sing is beyond troubling, where no law in the members struggles against the law of the mind, where no struggle of desire imperils the victory of charity.[121]

As in so many other matters, Augustine's teaching on authentic prayer represents a synthesis of the early church's thought. This doctrine has three interrelated components: (1) harmony of interior and exterior prayer, leading to (2) concord between members of the church and (3) conversion of self-love into love of God and neighbor. The first element of this triad is typically described as *apatheia* or *puritas cordis* by early Christians who write mainly under the influence of Scripture, but also of Stoic philosophy. Both terms appear to name an absence: an interior emptiness that remains after passions, disordered thoughts, and fleshly desires have been driven out. But emptiness leads to fullness of harmony, so that "there may be no discord" in the individual Christian and no discord in the body of Christ. Authentic prayer and authentic worship aspire to this "highest harmony" because "the Lord wants us to sing to him in such a way." Cooperation in harmony is the authentically liturgical "way of doing things."

---

[121] Augustine, *Sermo* 256, quoted in Erich Auerbach, *Literary Language and Its Public in Late Latin Antiquity and in the Middle Ages* (New York: Pantheon, 1965), 28–29.

*Chapter Four*

# The Authentic Performance of Prayer

By the time St. Benedict wrote down his monastic Rule, sometime around the middle of the sixth century, "a fear of hypocrisy and misunderstanding in worship, and a corresponding desire for sincerity and accuracy, were deeply rooted in Christian thought and tradition."[1] The desire for authentic liturgy and the fear of inauthentic performance were also *widely* rooted in different sources of the Christian tradition, including the Hebrew Bible and the New Testament, the writings of Christian apologists, bishops, and monks, and even the philosophy of the Stoics. Despite their diversity, these sources use a typical set of metaphors, often drawn from the human body, and they consistently presume a distinction between interior and exterior acts. Most significantly, the various early sources of Christian thought about liturgical authenticity all share the ideal of *harmony* between interior and exterior prayer. Both the fear of hypocrisy and the desire for authenticity "were often expressed as a dichotomy or a search for harmony between two associated aspects of the act of worship or prayer, one internal, such as the soul, spirit, heart, mind, thought, meaning, or sense, and the other external, such as the voice, tongue, lips, breath, words, or sound."[2]

How did this search for harmony between interior and exterior prayer evolve into modern ideas about authenticity? And if harmony

---

[1] Giles Constable, "The Concern for Sincerity and Understanding in Liturgical Prayer, Especially in the Twelfth Century," in *Classica Et Mediaevalia: Studies in Honor of Joseph Szövérffy*, ed. Helmut Buschhausen and Irene Vaslef (Leyden: Brill, 1986), 17.

[2] Constable, "Concern for Sincerity," 17.

of mind and voice is oriented toward unity among the members of the worshipping body, how could the quest for authentic liturgy become so divisive? How can many contemporary Christians reject *all* liturgical ritual as "not authentic for me" even as others claim that the authenticity of liturgy has nothing to do with whether its participants enjoy or understand what they are doing? I argue that present disagreements about the authentic performance of liturgical prayer reflect the gradual mutation of a gospel virtue. Performative authenticity is rightly and perennially lauded as "Christian sincerity," "purity of heart," or "minds in tune with voices." Since early modernity, however, "sincerity" and "authenticity" have often stood for ideals that presume the inauthenticity of collective ritual and look to the inward self as the sole source of authentic action.

Most studies of modern authenticity view the ideal as "the child of the Romantic period" and trace its more remote origins to the "crisis" of Western civilization in the sixteenth century.[3] In this chapter, however, I take a longer view to focus on the relationship between interior and exterior activity in the performance of prayer. In prayer, the ideal of authenticity articulated in the Rule of Benedict as a *harmony* of interior and exterior participation gradually metamorphoses into an ideal of *inwardness* or *interior feeling*. The desire to closely scrutinize the interior aspect of prayer was already present before the Middle Ages, as the case of Augustine shows. Benedict and other monastic founders continued to recommend inwardness as a way to promote harmony between the individual's mind and voice and concord between members of the community. Regrettably, confidence in this alliance between individual devotion and ecclesial unity gradually waned during the Middle Ages. Starting in early modernity, it became possible and eventually commonplace to think of outward conformity to the rituals of the church and interior conformity to Christ as separate and potentially competing concerns.

## "Incline the ear of your heart"

"As everyone knows," writes Nathan Mitchell, "the Benedictine Rule's first word is a cry for attention: Listen! It is significant, more-

---

[3] Brian J. Braman, *Meaning and Authenticity: Bernard Lonergan and Charles Taylor on the Drama of Authentic Human Existence* (Toronto; Buffalo: University of Toronto Press, 2008), 4; Charles B. Guignon, *On Being Authentic* (London: Routledge, 2004), 27.

over, that the Latin word for hearing and listening—*audire*—occurs no less than twenty-three times in RB."[4] An amalgamation of Proverbs 4:1 and 4:4 supplies the Rule's opening line. Benedict calls for filial attention that hears words spoken outwardly and treasures the words inwardly, repeating them often so they are not forgotten. "Listen, O my son, to the teachings of your master, and turn to them with the ear of your heart" (RB Prol. 1). It has often been said that the Rule's first line "serves as a synopsis or précis of monasticism."[5] The exhortation also concisely summarizes the disposition required for authentic liturgy, vividly evoking harmony of interior and exterior participation through a wonderfully mixed metaphor: "Incline the *ear* of your *heart*." This beginning characterizes the whole Rule in that "*the hearing heart* is what makes us most human, most Christian, most prayerful, most 'liturgical.' "[6]

The first thing to understand about the Rule of Benedict is that the entire rule is oriented toward liturgical living. The sections regulating manual labor, holy reading, shared meals, and relations among members of the community are no less liturgical than the sections ordering the singing of psalms and the praying of the daily Office. Although the Rule refers specifically to the Liturgy of the Hours as the "*opus Dei*," the "best description" of what it means by this term is much broader, says Mitchell, because the Benedictine is "devoted to listening and living *inside* those poems we call the psalms."[7] If, as Origen says, "the whole life of the saint is one, mighty, integrated prayer,"[8] then the poetic words sung aloud at fixed hours must be heard and repeated inwardly during the prosaic activities of the day. "The liturgical Work of God means, above all, letting God's Word and Wisdom speak in us, letting the Unsayable utter itself in our waking hearts as we sing the canticle of creation."[9]

For Benedict, as for Augustine, true prayer requires returning within ourselves. Inwardness teaches us that our thoughts, words,

---

[4] Nathan Mitchell, "Liturgy and Life: Lessons in Benedict," *Worship* 82, no. 2 (March 2008): 163.

[5] Anne M. Carpenter, " 'Incline the Ear of Your Heart,' " *Questions Liturgiques* 95, no. 3 (2014): 162.

[6] Mitchell, "Liturgy and Life," 163. Italics in original.

[7] Mitchell, "Liturgy and Life," 165. Italics in original.

[8] Origen, *Peri euchēs* 12.2, in Tertullian, Cyprian, and Origen, *On the Lord's Prayer*, trans. Alistair Stewart-Sykes (Crestwood, NY: St. Vladimir's Seminary Press, 2004).

[9] Mitchell, "Liturgy and Life," 165.

and deeds are most authentically our own when they originate from the God beyond ourselves. The Rule's emphasis on listening, therefore, isn't meant to shut lips but to open the ears and loose the tongue of the heart. Inwardly echoing what comes to us from participation in exterior prayer, we perceive that what resounds innermost are the words that come from the Word who is most other. The liturgical act is "rooted in our capacity to hear an other precisely as other and not simply as an echo of our own thoughts, wishes, and fantasies."[10] The monk's interiorization of prayer is therefore a movement toward community, not away from it. Singing the psalms together and praying in common develops this capacity for authentic inwardness tied to authentic community.

Common prayer, however, also gives occasion to the temptation to be admired by others, and pride presents the greatest obstacle to turning from self-love to love of God and neighbor. Benedict follows the same approach to this danger that Jesus takes in Matthew's gospel and that Cyprian follows in his catechesis on prayer.[11] He emphasizes that the audience for prayer is not one's fellow monks, but God. Chapter 19 of the Rule of Benedict, "on the discipline of psalmody," therefore reads in full:

> We believe that the divine presence is everywhere and *that in every place the eyes of the Lord are watching the good and the wicked* (Prov 15:3). But beyond the least doubt we should believe this to be especially true when we celebrate the divine office.
>
> We must always remember, therefore, what the Prophet says: *Serve the Lord with fear* (Ps 2:11), and again, *Sing praise wisely* (Ps 46[47]:8); and, *In the presence of the angels I will sing to you* (Ps 137[138]:1). Let us consider, then, how we ought to behave in the presence of God and his angels, and let us stand to sing the psalms in such a way that our minds are in harmony with our voices.[12]

---

[10] Mitchell, "Liturgy and Life," 164.

[11] See Matt 6:6; Cyprian, *De dominica oratione*, 4.

[12] In his translation and commentary on the Rule, Terrence Kardong points out that "RB 19 is not restricted to either psalms or singing, but the whole comportment of the participants in the Divine Office." He also more literally translates *mens nostra* as "our mind" and *voci nostrae* as "our voice." Terrence G. Kardong, *Benedict's Rule: A Translation and Commentary* (Collegeville, MN: Liturgical Press, 1996), 203–4.

Terrence Kardong describes chapter 19 of the Rule of Benedict as a "condensed version" of chapter 47 of the Rule of the Master (RM), a roughly contemporaneous but much longer monastic rule that was one of Benedict's most important sources.[13] Chapter 47 of the Rule of the Master "contains some disgusting material" regulating spitting and nose-picking during prayer,[14] but it also cites additional biblical and patristic precedents for bringing minds and voices into tune. These include Isaiah's critique of lip service (29:13), which the Rule of the Master interprets as a warning against inattention. "When we praise God with the tongue alone, we admit God only to the doorway of our mouth while we bring in and lodge the devil in the dwelling of our heart." The Master also casts Paul's instruction regarding glossolalia as a general teaching about harmony of mind and voice. "Let him who resounds in the voice also be in the mind of the singer. Let us therefore sing with voice and mind in unison; as the apostle says: 'I will sing with the spirit, but I will sing with the understanding also' (1 Cor 14:15). We must cry out to God not only with our voices, but with our hearts as well." For the Master, praying the psalms with understanding requires the singer to "pay attention to each and every verse he says." Chapter 19 of the Rule of Benedict doesn't include this instruction, and Kardong doubts that Benedict is asking for such strict attention.

What, then, is the "discipline" or "proper manner" of singing the psalms that Benedict is looking for?[15] What is the liturgical way of

---

[13] Kardong, *Benedict's Rule*, 204. On the relationship between the Rule of Benedict and the Rule of the Master, see Georg Holzherr, *The Rule of Benedict: An Invitation to the Christian Life*, trans. Mark Thamert, Cistercian Studies Series 256 (Collegeville, MN: Liturgical Press, 2016), xli–xliii. The following translations of chapter 47 of the Rule of the Master are from Adalbert de Vogüé, ed., *The Rule of the Master*, trans. Luke Eberle (Kalamazoo, MI: Cistercian Publications, 1977), 205–7.

[14] Kardong, *Benedict's Rule*, 204.

[15] Kardong notes that *disciplina* "appears frequently in RB, but usually in reference to punishments. Although it normally pertains to external behavior, the content of RB 19 makes it clear that here it refers to both external conduct and internal attitude." Kardong, *Benedict's Rule*, 204. Holzherr agrees that "the issue is not only the recitation of psalms in the narrow sense but also one's entire body-and-soul behavior when at prayer." Holzherr, *The Rule of Benedict*, 219. And Anselmo Lentini points out that chapters 8–18 establish the "body" of the Office, while chapter 19 of Benedict's Rule deals with its "soul." Anselmo Lentini, *San Benedetto: La Regola*, 2nd ed. (Monte Cassino, 1980).

doing things that allows the monks to "sing praise wisely" in the sight of God and the angels? The required attitude is not simply attentiveness, but *concordia*—harmony. Chapter 19 of the Rule of Benedict states the requirement adverbially: the monks are to pray "in such a way" that the mind harmonizes with the voice (*mens concordet voci*). As Viktor Warnach explains, Benedict treats *concordia* as both the beginning of authentic prayer and its aspirational goal. The verb *concordare* denotes more than mere agreement or compatibility; it means "becoming one heart together." So, "when St. Benedict connects *mens* and *vox* with the verb *concordare*, he wants to say that the spirit and voice should grow together in prayer into a living unity."[16]

If this all-encompassing *concordia* is the goal of the individual monk, it's also the goal of the whole monastic community that prays the psalms together. Benedict suggests this communal meaning of harmony by mixing plural possessives with singular nouns; the last line of the Rule of Benedict, chapter 19, urges us to sing in such a way that "*our mind* is in harmony with *our voice*" (*mens nostra concordet voci nostrae*). Warnach argues that Benedict says "our voice" because he is speaking here about participation in the liturgy, not the monks' private prayers. For their participation in communal psalmody not to "remain a purely external work," but instead to "become a spiritual sacrifice," the monks must share one mind and heart and one voice. Personal *concordia* and communal *concordia* grow in tandem. Only when a monk "is released from his own conflict and united in himself" does he "become capable of free and genuine fellowship with others." Each monk's personal quest for purity and wholeness in prayer promotes the authenticity of the whole community's liturgical offering. Likewise, prayer in common is a necessary aid to each monk's personal growth in harmony and holiness. "This twofold unity (*concordia*) of man in himself and with others, which is an essential outpouring of Christian *agape*, should be realized above all in prayer."[17]

[16] Viktor Warnach, "*Mens concordet voci*: Zur Lehre heiligen Benedikt über die geistige Haltung beim Chorgebet nach dem 19. Kapitel seiner Klosterregel," *Liturgisches Leben* 5 (1938): 169–90: 179. My translation.

[17] Warnach, "*Mens concordet voci*," 182.

## Medieval liturgical reforms

The formula of chapter 19 of Benedict's Rule—*mens concordet voci*—"was not exceptional in its meaning," but it became "exceptionally influential owing to its source."[18] The Rule of Benedict had become dominant in Western monasticism by the ninth century, thanks to its balance and adaptability. Benedict of Aniane, the reforming abbot who had the ear of Charlemagne, saw to the Rule's official imposition on all the monasteries of the Frankish Empire. It continued to shape the religious life of Europe long after the power of the Carolingians had dissipated.[19] Over the next few centuries, religious orders within the Western church would proliferate as efforts to reform monastic and canonical life in the eleventh and twelfth centuries were followed by the emergence of mendicant orders and other new forms of consecrated life in the thirteenth and fourteenth centuries. It's no exaggeration to say that every attempt to restore, update, purify, or invigorate Christianity in Europe would aspire to the Rule's ideal of a life in which outward acts of prayer and labor are harmoniously united to interior attention, intention, and understanding. The appearance of chapter 19 of Benedict's Rule in *Sacrosanctum Concilium* as a standard of authentic liturgy is neither sudden nor surprising. Since successive reforms have appealed to the Rule of Benedict as a guarantor of genealogical authenticity, the Rule's formula of "minds in tune with voices" has become an indispensable articulation of performative authenticity as a liturgical ideal.

Still, the influence of Benedict's Rule is exceptional but not singular. The monastic rule attributed to Augustine, for example, attracted renewed interest when reforms associated with Pope Gregory VII (1073–85) required cathedral and collegiate canons to renounce private property, remain celibate, and live in common. Simultaneously, "the surge of interest in community life involving active works in the eleventh and twelfth centuries led to the adoption of the Augustinian *Rule* as an alternative to the Benedictine," since it was "less minutely prescriptive than the Benedictine *Rule* and better adapted for a religious family wishing to pursue an active life in the service of God."[20]

---

[18] Constable, "The Concern for Sincerity," 19.

[19] See Holzherr, *The Rule of Benedict*, lviii–lxii.

[20] Gerald Bonner, "The Author of the Rules," in Augustine, *The Monastic Rules*, trans. Agatha Mary and Gerald Bonner (Hyde Park, NY: New City Press, 2004), 32.

As we have seen, Augustine's emphasis on both personal and communal harmony in prayer is at least as strong as Benedict's, even if the Rule of Benedict is far more detailed about the external form that common prayer ought to take.

The "concern for liturgical authenticity" remained strong as Benedictine monasticism itself experienced a dramatic surge of reformist energy in the twelfth century.[21] Cluniacs, Cistercians, Carthusians, and many other monks sought a renewed observance of the Rule of Benedict. In their view, the monasteries of Europe had become lax by allowing "custom" to supersede the pure "truth" of the Rule. In the rhetoric of abbots like Bernard of Clairvaux, Peter the Venerable, and Robert of Arbrissel, "truth, nature, reason, authenticity, and antiquity stood together as allies, and almost equivalents, in the battle of the reformers against custom, usage, novelty, and triviality."[22] In the realm of liturgy, this rhetoric of reform meant an alliance between the genealogical and performative meanings of authenticity. The monastic reformers were open to ritual change despite their interest in "protecting conformity and continuity." As Giles Constable explains, the "quality of timelessness, in which the real point of referral was the present rather than the past, endowed monastic ritual with a capacity to change." Nothing warranted exterior ritual change so much as the need for correspondence between minds and voices. "Reformers wanted the form of the ceremony to match the meaning of the words, which should reflect the inner attitudes of the participants."[23] At the abbey of Cluny, for example, Peter the Venerable didn't hesitate to eliminate or change parts of the Office he deemed meaningless, inelegant, or repetitive. He defended his adjustments to the liturgy's external forms not as concessions to convenience but as adherence to the truth. To avoid singing the hymn *Iam lucis orto sidere* ("Now that the daylight fills the sky") in the dark, he delayed the celebration of Prime during the winter months, insisting that "the

---

[21] Constable, "Concern for Sincerity," 20.

[22] Giles Constable, *The Reformation of the Twelfth Century* (Cambridge: Cambridge University Press, 1996).

[23] Giles Constable, "The Ceremonies and Symbolism of Entering Religious Life and Taking the Monastic Habit, from the Fourth to the Twelfth Century," in *Segni e ritti nella chiesa altomedievale occidentale, Spoleto, 11–17 Aprile 1985,* Settimane di studio del centro italiano di studi sull'alto medioevo 33 (Spoleto, 1987), 774–75.

children of light should no longer proclaim so great a lie in the presence of God."[24] Similarly, the Cistercians led by Bernard of Clairvaux carefully revised their liturgical books so the monks would use only the chant "that is found to be the most authentic"—in which the "undoubted meanings" of the words "shine with truth" and "bring a light to the mind," while the melodies "nourish rather than empty the sense of the letter."[25]

These medieval efforts to return to authentic sources and to authentic performance of the liturgy resulted in more variety, not less. Diversity in the exterior forms of religious life and liturgical ritual increased during the high Middle Ages. The reformers "were equally concerned for harmony between the inner and outer aspects of prayer and insisted no less strongly than the fathers of the church and the early monastic writers that Christians should understand the meaning and intend the consequences of their words and actions in prayer."[26] The "problem of the reformers," Constable says, was that they "wanted to promote both unity and devotion and were faced with the countless differences between individual monasteries and churches." From the Rule of Benedict and other shared sources, they had inherited confidence in the alliance between communal harmony and individual attunement of mind and voice. But despite its deep roots in the Bible and in the early church, this confidence in *concordia*'s twofold nature was waning. Though all were committed to the renewal of authentic prayer, the reformers found themselves "caught" by a liturgical tradition "that bound them, whether they liked it or not, to other religious men and women whose way of life they criticized and condemned and yet who resembled them, and whom they resembled, in many ways."[27] In this respect, twelfth-century divisions between monks were a harbinger of sixteenth-century divisions between Protestants and Catholics who laid claim to the same tradition and the same commitment to praying with both minds and voices.

[24] Peter the Venerable, *Statutes*, 61, trans. in Constable, "The Concern for Sincerity," 21. See also Constable, *Reformation of the Twelfth Century*, 154, 202–3.

[25] Bernard of Clairvaux, *Epistula* 398.2, trans. in Constable, "The Concern for Sincerity," 22, 24.

[26] Constable, "Concern for Sincerity," 26.

[27] Constable, *Reformation of the Twelfth Century*, 207.

Medieval liturgical reforms also reveal that "modern feelings about ritual began to emerge" long before the sixteenth-century reformations.[28] In the high Middle Ages, ritual differentiation and mutual antagonism regarding outward practices increased among Christians even as the emphasis in Christian spirituality was shifting inward. The apparent paradox is explained by another loss of confidence, related to the one just described, in the alliance between corporate ritual and authentic interior prayer. Christian piety had always denounced external ritual without interior prayer, but the ritualization of prayer as such wasn't the problem. Hypocrisy, disharmony, or impurity of heart was the underlying disease. At worst, learning to pray by rote was a symptom, and even then the disease was visible not in the rote-learning itself but in the lack of corresponding ethical behavior that could verify the interior worship of the heart.[29] When the body of worshippers was healthy, a liturgy that emphasized the memorization and recitation of the psalms and other texts was an aid to authentic internal participation:

> For the early Christians meditation was, like digestion and rumination, an activity which involved all aspects, internal and external, of the body, since a text had to be spoken or heard before it could be memorized, understood and put into practice. This is what was intended in the Rule of Benedict when it said that in psalmody the mind should be in agreement with the voice, which provided the material for the formation of the monk's inner *persona*, his heart, mind, soul, and spirit.[30]

But "the balance and priority of these activities shifted as the Middle Ages progressed, and relatively greater importance was given to the interior aspects of prayer as confidence in the outer aspects waned." Although "the ideal of harmony remained close to the hearts of liturgical reformers"—and although the Rules of Benedict and Augustine would remain the preeminent articulations of that ideal even into the modern era—"the emphasis was changing and preparing

---

[28] Constable, "Ceremonies and Symbolism," 775.
[29] See Isa 29:13; Mark 7:6; Matt 15:8.
[30] Constable, "Concern for Sincerity," 20.

the way for the Franciscan formula 'that the voice should be in agreement with the mind' " (*vox concordet menti*).[31]

## The prayer of the heart and the rites of the church

Constable hastens to add that we should not make too much of the inversion of *mens* and *vox* in the formula attributed to St. Francis—or in a slightly earlier example from Adam of Dryburgh, a Norbertine canon who resigned his abbacy to become a Carthusian monk. Writing near the end of the twelfth century on exercising the will in prayer, Adam advised, "You should experience in your heart what you say with your mouth, so that your voice may be in agreement with your mind (*ut concordet vox tua cum mente tua*), and the latter may think about what the former sounds."[32] Adam's "principal concern was that worshippers should think about and try to understand what they said, not that they should put into words what was in their minds." Still, by "reversing for the first known time the formula in the rule of Benedict," Adam "pointed the way towards the time when more attention was given in prayer to what was thought than what was said."[33] Francis of Assisi's similar statement that the voice should accord with the mind didn't represent a departure from the ideal of harmony between exterior and interior prayer. Although the spirituality and discipline of the mendicant orders deemphasized the singing of the Office, the Franciscan ideal of authentic prayer wasn't opposed to chapter 19 of Benedict's Rule or to liturgical ritual, as some have argued.[34]

[31] Constable, "Concern for Sincerity," 20, 25. The Franciscan formula appears in Francis of Assisi, *Opuscula sancti patris Francisci Assisiensis* (Quarachhi: Collegium S. Bonaventurae, 1904), *Epistola* 2a, 105–6.

[32] Adam of Dryburgh, *De quadripartito exercitio cellae*, 35, in *PL* 153, col. 878–79, quoted in Constable, "Concern for Sincerity," 25–26. The same passage is quoted at greater length in Bertilo de Boer, "La soi-disant opposition de saint François d'Assise à saint Benoît," Études franciscaines N.S. 9 (1958): 61–62. De Boer argues that this "very remarkable" text has not received sufficient attention, especially since Adam repeats the same idea "at least ten times" in the span of a few sentences, proposing "the mind (*mens*) as the measure of the voice" (620). My translation.

[33] Constable, "Concern for Sincerity," 26.

[34] See Stephan Van Dijk, "The Liturgical Legislation of the Franciscan Rules," *Franciscan Studies* 12, no. 2 (1952): 176–95; Van Dijk, "Liturgy of the Franciscan Rules (Continued)," *Franciscan Studies* 12, no. 3/4 (1952): 241–62. On the opposition or

Still, the reversal of *mens* and *vox* "reflected an important tendency in contemporary spirituality" to regard mental prayer as primary.[35] Earlier in the twelfth century, the itinerant preacher and founder of Fontevraud abbey, Robert of Arbrissel, had written to Ermengarde, the unhappily married Countess of Brittany.[36] While he had to refuse Ermengarde's desire for the life of a vowed religious, Robert assured her that her continued life in the world didn't have to be an obstacle to true prayer:

> Prayer from the heart, not the lips, is acceptable to God. God does not pay heed to words, but to the heart of the one who prays. All good works of the just are prayer. We can always pray in our hearts, not always with our mouths.[37]

Robert's preference for the prayer of the heart and the prayer of good works over the prayer of the lips reiterates the teaching of Scripture and the early church.[38] But viewed in light of changes that were already underway in the religious life of Europe, Robert's comments reveal that for him "and for many who came after him, true prayer came from the heart and was expressed in works rather than in words."[39]

The "works" that Robert and subsequent preachers increasingly thought of as prayer were works of private devotion, not public

---

compatibility of the Franciscan and Benedictine ideals, see H. Dausend, "Der Franziskanerorden und die Entwicklung der kirchlichen Liturgie," *Franziskanische Studien* 11 (1924): 165–78; Odo Casel, "Response to H. Dausend, 'Der Franziskanerorden und die Entwickelung der Liturgie,'" *Jahrbuch für Liturgiewissenschaft* 4 (1924): 219–20; Warnach, "*Mens concordet voci*"; de Boer, "La soi-disant opposition."

[35] Constable, "Concern for Sincerity," 26.

[36] For the full history of Ermengarde's interaction with Robert of Arbrissel, see Jacques Dalarun, *Robert of Arbrissel: Sex, Sin, and Salvation in the Middle Ages*, trans. Bruce L. Venarde (Washington, DC: Catholic University of America Press, 2006), 93–101.

[37] J. de Petigny, "Lettre inédite de Robert d'Arbrissel à la comtesse Ermengarde," *Bibliothèque de l'École des Chartres*, ser. 3, t. 5 (1854): 209–35, para. 11, trans. in Bruce L. Venarde, *Robert of Arbrissel: A Medieval Religious Life* (Washington, DC: Catholic University of America Press, 2003), 78.

[38] To introduce these comments, Robert cites Matt 6:2–7, 16. His claim that "all the works" of a saint are prayers closely resembles Origen's teaching in *De oratione*, 12.2; 22.3–5.

[39] Constable, "Concern for Sincerity," 26.

charity. Although Robert endorses almsgiving—above all to "servants of the faith" like himself—he won't allow Ermengarde to hand over all her worldly possessions and become outwardly poor herself. "Many clerics are hypocrites," he tells her. "Monks and hermits," too, "pretend to make long prayers that they might be seen by men." Ermengarde's "voluntary poverty" should be more authentic, "far removed from all vanity and pretense," in which the soul withdraws from the world even as the body remains "amidst positions and honors, amidst riches and silk garments, amidst husband and beloved children and splendid parents." *Within herself* she will find the place from which to make a sincere and worthy offering:

> Settle in the land of your heart (*inhabita terram cordis tui*) and *feed on its riches. Take delight in the Lord, and he will give you your heart's desire* [Ps 36/37:3-4]. Rejoice in tribulations because *tribulation gives rise to patience, patience to testing, testing to hope. Hope does not confound, because the love of God is poured out into our hearts through the Holy Spirit that has been given to us* [Rom 5:3-5].
>
>   You live for the time being amongst savage men; flee their wicked works in your heart. Lift up your heart to your God, and let your conversation always be in heaven [Phil 3:20].[40]

Robert reminds Ermengarde of Christ's teaching: "*When you pray, go into your room, and pray to your Father with the door shut. And your Father, who sees all that is done in secret will reward you* [Matt 6:6]." She requires no monastic cell to fulfill the command, for even while "occupied with much business," she can pray her *Pater noster* "from memory, always." This inward "prayer from the heart" is apparently worth more than vocal participation in the canonical hours, which Ermengarde should only "hear." Robert doesn't even mention the Eucharist in his advice to the pious noblewoman.[41]

  If Robert's letter to Ermengarde was an idiosyncratic response to the peculiar situation of a woman consigned to remain in the world instead of retiring to a monastery, it was also a "bell-wether" of a gathering reaction against further elaboration and enlargement of

---

  [40] De Petigny, "Lettre inédite de Robert d'Arbrissel," paras. 9–10, trans. in Venarde, *Robert of Arbrissel*, 77.
  [41] De Petigny, "Lettre inédite de Robert d'Arbrissel," paras. 10–12, trans. in Venarde, *Robert of Arbrissel*, 77–78.

the liturgy.[42] Increasingly, preference for the prayer of the heart induced suspicion of lengthy prayers sung or spoken in common. In the early Middle Ages, the fixed and repetitive nature of liturgical prayer had been an aid to the harmonization of mind and voice, especially in monastic life. "The inner *persona* of the monk or nun was shaped by the outer ceremonies and signs, and the essence of their religious life was expressed by its symbols."[43] But if exterior liturgical participation was still an opportunity to shape a person's interior, in the later Middle Ages it would also come to be seen as an occasion for pretense.[44] Time spent praying the Office or hearing Mass could be time taken away from interior prayer, while even in monasteries the liturgy itself "became more of a personal devotion than an institutional commitment." As a practical consequence of these shifts, some questioned daily celebration of Mass, but the prolix monastic Office was the primary target for abbreviation. Benedictine abbots meeting at Reims in 1131 proposed reducing the number of psalms, "citing 1 Corinthians 14.19 that five words spoken with understanding were better than ten thousand words without understanding."[45]

Since five hundred years would pass before John Bunyan would quote from the same passage to launch a Puritan attack on scripted prayer,[46] it's striking to see Benedictine abbots compare routine recitation of the Office to the mindless utterance of tongues criticized by Paul. Although the early modern "repudiation of ritual," "rejection of liturgy," and "stripping of the altars" were still far off,[47] the slow

[42] Constable, *Reform of the Twelfth Century*, 201.

[43] Constable, "Ceremonies and Symbolism," 833.

[44] Robert of Arbrissel's letter opens with a remarkable denunciation of "pretense" (*simulatio*), in which he declares that false humility, sanctity, charity, mercy, abstinence, and chastity are worse than pride, vainglory, envy, greed, gluttony, and lust (de Petigny, "Lettre inédite de Robert d'Arbrissel," 225).

[45] Constable, *Reform of the Twelfth Century*, 201–3. For the acts of the Council of Reims, see Ursmer Berlière, ed., *Documents inédits pour servir a l'histoire ecclésiastique de la Belgique* (Maredsous: Abbaye de Saint-Benoit, 1894), 109.

[46] John Bunyan, *I Will Pray with the Spirit, and I Will Pray with the Understanding Also: Or, A Discourse Touching Prayer, From I Cor. 14.15*, 2nd ed. (London: Printed for the Author, 1663).

[47] These descriptions are from Peter Burke, "The Repudiation of Ritual in Early Modern Europe," in *The Historical Anthropology of Early Modern Italy: Essays on Perception and Communication* (Cambridge: Cambridge University Press, 1987), 223–38; Lori Branch, *Rituals of Spontaneity: Sentiment and Secularism from Free Prayer to Wordsworth*

loss of confidence in external prayer was underway well before the end of the Middle Ages:

> Some time after the turn of the millennium, for reasons which are far from clear, this confidence in the meaning and efficacy of ritual began to wane. There are signs of a sense of division between the essence and forms of religious life, and a growing belief that to be a monk it was no longer enough to live and look like one. This was reflected both in the emphasis on formality in the entry to religious life, as in the requirement of profession and consecration, and in the concentration on the inner feelings of which the outer actions and appearances should be an expression. In prayer, the mind was no longer expected to conform to the words so much as the words to the mind and heart, where God's real concern lay.[48]

In Constable's estimation, this shift is no less important to the modern understanding of ritual than the changes wrought by the Protestant Reformation five centuries later. "The breakdown of the early medieval sense of coherence between inner and outer forms, and its expression in ritual, marked a turning point in the history of monasticism as it did in the history of the church and of Christian society as a whole."[49]

This gradual "breakdown" of confidence in the performative authenticity and *formative* efficacy of liturgical ritual paradoxically coincided with heightened confidence in the *sacramental* efficacy of certain ritual performances. Above all, this confidence applied to the ritual consecration of the Eucharist at Mass, followed closely by the other sacraments. Scholastic theologians defended and systematized the efficacy of the sacraments more thoroughly than ever. But reliance on the efficacy of liturgical performances extended beyond the list of seven sacraments, only then becoming standard. Constable's analysis of monastic reform, for example, shows that the emerging emphasis on interior prayer coexisted with increased formalization of liturgical rites like monastic profession and consecration. In the Byzantine East,

---

(Waco, TX: Baylor University Press, 2006), 35–61; Eamon Duffy, *The Stripping of the Altars: Traditional Religion in England, 1400–1580*, 2nd ed. (New Haven, CT: Yale University Press, 2005).

[48] Constable, "Ceremonies and Symbolism," 833.
[49] Constable, "Ceremonies and Symbolism," 834.

where monk-theologians "were on their own path to a septenarium of sacramental rites" that *included* monastic tonsure, there was a similarly "unremitting focus" on both the precision of external ritual and the purity of interior prayer.[50] God might pay attention to the prayer of the heart, but to the human participants in liturgy, outward ceremony and solemnity were signs of an effective rite.

There is a significant element of truth to Lori Branch's claim that the meaning and efficacy of liturgical ritual weren't questioned by Christians before the early modern period:

> When the earliest rumbles of the Reformation sounded among Wycliffites, Lollards, and Hussites in fourteenth- and fifteenth-century England and Bohemia, Christianity in both the East and West had been a liturgical religion for nearly a millennium and a half. A rich practice and literature of worship had blossomed from Sarum to Kiev with no hint of the coming critique of ritual and the ethos of spontaneity that would remake worship entirely.[51]

The new forms of religious life and spirituality that developed in Western Europe in the intervening period of the later Middle Ages readily accepted the efficacy of the sacramental rituals and held the Mass and the Office in high esteem. Confidence in the Eucharist as the effective sign of Christ's real presence caused some of the most inwardly oriented mystics and religious orders to make contemplation of the sacrament central to their spirituality. While reception of communion became infrequent, especially among the laity, pious fear of the sacrament's power was the motive for reluctance. The concomitant rise of "spiritual communion" as an alternative to sacramental reception proves neither a lack of faith in the Eucharist nor a magical understanding of the Mass.[52]

---

[50] Yury P. Avvakumov, "Sacramental Ritual in Middle and Later Byzantine Theology: Ninth–Fifteenth Centuries," in *The Oxford Handbook of Sacramental Theology*, ed. Hans Boersma and Matthew Levering (Oxford: Oxford University Press, 2015), 249–66, at 253–57.

[51] Branch, *Rituals of Spontaneity*, 36.

[52] See Gary Macy, *The Theologies of the Eucharist in the Early Scholastic Period: A Study of the Salvific Function of the Sacrament According to the Theologians, c. 1080–c. 1220* (Oxford: Oxford University Press, 1984); Virginia Reinburg, "Liturgy and the Laity in Late Medieval and Reformation France," *The Sixteenth Century Journal* 23, no. 3 (1992): 526–47; Duffy, *Stripping of the Altars*.

Instead, as Gerard Rouwhorst argues, the high regard that theologians and ordinary Christians had for spiritual communion "points to the existence or the emergence of a new form of liturgical participation by the laity in the ritual of the Mass celebrated by the clergy in Latin: an inward, spiritual, and more individual participation from a 'distance.'" *Distance* from the ritual doesn't imply disdain for the ritual. Medieval eucharistic spirituality "remains connected with the ritual of the Mass, but also betrays a tendency to develop separately from this ritual, at least separately from its textual elements." The increasing distance between interior participation and exterior participation also "reflects a new attitude towards the individual believer which is remarkably paralleled by numerous other phenomena characteristic of the same period, for instance, the central role ascribed to private confession and the definitive decline of public penance, the interiorization of guilt." Thus, while the efficacy of liturgical ritual wasn't directly called into question, the later Middle Ages witnessed a "growing separation of communal liturgy and personal spirituality."[53]

## Sacramental efficacy and the crisis of representation

In retrospect, we can detect more than a hint of the modern critique of ritual in the medieval sharpening of the distinction between interior and exterior participation. "An ideal of inner conformity did not replace one of outer conformity," Constable says, "since there had been no clear division between the two in the early Middle Ages." Yet participation in the outward forms of religious life "took on a new significance as they were seen as distinct from, and sometimes at variance with, the inner life of monks and nuns."[54] The distinction between interior and exterior—and the potential for discrepancy—probably became even more pronounced among secular clergy and laypeople. But a potential for disharmony was also an opportunity for new, more intentional efforts to reconcile internal and external participation. Among theologians, these efforts appeared from the twelfth century on in sacramental doctrine that distinguished and

---

[53] Gerard Rouwhorst, "The Mystical Body Falling Apart? Reflections on the Emergence and Development of Eucharistic Spirituality in the Western Middle Ages," *Religion & Theology* 23, no. 1–2 (2016): 53–54.

[54] Constable, "Ceremonies and Symbolism," 833–34.

then negotiated the difference between valid administration and fruitful reception, between the visible *sacramentum* and the hidden *res*, and between the ritually required *opus operatum* and the spiritually required *opus operantis*.

This refinement of sacramental doctrine is best understood as part of a broader refinement of religious discipline, as Talal Asad demonstrates in his important essay on medieval monasticism. Asad summarizes the interior-exterior distinction in the medieval concept of *disciplina* as "a tension between the idea of learning and exercising a virtue and the idea of respecting and obeying the law." Ideally, the two goals would coincide, but the formation of virtuous dispositions implies internal self-regulation while satisfaction of the law implies submission to an external rule:

> For in relation to virtues, defects can be described in intrinsic terms as inabilities: thus an ungenerous act is the behavior of an agent who has failed to exercise the moral virtue of generosity appropriate to his social role. In the context of the law, however, faults are identified by reference to an external (i.e., transcendental) rule; a transgression is what it is essentially because it disobeys the law, which commands or forbids something. The requirements of the law and those of the conditions for exercising the virtues are not always easy to reconcile.[55]

Often, late medieval Christianity didn't reconcile satisfaction of external law and cultivation of interior virtue so much as it established separate disciplinary procedures and theological doctrines to deal with the requirements of each. Asad points to the evolution of the sacrament of penance in medieval monasteries as an example. In the earlier ritual structure involving public accusation of fault, the exterior acts of penance served the dual purpose of outwardly satisfying the law's demand for justice while also evoking interior feelings of remorse. This interior sorrow for sin—"contrition"—was the necessary condition of a changed disposition, in which the sinner desired to be free of sin and resolved to avoid repeating it. The expression of contrition was usually sufficient reason to lift the imposed penance

---

[55] Talal Asad, "On Discipline and Humility in Medieval Christian Monasticism," in *Genealogies of Religion: Discipline and Reasons of Power in Christianity and Islam* (Baltimore: Johns Hopkins University Press, 1993), 158.

and reconcile the sinner to the monastic community, since the exterior satisfaction of God's law was seen to coincide with the interior transformation of the penitent's dispositions—the latter being "necessary both for the learning of individual virtues and for orderly community life." But as private confession of sins displaced public accusation, performing penance lost much of its connection with forming contrition, since sorrow for sin now *preceded* penance as the motivation for self-accusation. "Where [penance] remains to be carried out *after* remorse, as in the case of self-accusation, the dual function of reconciliation splits apart: the construction of virtuous dispositions may be seen to be quite a different matter from the power of divine law to forgive an offense." It also seemed unacceptable to restrain God's power to forgive a contrite sinner until after the formal completion of penance. So, following "a profound theological debate in the twelfth century," the orthodox practice and theology of penance came to emphasize the confessor's absolution from further liability for confessed sins by the "power of the keys," which the priest held as God's legal representative on earth.[56]

The "split" in the functions of penance is emblematic of a distinction, which grew over time, in the medieval understanding of the efficacy of sacraments and other rites of prayer. As private confession became the norm in monasteries and beyond, the ritual of absolution satisfied the *exterior* requirements of divine law, and the theology of the judicial confessor explained how the rite caused the sinner's reconciliation with God. The *interior* cultivation of virtue and the reintegration of the sinner into the community had to be brought about through disciplines of humility and obedience that were performed separately from the sacrament of penance. Gradually, the function of contrition also split. Remorse for sin remained the condition of effective interior conversion from vice to virtue, but the emphasis in theology and practice had shifted to seeing contrition as the condition of effective conferral of absolution. The split is reflected

---

[56] Asad, "Discipline and Humility," 161–64. Asad acknowledges but does not emphasize the historical evolution of the sacrament away from public penance and toward private confession. His account, though greatly abbreviated and limited to monasteries, agrees with the detailed history of medieval penance in James Dallen, *The Reconciling Community: The Rite of Penance* (Collegeville, MN: Liturgical Press, 1986), 100–167.

in scholastic theology's eventual dissection of contrition into the
remote disposition of the penitent required for an effective conferral
of absolution—a fear of punishment called "attrition"—and the proxi-
mate disposition of genuine sorrow for having offended God, which
the grace of the sacrament brings about and which becomes the condition of renewed growth in virtue. Thomas Aquinas synthesized the
two functions of contrition, arguing that "the forgiveness of sin is the
effect of penance as a virtue, but still more of Penance as a sacrament."[57] Later theologians, however, further de-emphasized the effectiveness of penance as a virtue. James Dallen argues that "the ritual
expression of the Church's judgment came close to replacing personal
conversion in late medieval theology."[58] It's a fair summary regarding
the *sacrament* of penance. Popular religion, however, offered new
ways to evoke contrition and cultivate penance as a *virtue*, often by
meditating on the suffering of Christ, the sorrows of Mary, or the
pains of hell. While the visual images and bodily mortification associated with popular penitential piety could be striking and highly
public, the goal was to evoke strong interior feelings of guilt and
sorrow for sin.[59] The goal of performing penance within the sacrament was harder to explain—perhaps dangerously so, considering
the abuses of the penitential system and the corresponding attacks
upon it that were to come.

---

[57] ST III, q. 86, a. 6, co. See Joseph P. Wawrykow, *The Westminster Handbook to Thomas
Aquinas* (Louisville, KY: Westminster John Knox Press, 2005), 104–6; Dallen, *Reconciling Community*, 146–48. Wawrykow emphasizes that Aquinas, "unlike some later
theologians," does not consider mere self-interested fear of punishment a sufficient
beginning of contrition for absolution to be effective. "If there is sham . . . such that
the external actions do not signify repentance . . . the spiritual effects will be blocked
by an impediment in the one who is confessing (III.84.3 ad 5)" (105).

[58] Dallen, *Reconciling Community*, 148. The case in point for Dallen's argument is
that the "act of contrition" would come to mean for Catholics *not* interior repentance
itself, but the typically memorized prayer whose recitation before or even *during* the
priest's absolution testified that the penitent was properly disposed to receive forgiveness. While the act of contrition did not become an ordinary part of the rite of penance
until after the Council of Trent, its wording was usually "modeled on the scholastic
description of the contrite attitude." Dallen, *Reconciling Community*, 180.

[59] See Jean Delumeau, *Sin and Fear: The Emergence of a Western Guilt Culture, 13th–
18th Centuries* (New York: St. Martin's Press, 1990); Michael S. Driscoll, "Penance in
Transition: Popular Piety and Practice," in *Medieval Liturgy: A Book of Essays*, ed. Lizette
Larson-Miller (New York: Garland, 1997), 121–63.

Curiously, reliance on the efficacy of interior prayer continued to increase in the late Middle Ages even as sacramental theology and practice emphasized the *ex opere operato* effectiveness of the church's external liturgical rituals. This wasn't necessarily an omen of the brutal conflicts over worship to come. The "splits" in the discipline of penance, for instance, might have mattered little to the history of Christianity had they only taken place within monasteries—or if other parts of medieval religion didn't similarly experience the "conflicting pulls of forming virtues and upholding the law." In liturgical prayer, which fulfills a duty to God and aims at personal sanctity, this tension could be managed as long as the ritual performances were "part of an entire disciplinary program," in which the "dynamic relation" between exterior sign and interior disposition could be "regulated and shaped by authoritative discourse in order to secure its authentic meaning." But even in a monastery, "effective performance" of rites whose primary aim was to transform self-love into worship and sinners into saints "depended on many contingent factors." The "possibilities of failure" increased in secular society, where "the conditions of discipline were less predictable."[60]

Above all, the performance of prayer can fail to convince both participants and onlookers when the external ritual action is no longer seen to imply a corresponding interior transformation. Because the disjunction is between a ritual signifier and a signified spiritual reality, historians speak of a *crisis of representation* that came to a head in the sixteenth century. At this time, "the term *ceremony*, for instance, first began to acquire negative connotations of hollowness and superstition."[61] Similarly, "ritual became a bad word in parts of western Europe in the course of the early modern period,"[62] and the same connotation of emptiness applied when "pageant," "performance," "show," or "act" were used to describe the liturgy. In almost every instance, the primary contrast drawn in the early modern critique of ritual was between real internal prayer and feigned or frivolous external prayer.

---

[60] Asad, "Discipline and Humility," 155, 165.

[61] Branch, *Rituals of Spontaneity*, 37. See Thomas M. Greene, introduction to *Ceremony and Text in the Renaissance*, ed. Douglas F. Rutledge (Newark: University of Delaware Press, 1996), 11–18, at 12–13.

[62] Burke, "Repudiation of Ritual," 224.

Despite the medieval West's apparent confidence in sacramental efficacy, the storm had been gathering for some time, so that when it broke, "early modern Protestant *and* Catholic reformers *both* insisted upon a dichotomy between 'true' worship and 'false' worship, the falsifying element being in most instances ritual."[63] Yet the subsequent rise of "sincere" worship as an alternative to "false ritual" is often wholly attributed to Protestantism. There is a natural association between the "condemnation of ritual" and the Protestant "critique of 'works.'"[64] Contemporary scholars therefore blame our present "overwhelming concern with sincerity at the expense of ritual" on "the strong role of Protestant Christianity in the making of our modern world and of contemporary culture."[65] But this ignores the "evidence of an increasingly critical attitude within the [Catholic] church towards some traditional claims for ecclesiastical ritual." Even in the sixteenth and seventeenth centuries, Catholic theologians and pastors tried to counter superstitious uses of liturgy and "chip away at the encrustations of popular, unofficial beliefs and ceremonies which had accumulated around the theology and ritual of the church."[66] It's true that the Council of Trent solemnly affirmed the church's institution and use of "certain rites," "ceremonies," and other "external aids" in offering the sacrifice of the Mass. Yet the need to articulate this as an explicit doctrine suggests it was no longer self-evident that "the minds of the faithful are aroused by those visible signs (*signa*) of religion and piety to contemplation of the highest realities (*rerum*) hidden in this sacrifice."[67]

[63] Andrew E. Barnes, "Religious Reform and the War Against Ritual," *Journal of Ritual Studies* 4, no. 1 (1990): 127. Emphasis added. See the seminal studies that Barnes reviews in this essay: John Bossy, *Christianity in the West, 1400–1700* (Oxford: Oxford University Press, 1985); William A. Christian, *Local Religion in Sixteenth-Century Spain* (Princeton, NJ: Princeton University Press, 1981); Carlos M. N. Eire, *War Against the Idols: The Reformation of Worship from Erasmus to Calvin* (Cambridge: Cambridge University Press, 1986).

[64] Burke, "Repudiation of Ritual," 226.

[65] Adam B. Seligman et al., *Ritual and Its Consequences: An Essay on the Limits of Sincerity* (Oxford: Oxford University Press, 2008), 9.

[66] Burke, "Repudiation of Ritual," 230–32.

[67] Council of Trent, Session 22 (17 Sept 1562), *Doctrina et canones de sanctissimo missae sacrificio*, ch. 5, in Norman P. Tanner, ed., *Decrees of the Ecumenical Councils* (London: Sheed & Ward, 1990), vol. 2, 734. My translation.

As Gary Macy says, "the modern Roman Catholic Church started in the sixteenth century just as surely as the Lutheran and Calvinist churches."[68] Likewise, the modern Catholic attitude toward liturgical ritual isn't a holdover from the Middle Ages, and Catholics contributed in no small way to the rise of sincerity and authenticity as quintessentially modern values. Most important, as modernity progressed, both Protestants and Catholics found it easier for the *self*, the *subject* of religious action, to be "conceived of without ritual."[69] Already, the split of the medieval concept of *disciplina* into distinct activities for satisfying the external law and acquiring internal virtue had introduced a gap between being an authentic participant in the church's liturgy and becoming an authentic individual subject of prayer. As this gap widened, Catholics and Protestants would focus less on the harmony of interior and exterior prayer and emphasize instead the quality and intensity of interior feeling and devotion.

## Sincerity and spontaneous prayer

As Charles Guignon explains, the "social virtue" of sincerity became a pressing concern in the sixteenth and seventeenth centuries because "radical transformations in Western civilization" destabilized assumptions about the social, cosmic, and moral contexts in which knowing oneself and being true to oneself made sense. Guignon identifies these transformations as three sharp divisions: between society and one's "natural" self, between an arbitrary universe and meaning-making subjects, and between interior motives and external works.[70] Sixteen centuries earlier, according to Charles Taylor, Christianity had initiated a "break" in the social and cosmic embedding of the self, but for a long time the boundaries had remained highly "porous."[71] Now, for the first time, many people made "a sharp distinction between the way one appears in public life and what one truly is in one's inner life."[72] This inward turn to the subject had a

---

[68] Gary Macy, *The Banquet's Wisdom: A Short History of the Theologies of the Lord's Supper* (New York: Paulist Press, 1992), 135.

[69] Branch, *Rituals of Spontaneity*, 37.

[70] Guignon, *On Being Authentic*, 26–48.

[71] Charles Taylor, *A Secular Age* (Cambridge, MA: Belknap Press of Harvard University Press, 2007), 146–58.

[72] Guignon, *On Being Authentic*, 35.

profound effect on both Protestant and Catholic religious sensibilities in Europe.

It's true that inwardness has always played an important role in Christian spirituality. Guignon cites Augustine's *Confessions* as a paradigmatic example of concentrated self-reflection. But "Augustine does not even see the self as a unified, self-subsistent source of agency in the way we do."[73] While he seeks to clarify his own intentions and purify his motives for acting, Augustine repeatedly concludes that it is really God who acts through him, with purposes and designs that are "secret."[74]

In the modern Christian sensibility, personal motives and intentions appear all-important. An individual's interior purpose in acting outweighs the significance of the exterior actions and their external consequences. This shift is easily recognizable in a *sola fide* spirituality, in which "salvation depends not on external acts (such as buying indulgences or participating in rituals), but rather on the inner condition of the soul in relation to God." Yet Catholic spirituality made a similar turn to the subject in early modernity, evident especially in the new emphasis on examination of one's conscience to prepare for confession.[75] Rites for the public reconciliation of sinners remained in some liturgical books but were practically forgotten. Far from reviving it, the Council of Trent affirmed secret confession of all mortal sins to a priest, after penitents had made "a careful self-examination," with special attention to hidden sins of lust and envy, "since these may often quite seriously damage the soul and are more dangerous than those which are openly admitted."[76] While Trent admonished the faithful to receive communion more often, it did so mainly by exhorting them to "be on guard" and prove themselves individually worthy of receiving the Eucharist. They were to approach the sacrament only with a clean conscience and "with such constancy and firmness of faith, such dedication of mind, such devotion and worship, that they may be able to receive frequently that life-supporting

---

[73] Guignon, *On Being Authentic*, 16.

[74] E.g., Augustine, *Confessions*, 4.14.23, 5.6.11, 5.8.14, 6.7, 9.10.23, 10.5.7.

[75] Guignon, *On Being Authentic*, 28–29.

[76] Council of Trent, Session 14 (25 Nov. 1551), *Doctrina de sanctissimis poenitentiae et extremae unctionis sacramentis*, ch. 5, in Tanner, *Decrees of the Ecumenical Councils*, vol. 2, 706.

bread."[77] Catholic devotional life also turned away from late medieval enthusiasm for public dramas and spectacles—like the popular Corpus Christi plays—and toward interior spiritual exercises like those of Thomas à Kempis, Ignatius of Loyola, and Teresa of Avila.

Still, the Protestant critique of Catholic liturgy was real, strident, and heavily focused on the external ceremonies of the Mass and the sacraments. Jonas Barish points out that the repudiation of "popish" liturgy in England, for example, often took the form of an unflattering comparison to the theater of the stage:

> From [William] Tyndale onward . . . popish liturgy is scornfully likened to the theater, and much picturesque invective mustered to drive the point home. Tyndale himself never wearies of referring to traditional priestly vestments as "disguises." . . . [Thomas] Becon's whole treatise, indeed, *The Displaying of the Popish Mass*, amounts to a sustained attack on the theatricality of traditional worship. The detailed contrast between the Last Supper and its liturgical reenactment turns on the claim that by introducing ceremonial costume, ritual gesture, and symbolic decor, and by separating the clergy from the laity, the church has perverted a simple communal event into a portentous masquerade, a magic show designed to hoodwink the ignorant.[78]

The anti-theatrical prejudice in Western moral thought is at least as old as Plato, and it is strongly expressed in Christian terms by Tertullian, John Chrysostom, Origen, and Augustine.[79] But in the early modern period, "theatrical" becomes an epithet applied not just to individual displays of piety but to all liturgical ritual.

A paradox was that fierce critics of Catholic ritualism nevertheless created their own "rituals of spontaneity" as they struggled to attain free prayer of the mind and heart. Intense interior emotion, outwardly manifested in extemporaneous prayer, became the mark of sincere devotion and the authentic currency with which an acceptable offering could be made to God. Despite Protestant condemnations of

---

[77] Council of Trent, Session 13 (11 Oct. 1551), *Decretum de sanctissimo eucharistae sacramento*, ch. 7–8, in Tanner, *Decrees of the Ecumenical Councils*, vol. 2, 696–97.

[78] Jonas A. Barish, *The Antitheatrical Prejudice* (Berkeley: University of California Press, 1981), 155–61.

[79] Barish, *Antitheatrical Prejudice*, 1–65.

works-righteousness, free-prayer literature held that both the words and the emotions of prayer had to be *produced* through the work of performance. As Branch explains, spontaneous prayer was not only expected, but *prescribed*:

> In the consolidation of the discourse and practice of free prayer, we see the culmination of Renaissance crises of representation and the fruition of the dramatic Reformation attacks on ritual, when under increasing pressures toward certainty and ever more entrenched economic logics, spontaneity becomes policy: not an option, but, for growing numbers of Protestants, paradoxically an obligation and the *sine qua non* of valid prayer and a saved subjectivity.[80]

John Bunyan, for example, takes Paul's frequently cited injunction to "pray with the spirit" but "with the mind also" (1 Cor 14:15) as *encouragement* to spontaneous, emotional prayer. An acceptable prayer isn't the product of a liturgical script, but the product of powerfully felt emotion. Bunyan considers how two kinds of "begging" appear to God:

> There are some who out of custome and formality, go and pray; there are others, who go in the bitterness of their spirit: The one he prayes out of bare notion, and naked knowledge; the other hath his words forced from him by the anguish of his soul. Surely, that is the man that God will look at.[81]

Interestingly, Bunyan's criticism of formal prayer admits that the ritualist *does* possess the "bare notion" and "naked knowledge" of what a beggar should say to implore God's mercy. Learning to pray by rote hasn't created a deficit of intellectual *knowledge* so much as a lack of sincere *feeling*. The beggar untutored in the external forms of prayer "speaks with more sence, feeling, and understanding" of the poverty and misery routinely "mentioned" in the other's carefully rehearsed prayer.[82]

---

[80] Branch, *Rituals of Spontaneity*, 42.
[81] Bunyan, *I Will Pray with the Spirit*, 67.
[82] Bunyan, *I Will Pray with the Spirit*, 67.

On the surface, the rise of free prayer and the rejection of liturgy seem to change the standard for determining the authenticity of prayer. Harmony of mind and *heart* appears to replace harmony of mind and *voice*. The essential criterion of authenticity becomes correspondence of intellect and emotion instead of correspondence of interior and exterior. "The hypocrisy God detests, then, is importantly not a matter of saying one thing and doing another, but of saying one thing and feeling another: of a disjunction between the logocentric intellect and the heart, between the propositional truths of abstract doctrine and the emotions which are substantively to mirror and confirm it."[83]

While the Protestant Reformation is often held to represent a rationalizing, logocentric triumph of written words over rituals, Branch's examination of free-prayer literature shows that the reality was more complex. Often, written words were presumed to be unsuitable for authentic prayer, even when the prayer was offered in common:

> Again and again, free-prayer tracts inveigh against liturgical prayer as emotionally "cold" or "lukewarm," mere "lip-labor" born of "custom and formality." Even more than doctrinal correctness—contend these pamphlets—the element of true prayer lacking in those who use forms is emotional authenticity and sincerity, to which spontaneous, unwritten, and unpremeditated verbal prayer testifies and to which the formulaic repetition of liturgy is inimical.[84]

The fear of formulaic written words could not, of itself, supply suitable extemporaneous spoken words for worship. So, besides polemical tracts, Nonconformists of the seventeenth and early eighteenth centuries produced books for public worship that claimed to be free of "forms" and scripted prayers, even while describing the contents of each oration in minute detail.[85]

The paradox of prescribing and then regulating spontaneity shows that emotional intensity in prayer didn't simply replace correspondence of interior and exterior prayer as a criterion of authenticity.

[83] Branch, *Rituals of Spontaneity*, 44.
[84] Branch, *Rituals of Spontaneity*, 43.
[85] Branch, *Rituals of Spontaneity*, 45, 52–56.

Rather, the problem of authentic performance stood out more sharply than ever. Advocates of free prayer, Branch argues, couldn't avoid feeling "anxiety" about having to produce a spontaneous and emotionally intense performance.[86] In 1661, Henry Dawbeny, a Puritan tract-writer, described the "duty of prayer" as a "spiritual performance" and wrote of the exacting "directions which our *Holy Father* hath given in his Word for the *acceptable performance* of it":

> What God hath set us . . . obligeth us to a performance of it under such *Circumstances,* as shall neither divert the *intention of our mind,* nor cool the *fervour of our Spirits,* which two things are most essentially necessary to the acceptable performance of our duty in it, and so excellently becomes that most sacred performance; and without which our performance is but *lip-labour,* and *lost labour;* yea, no other than a most gross *Hypocrisie,* and *mocking* of him *who cannot be mocked.*[87]

Dawbeny's "central metaphor figures the suppliant as a busy craftsman, servant, or errand-boy in a spiritual marketplace, bringing his labor in the form of phrases, praises, and requests, before a merchant-God who presumably evaluates the labor and pays wages by granting or denying the laborer's requests."[88] The metaphor's seeming embrace of works-righteousness reveals a "modern religious subjectivity" in which the worshipper is "driven back to theatricality even by [the] effort to escape it."[89] However heavily one might emphasize interior participation in prayer, it proves impossible to avoid the exteriority of "language, in all its iterable liturgicality."[90]

Branch perceives that rising anxiety about the spontaneity and fervor of prayer is "profoundly interconnected" with emergent secular logics of capitalism and empiricism, which were "coming to

[86] Branch, *Rituals of Spontaneity,* 56–61.

[87] Henry Dawbeny, *A Sober and Temperate Discourse, Concerning the Interest of Words in Prayer: The Just Antiquity and Pedigree of Liturgies, or Forms of Prayer in Churches: With a View of the State of the Church, When They Were First Composed, or Imposed* (London: Printed for W.A., 1661), 1–2. Emphasis in original. Partially quoted in Branch, *Rituals of Spontaneity,* 49.

[88] Branch, *Rituals of Spontaneity,* 57.

[89] Branch, *Rituals of Spontaneity,* 58–59. Branch quotes William J. Bouwsma, *John Calvin: A Sixteenth-Century Portrait* (New York: Oxford University Press, 1988), 180.

[90] Branch, *Rituals of Spontaneity,* 58.

permeate all forms of rational thought"—including religious thought—"as unarguable common sense or an inevitable bottom line."[91] Far from opposing the calculation of prayer's value from external measurements of devotion, free-prayer advocates imagined "the heart as both a scientific object and an object of trade, the substance and value of which can be abstracted into the currency of words in prayer." The long-term effect, Branch argues, is a "modern religious subject" isolated from her fellow worshippers and alienated from her own "labor and performance" in prayer. The "Reformation crisis of representation" inexorably eroded "faith in the possibility of communing with God through the action of a community rather than the isolated self." Opponents of free prayer—not just Catholics and high-church Anglicans, but increasingly secular humanists— charged the tradition of spontaneous worship with the same accusation of performative inauthenticity that Puritans and other Nonconformists leveled against the "liturgical" traditions. "The cult of true sincerity and spontaneity led to a profound skepticism that dismissed all prayer and worship as what it can only be, in some manner constructed, volitional, and performative."[92] Liturgy, like all prayer, is a performance; to reject performance itself as inauthentic is to foreclose any possibility of authentic communal prayer.

## From sincerity to authenticity

Still, as Ramie Targoff convincingly demonstrates, the modern urge to deny the connection between external displays of piety and real interior devotion always stood in tension with a "firm commitment to the authenticity of the body's physical signs," both as an indicator of inward dispositions and, crucially, as an effective means of *transforming* those dispositions. Not only Catholics, but "mainstream Renaissance Protestants frequently imagined performative

---

[91] Branch, *Rituals of Spontaneity*, 59. Branch notes that her conclusion about the reciprocal influence between Puritanism and capitalism stands "someplace between those of Marx and Weber," resisting both materialistic and idealistic determinisms. She attributes a similar position to David Zaret, *The Heavenly Contract: Ideology and Organization in Pre-Revolutionary Puritanism* (Chicago: University of Chicago Press, 1985), 10.

[92] Branch, *Rituals of Spontaneity*, 59–61.

behavior to have a causal as well as reflective relation to the internal self: according to such accounts, the individual's assumption of external gestures prompted the corresponding internal conditions." The same reformers who dismissed the Mass as ineffectual theater could attack the Elizabethan stage for being all too effective in forming the morals of players and audiences.[93]

The cult of sincerity was slow in developing, and it's a mistake to think that either the Protestant or Catholic reforms of the sixteenth century simply aimed to replace external ritual performances with interior acts of religion. Targoff's study of devotional language in early modern England proves that it is especially facile to associate "Catholicism and publicness on the one hand, and Protestantism and privacy on the other."[94] Instead, the Protestant *and* Catholic reforms of the sixteenth century helped to solidify the boundary between public and private devotion. The common emphasis on inwardness, combined with efforts on all sides to enforce liturgical uniformity, further sharpened the distinction between interior, "private" acts of religion and exterior, "public" ones. This also made it harder for Catholics and Protestants to assume any reliable correspondence between the external ritual forms of the liturgy and the internal dispositions required for authentic, fruitful participation by the laity. In the clergy's efforts to better catechize the faithful, the Catholic emphasis on an individual being in the state of grace and the Protestant emphasis on personal conviction of salvation were two sides of the same coin. Both sought to increase interior devotion, but "whereas Protestants sought to break down the auricular barriers between the clergy and the congregation, Catholics insisted that these barriers were actually conducive to a genuine devotional practice." According to Targoff, "[W]hat emerges in the aftermath of the Reformation is less a triumphant embrace of the individual's private and invisible self than a concerted effort to shape the otherwise uncontrollable and unreliable internal sphere through common acts of devotion."[95]

The sixteenth and seventeenth centuries laid the groundwork, however, for the religious use of collective ritual to be seen either as wasted effort or as external imposition on the private beliefs of indi-

[93] Targoff, "Performance of Prayer," 49–69.
[94] Targoff, *Common Prayer*, 5.
[95] Targoff, *Common Prayer*, 14, 6.

viduals. The late modern ethic of authenticity grew out of the early modern virtue of sincerity and eventually came to eclipse it in many spheres of social life, including art, politics, and religion. According to Lionel Trilling's seminal analysis, authenticity is the descendant of sincerity, which gained prominence in the moral and political life of Europe beginning in the sixteenth century.[96] As feudalism declined and the church's authority waned, new social mobility and rapid urbanization fed a desire to more closely scrutinize both society and the self. "The sixteenth century was preoccupied to an extreme degree with dissimulation, feigning, and pretence." "Sincerity" came to mean honesty and transparency in self-expression, whereas the word previously denoted the general wholesomeness or purity of a person's life.[97] Trilling highlights a classic formulation of sincerity in the English language, the surprisingly lucid advice that the foolish old courtier Polonius gives to his son in Shakespeare's *Hamlet*:

> This above all: to thine own self be true
> And it doth follow, as the night the day,
> Thou canst not then be false to any man.[98]

Trilling stresses that the "essential condition of virtue" articulated here is truthfulness to *others*; being true to oneself is enjoined as a *means* to that "public end."[99]

In our own time, however, we recall only the first line of the sentence. "Sincerity has lost its former status," so that "the word itself has for us a hollow sound and seems almost to negate its meaning." We think being true to oneself is a virtue in its own right. "If one is true to one's own self for the purpose of avoiding falsehood to others, is one being truly true to one's own self?"[100] Some recent critics of modernity see only narcissism in such a question, but Taylor argues that "there is a powerful moral ideal at work here, however debased and travestied its expression might be." That ideal, "brilliantly defined"

---

[96] Lionel Trilling, *Sincerity and Authenticity* (Cambridge, MA: Harvard University Press, 1972).

[97] Trilling, *Sincerity and Authenticity*, 12–25.

[98] William Shakespeare, *Hamlet*, 1.3.564–66, quoted in Trilling, *Sincerity and Authenticity*, 3.

[99] Trilling, *Sincerity and Authenticity*, 3.

[100] Trilling, *Sincerity and Authenticity*, 9.

by Trilling, is *authenticity*—"being true to oneself, in a specifically modern understanding of that term."[101] Moderns understand being true to themselves not as "egoism" or "permissiveness," but as a *calling* to discover within themselves the "source" of meaning and morality. The modern ethic of authenticity "can be seen just as a continuation and intensification of the development inaugurated by Saint Augustine, who saw the road to God as passing through our own reflexive awareness of ourselves." The "first variants" of authenticity retained the ideal's theistic and Stoic roots. Being true to oneself meant resisting "pressures towards outward conformity" that opposed following the "voice within," which "is most often drowned out by the passions," chiefly pride.[102] Avoiding overt falsehood remained important, but "above all," it was necessary to discern and be true to that inner voice, regardless of what others thought.

Daniel Dahlstrom begins one of the most recent and persuasive philosophical investigations of authenticity with the same famous quote from Shakespeare. Despite calling Trilling's narrative "remarkably parochial," Dahlstrom grants that it shows an important evolution in modern moral reasoning.[103] Although the personal virtue of being true to oneself is unattainable without the social virtue of being true to others, it's a fact that over the past five centuries, "these ideas have been seen to come apart." Social and institutional demands for sincere self-expression appear to many as obstacles to self-realization.[104] In late modernity, the imperatives of inwardness and sincerity exert a combined social pressure on the individual to *appear* sincere in the eyes of others. Therefore, "we sincerely act the part of a sincere person." We want our audience to believe we "have that within which passeth show," so we make a show of sincerity, "with the result

---

[101] Taylor, *Ethics of Authenticity*, 15. For criticism of modern authenticity, see Daniel Bell, *The Cultural Contradictions of Capitalism* (New York: Basic Books, 1976); Allan Bloom, *The Closing of the American Mind: How Higher Education Has Failed Democracy and Impoverished the Souls of Today's Students* (New York: Simon and Schuster, 1987); Christopher Lasch, *The Culture of Narcissism: American Life in an Age of Diminishing Expectations* (New York: Norton, 1978); Lasch, *The Minimal Self: Psychic Survival in Troubled Times* (New York: W. W. Norton, 1984).

[102] Taylor, *Ethics of Authenticity*, 16–17, 26–27.

[103] Daniel O. Dahlstrom, *Identity, Authenticity, and Humility* (Milwaukee, WI: Marquette University Press, 2017), 98.

[104] Dahlstrom, *Identity, Authenticity, and Humility*, 103.

that a judgement may be passed upon our sincerity that it is not authentic."[105]

The "mutation in human nature" that gradually makes being true to oneself seem more important than being true to others is, according to Trilling, the emergence of the modern idea of "society."[106] While Christians had long viewed earthly social orders as fallen and in need of redemption, only in the late sixteenth and early seventeenth centuries did the sense emerge of "society as something man-made, as a product of human decision and contractual arrangements rather than as something natural or preordained."[107] With society disembedded from the cosmic chain of being that extended from God and the angels down through earthly kings and princes to the lowliest peasant, individual persons could survey society as an object of criticism and reform. Along with a class of intellectuals who made it "their business to scrutinize the polity,"[108] a widespread "social imaginary" emerged in which the only legitimate reason for a society's existence was to serve the temporal and spiritual flourishing of its citizens.[109]

This new readiness to question, debate, and refashion whole social orders fueled political and economic revolutions. Religion wasn't immune from similarly rigorous scrutiny and radical transformation. Intellectuals, clerics, and ordinary worshippers associated the exterior, ecclesial forms of public prayer—both scripted and spontaneous—with the expectations of society. But when the social forms of prayer failed to inculcate or express personal devotion, the proposed remedies could be strikingly different. The seventeenth and eighteenth centuries witnessed an even "greater flowering of inward religion" in the devout humanism of France, the Pietist movement in Germany, and Methodism in England. Yet a contrary "emphasis on external conduct, both moral and ritual," also flourished—a "stream of spirituality that we call Jansenist," though "the outlook was much wider than the sect." The "paradoxical pairing" of Jansenism and devout humanism shows that the expanding distance between self and society could engender religious cultures that were

---

[105] Trilling, *Sincerity and Authenticity*, 11; Shakespeare, *Hamlet*, 1.2.85.
[106] Trilling, *Sincerity and Authenticity*, 20.
[107] Guignon, *Being Authentic*, 33.
[108] Trilling, *Sincerity and Authenticity*, 26.
[109] See Taylor, *A Secular Age*, 170–71.

narrowly moralistic and ritualistic, while also giving rise to humanist reactions against the claims of established religion.[110]

A famous example of the latter reaction comes from a man widely acknowledged to be the most important articulator of the modern ethic of authenticity, Jean-Jacques Rousseau (1712–1778).[111] The "Profession of Faith of the Savoyard Vicar" in book 4 of *Émile* is a defense of natural religion against the doctrinal impositions of Christianity, and it led to the book being condemned in both Catholic Paris and Calvinist Geneva. Later in the eighteenth century, however, readers of *Émile* would "admire above all the deep authentic sentiments of the characters,"[112] including the Savoyard vicar who turns traditional Christian teaching on the superiority of interior prayer into a weapon with which to attack liturgical "vanity":

> Let us not confuse the ceremony of religion with religion itself. The worship God asks for is that of the heart. And that worship, when it is sincere, is always [already] uniform. One must be possessed of a mad vanity indeed to imagine that God takes so great an interest in the form of the priest's costume, in the order of the words he pronounces, in the gestures he makes at the altar, and in all his genuflexions. Ah, my friend, remain upright! You will always be near enough to the earth. God wants to be revered in spirit and in truth. This is the duty of all religions, all countries, all men. As to external worship, if it must be uniform for the sake of good order, that is purely a question of public policy; no revelation is needed for that.[113]

The fictional priest who utters these words believes that "the true duties of Religion are independent of the institutions of men."[114] He trusts only reason unaided by any institutionally mediated tradition

[110] Taylor, *A Secular Age*, 227–28.

[111] See Taylor, *Ethics of Authenticity*, 27–28; Guignon, *On Being Authentic*, 55–60; Lindholm, *Culture and Authenticity*, 8–10; Trilling, *Sincerity and Authenticity*, 53–80; Alessandro Ferrara, *Modernity and Authenticity: A Study in Social and Ethical Thought of Jean-Jacques Rousseau* (Albany: State University of New York Press, 1993); Alessandro Ferrara, *Reflective Authenticity: Rethinking the Project of Modernity* (London: Routledge, 1998).

[112] Taylor, *A Secular Age*, 488.

[113] Jean-Jacques Rousseau, *Émile, or, On Education*, ed. Christopher Kelly, trans. Allan David Bloom (Hanover, NH: University Press of New England, 2010), 460.

[114] Rousseau, *Émile*, 479.

of revealed knowledge. Provocatively, Rousseau claims that his priest can still offer Mass sincerely and reverently. The vicar must make a concentrated act of will to bring his internal feelings into agreement with the external ritual, which he is determined not to perform out of long habit. To Rousseau, the priest is a hero of conscience for trying to perform the rites with sincerity, knowing that the "simple people" are given no other way to express their religious sentiments.[115] The theory of religious interiority articulated here remains very influential in popular and scholarly understandings of ritual. Rousseau's "view of the unique privatized subject whose essence cannot be captured in the social conventions of a given society seems to resonate with the conception of ritual action as necessarily devoid of 'authentic, individualized' emotions."[116]

## From amnesia to renewed anamnesis

A privatized understanding of the subject who performs authentic acts of prayer didn't become widespread due to Rousseau's influence alone. Intellectual attacks on the artificial character of social convention made headway because changes in social life accelerated for more than a small elite. Beginning in the late eighteenth century, unprecedented urbanization, industrialization, and political revolution contributed to the "crumbling" of what Danièle Hervieu-Léger calls "societies of memory." Societies of memory understand themselves as belonging to a lineage whose "continuity transcends history" and whose permanence is "affirmed and manifested in the essentially religious act of recalling a past which gives meaning to the present and contains the future." In early modern Europe, parishes, monasteries, and families firmly rooted in one location for as long as anyone could remember still formed "a framework of collective memory

---

[115] Rousseau, *Émile*, 475–77. Part of what Rousseau contributes to the modern understanding of authenticity is a reorientation of the *telos* of the older ideal of sincerity away from others and toward oneself. The attempt to change one's own feelings or dispositions in order to more sincerely play a role that others have assigned comes to be judged as inauthentic, even if the blame redounds, as in the example of the Savoyard Priest, more to society's account than to one's own. See Trilling, *Sincerity and Authenticity*, 10–11; Ferrara, *Reflective Authenticity*, 86–87.

[116] Saba Mahmood, *Politics of Piety: The Islamic Revival and the Feminist Subject* (Princeton, NJ: Princeton University Press, 2005), 129 n. 18.

which provided every individual with the possibility of a link between what comes before and his or her own actual experience." The "central factor" in the disintegration of this framework—but also the slowest to develop—was the subordination of family continuity to the demands of industrial production, national identity, and "individual well-being and fulfillment."[117]

The disintegration of monastic life in Europe outpaced that of parochial life, foreshadowing the crumbling of societies of memory. "Monasteries were often the first and most dramatic victims of historical change between 1790 and 1914," R. W. Franklin notes. "In 1790 in western Europe there were over 1,000 monasteries for Benedictine men and over 500 for women. Fourteen years later, less than two percent of these houses remained and by 1845 only five percent had been restored."[118] Before this collapse, monks were among the scholars studying the liturgical tradition with new methods that relied less on living memory than on documentary research. Through their efforts, *genealogical* authenticity became a domain in which historical science could assert its expertise. Few ordinary Christians had access to the groundbreaking work of cleric-scholars like Jean Mabillon, OSB (1632–1707), Giuseppe Maria Tomasi (1649–1713), and Lodovico Antonio Muratori (1672–1750). Still, for those with the education to read it, historical research provided a new way to form an image of how earlier generations had celebrated the liturgy.

Historical scholarship would spur efforts to reform the liturgy and increase lay participation,[119] but it couldn't halt the gradual erosion of a socially imagined past. Liturgical history, as Robert Taft says, studies "tradition, which is *a genetic vision of the present*."[120] The vision can only be supplied by a living tradition in which the experience of monastic, parochial, and domestic life provides "social evidence of

[117] Danièle Hervieu-Léger, *Religion as a Chain of Memory* (New Brunswick, NJ: Rutgers University Press, 2000), 122–30.

[118] R. W. Franklin, "Nineteenth Century Liturgical Movement," *Worship* 53, no. 1 (January 1979): 13.

[119] See Keith F. Pecklers, "The Jansenist Critique and the Liturgical Reforms of the Seventeenth and Eighteenth Centuries," *Ecclesia Orans* 20 (2003): 330–32; Ulrich L. Lehner, *On the Road to Vatican II: German Catholic Enlightenment and Reform of the Church* (Minneapolis: Fortress, 2016), 174–75.

[120] Robert Taft, "Structural Analysis of Liturgical Units: An Essay in Methodology," *Worship* 52, no. 4 (July 1, 1978): 318. Emphasis in original.

continuity."[121] History's refinement as a science coincides with the transition from societies of memory to societies of change. It serves, in Taft's view, to "recover" elements of "authentic tradition" that have been "washed away by the tides of time" and to form in modern people "a sense of relativity, of seeing the present as always in dynamic tension between past and future."[122] Such modern historical consciousness becomes essential for communities that claim a liturgical tradition when ordinary experience no longer offers unquestionable social evidence of the present's genetic link to the past. The crumbling of collective memory and the shift to a self-consciously historical understanding of genealogical authenticity didn't happen all at once. In French parochial society, Hervieu-Léger says, "the underlying structure of imagined continuity . . . remained more or less in place until the First World War."[123]

Gradually, however, *performative* authenticity in prayer was freed (or robbed) of the social and cosmic context in which it had been embedded. As a counterpart to social, economic, and political modernity, a "psychological modernity" emerged, in which individuals set some "distance . . . between a norm imposed from outside and the authenticity of personal experience."[124] The injunction "to thine own self be true" still held, but authenticity was now seen as an end in itself, separate from a duty to "not be false to any man" and possibly at odds with society's demand for external signs of Christian sincerity. Such a demand, combined with the emphasis on the prayer of the heart, appears inimical to authenticity because performing sincere devotion to satisfy others' expectations "is inevitably co-opted by the social trappings of its expression."[125]

In public prayer, I am in a bind whether I rigorously keep to a liturgical script or spontaneously assemble memorized phrases from Scripture. Whether I'm Catholic or Protestant, if I don't look the part and satisfy my church's expectations for outward religiosity, my performance of prayer is deemed insincere, especially by myself. But if I strive to be a model of ceremonial exactitude or a fountain of free

---

[121] Hervieu-Léger, *Religion as a Chain of Memory*, 134, 123.
[122] Robert Taft, "Liturgy as Theology," *Worship* 56 (March 1982): 116.
[123] Hervieu-Léger, *Religion as a Chain of Memory*, 133.
[124] Hervieu-Léger, *Religion as a Chain of Memory*, 132.
[125] Dahlstrom, *Identity, Authenticity, and Humility*, 103.

prayer, am I not guilty of praying so I "may be seen by others" (Matt 6:5), precisely as a "sincere" Christian? Like Dahlstrom, I believe there are "several things wrong" with the conclusion that the exterior "trappings" of Catholic or Protestant worship make inauthenticity inevitable, but even he thinks that "inauthentic sincerity is all too common," feeding like a parasite off "episodes of authentic sincerity."[126]

In the eighteenth and nineteenth centuries, judgments about the authenticity of public prayer increasingly rested on whether one thought society's influence on the individual worshipper was salutary or corrupting. Rousseau's basic faith in individual conscience, acting in the freedom of self-love elevated by sympathy and connection with the interior source of meaning, found many echoes in Romanticism's rebellion against Enlightenment rationalism.[127] Other cultural elites took a pessimistic view of untutored human nature and assumed that contemporary "customs and morals were refined in comparison to previous, more coarse centuries." Enlightenment theologians shared the latter view and concluded that popular religion, both Catholic and Protestant, was out of step with "polite society."[128]

Some nascent Catholic efforts at liturgical renewal came from Italian and German theologians who perceived a lack of moral and ritual refinement among the uneducated faithful. Noting progress in commerce, art, science, and manners, these "Catholic Enlighteners" worried that "the liturgy had remained the same, and that a growing number of the faithful stopped participating in it, but nevertheless, still practiced superstitious rituals." Revisiting the "forgotten" liturgical reforms promoted by these clerics, Ulrich Lehner identifies three common threads: "a simplification of worship, an emphasis on the community of the faithful, and an increase in the intelligibility of the devotional character of the liturgy." For the Enlighteners, authentic liturgy had to "meet the standards of reason and utility," because "liturgy is not only an expression of worship, but is also in the service of moral education." To combat "superstition" and distraction, priests like Vitus Anton Winter (1754–1814), Johann Josef von Pehem (1740–99), and Beda Pracher (1750–1819) sought to remove exorcisms from the rite of baptism, to discourage praying the rosary during Mass,

---

[126] Dahlstrom, *Identity, Authenticity, and Humility*, 103–4.
[127] See Taylor, *Sources of the Self*, 355–90; Braman, *Meaning and Authenticity*, 3–4.
[128] Lehner, *On the Road to Vatican II*, 172. See Taylor, *A Secular Age*, 234–42.

and to greatly reduce the cult of the saints and their relics. With protection from the Habsburg emperors Joseph II and Leopold II, Catholic Enlighteners also argued for fewer private Masses, an end to simultaneous celebration at multiple altars, communion of the laity with the priest, and more radical reforms aimed at active and intelligent participation by the faithful.[129] In Germany, for example, Benedict Werkmeister (1745–1823) advocated a vernacular liturgy so the laity could join with the priest and one another to "constitute one moral person," possessing "one mouth and heart."[130]

Attempted reforms of the Catholic liturgy, however, were localized, short-lived, and tangled in struggles over papal, episcopal, and national power. Within a few years of the 1786 Synod of Pistoia, Pope Pius VI condemned its liturgical agenda of radical simplification and declared many of its teachings heretical, including one that had censured extending the church's authority "beyond the limits of doctrine and of morals" to "exterior matters."[131] The *Punctuation of Ems*, published by German archbishops in the same year as Pistoia, encouraged vernacular hymn-singing by the congregation and other less provocative liturgical innovations, though these too were ultimately suppressed in 1855.[132] With few exceptions, the Catholic Enlighteners failed to effectively disseminate their ideas among the faithful because of the "pastoral insensitivity" of these liturgists who "wanted sweeping reforms and despised the simple prayer life of the rural population." Lehner gives them credit, however, for firmly establishing liturgical studies as a discipline in the theological academy with its own tradition of uncovering the "forgotten treasures of liturgical history" and using them as a source for liturgical reform.[133]

The difficulty that the Catholic Enlighteners experienced in gaining popular support for their liturgical reforms illustrates the challenge of integrating the genealogical and performative meanings of

---

[129] Lehner, *On the Road to Vatican II*, 171–89.

[130] Benedict Werkmeister, *Beyträge Zur Verbeserung der Katholischen Liturgie in Deutschland* (Ulm, 1789), 346. Quoted in Lehner, *On the Road to Vatican II*, 181.

[131] Pius VI, Constitution *Auctorem fidei*, August 28, 1794, no. 4, trans. in *Enchiridion Symbolorum: Compendium of Creeds, Definitions, and Declarations on Matters of Faith and Morals*, ed. Heinrich Denzinger et al., 43rd ed. (San Francisco: Ignatius Press, 2012), 529, no. 2604.

[132] Pecklers, "Jansenist Critique," 336–38; Lehner, *On the Road to Vatican II*, 176.

[133] Lehner, *On the Road to Vatican II*, 174, 189.

authenticity in the modern age. Historical research can authenticate the origin and lineage of external liturgical forms, but simply using earlier forms as replacements or models for current forms doesn't guarantee that the exterior prayer will harmonize with the interior prayer of the faithful. And while Enlightenment rationalism was honing the historical tools for authenticating the exterior texts and rites of the liturgy, the "Romantic rebellion in its various forms" was looking in the opposite direction for a new wholeness and harmony of life. The "crucial justifying concepts" of Romanticism, Taylor says, were "the idea that we find the truth within us, and in particular in our feelings," and the "Rousseauian notion" that what we find within ourselves is an intuitive sense of the "larger natural order" into which God (or nature itself) has placed us.[134] Social convention—including religious ritual—is precisely *not* the place to look for this providential order, because society corrupts our natural instincts and moral sentiments.

In one sense, this is the logical conclusion of a movement at least as old as Augustine's exhortation to "return within yourself." But as Guignon explains, the "true goal of the Romantic quest" isn't "getting in touch with nature" or with God, but achieving "spiritual autonomy":

> The ultimate destination is the recognition of the absolute priority of the creative powers of the human imagination over both the natural self and nature. At the culmination of the Romantic quest, organic energy is superseded by creative energy. Romanticism aims not at humanity's oneness with nature, but at the ultimate humanization of nature in the apotheosis of human creativity.[135]

In the Romantic understanding of liberated human creativity, performative authenticity means "following an inner voice or impulse," heedless of any higher claims that society purports to make in the name of God or humanity. The overriding imperative is to "give authentic expression" to one's intuitions and sentiments.[136]

---

[134] Taylor, *Sources of the Self*, 368–69.
[135] Guignon, *Being Authentic*, 61.
[136] Taylor, *Sources of the Self*, 368–69.

As inimical as various forms of Romanticism were to liturgical prayer, Thomas O'Meara claims that "only ignorance or prejudice" could deny the link between Romanticism and nineteenth-century movements to restore Catholic life, especially in Germany, where the liturgical movement would become strongly rooted in the twentieth century.[137] "The nineteenth century was an age of revivals," R. W. Franklin explains.[138] The liturgies of earlier generations appealed to the Romantic spirit not as the cold, documentary evidence of a dead past but as the living roots of present tradition, enfeebled by centuries of neglect but still vital. As monasteries had been some of the first victims of the Age of Revolutions, so the revitalization of Catholic liturgy was closely linked in its first steps to the restoration of monastic life, specifically in the first-generation communities of Solesmes, Beuron, and Maria Laach.[139] These monasteries were new foundations, not replicas of earlier communities, and the project of restoring the liturgy was similarly marked by the methods and ideals of its own time, which included both Enlightenment rationalism and Romantic expressionism.

Under the leadership of Prosper Guéranger, OSB (1805–75), for example, the monks of Solesmes sought to uncover the "pure" tradition of Gregorian chant using modern techniques of historical and paleographic research. Guéranger's own commentaries on the liturgical year, however, display "the romantic apparel and expansive lyricism which reveal his debt to Chateaubriand and the French Romantics."[140] One project investigated the *genealogy* of the liturgy; the other taught the right manner of *performing* the liturgy. Both were deeply concerned with the *authenticity* of the liturgy.

Unlike the secular humanism that also took many cues from Romanticism, Catholic revivalism and its Protestant counterparts resisted the step that took inwardness beyond the quest for harmony with the cosmos to the struggle for spiritual autonomy. The Eucharist

[137] Thomas F. O'Meara, "The Origins of the Liturgical Movement and German Romanticism," *Worship* 59, no. 4 (July 1985): 332. See also R. W. Franklin, "Response: Humanism and Transcendence in the 19th Century Liturgical Movement," *Worship* 59, no. 4 (July 1985): 342–53.
[138] R. W. Franklin, "Guéranger and Pastoral Liturgy: A Nineteenth Century Context," *Worship* 50, no. 2 (March 1976): 146.
[139] Franklin, "Nineteenth Century Liturgical Movement," 12.
[140] Franklin, "Nineteenth Century Liturgical Movement," 15, 18.

became a focus first among Catholics, but also among Protestants influenced by the Benedictine liturgical movement, for "eucharistic humanism was a humanism of community in an era when secular humanism tended to revel in individualism and was attracted by the image of the solitary, autonomous hero."[141]

As the seeds of liturgical renewal planted in the long nineteenth century took root, the nascent movement would need to take the modern passion for being true to oneself and harness it to a corporate vision of the church. As change displaced memory in the social experience of Christians around the globe, the church would need to employ new historical methods to recover the authentic sources of the liturgy. And for the liturgy to become again the "indispensable fount" of the "true Christian spirit,"[142] the faithful would need to relearn a liturgical "way of doing things" that values "not only a spiritual inwardness,"[143] but an authentic harmony of minds and voices.

[141] Franklin, "Response: Humanism and Transcendence," 343.

[142] Pius X, *Tra le sollecitudini, Motu Proprio* on the Restoration of Church Music, November 22, 1903, trans. in *The Liturgy Documents, Volume Three: Foundational Documents on the Origins and Implementation of Sacrosanctum Concilium* (Chicago: Liturgy Training Publications, 2013), 25–32.

[143] Romano Guardini, "A Letter from Romano Guardini," *Herder Correspondence* 1, no. 8 (August 1964): 237.

*Chapter Five*

# Authenticity and Liturgical Reform

"The church is constantly reforming itself." This was a provocative claim as recently as 1950, when it appeared as the first sentence in Yves Congar's pioneering study, *True and False Reform in the Church*.[1] After four centuries of mutually exclusive Protestant and Catholic claims to have already enacted authentic reform back in the sixteenth century, it isn't surprising that such words put Congar's book and its author on the wrong side of the Vatican's Holy Office from the time it was published until the Second Vatican Council.[2] But a broader understanding of ecclesial reform greatly predates modernity. The semantic narrowing of "reform" and "reformation" to refer only to modern religious change is itself a modern novelty. When Congar and other twentieth-century theologians wrote of a church "constantly reforming itself,"[3] they were returning to language used before:

[1] Yves Congar, *True and False Reform in the Church*, trans. Paul Philibert (Collegeville, MN: Liturgical Press, 2011), 19.

[2] See especially the council's Dogmatic Constitution on the Church (*Lumen Gentium*) 8 and the Decree on Ecumenism (*Unitatis Redintegratio*) 6. For a detailed study of the language of reform chosen by the council, see Peter De Mey, "Church Renewal and Reform in the Documents of Vatican II: History, Theology, Terminology," *The Jurist* 71, no. 2 (2011): 369–400. On the censure of the first edition of Congar's book, see Paul Philibert, "Translator's Introduction," in Congar, *True and False Reform*, xi.

[3] The famous adage *Ecclesia semper reformanda*, "which most probably was used for the first time by Voetius at the Synod of Dordt in 1609, is not found in the documents of the Second Vatican Council," but "the council comes very close" in *Lumen Gentium* 8 and *Unitatis Redintegratio* 6. De Mey, "Church Renewal and Reform," 369.

The terms most frequently used for religious change in the eleventh and twelfth centuries were *reformare* and *reformatio*. These, like reform today, were multi-purpose words and could refer either to restoration and revival, in a backwards-looking sense, or to rebirth and re-formation, as a forwards-looking change. In its traditional Christian sense, as Paul used it in Romans 12.2, *reformatio* described the ideal of personal renewal, but in the eleventh and twelfth centuries it was also applied to institutions, including the church, the empire, and society as a whole.[4]

As we have seen in the preceding chapters, Christians in *every* era have pursued transformations that encompass both interior and exterior change, that aim to update, not just restore, and that emphasize institutional renewal as much as personal conversion. These efforts at integral reform are especially evident in the realm of liturgical prayer, where the church constantly seeks greater harmony of minds and voices through ongoing adjustments to the internal and external activities of worship.

Still, the aim of this chapter is to show that authenticity is a distinctive concern of the liturgical reform proposed by the Second Vatican Council. If this isn't immediately obvious, it may be because the question of authenticity is usually addressed under the heading of "full, conscious, and active participation," the most characteristic theme of *Sacrosanctum Concilium*.[5] The meaning of active participation (*participatio actuosa*) is among the most hotly contested questions in debates about how the liturgical reform has been implemented. Martin Stuflesser gets to the heart of the matter, though, by asking how we are to understand the relationship between "interior participation" and "exterior participation."[6] He shows that *Sacrosanctum Concilium* proposes "a tension-laden unity" in which "neither meaningless actionism nor pure interiority" define *participatio actuosa*. This key term is best translated as "real participation," he argues, though

---

[4] Giles Constable, *The Reformation of the Twelfth Century* (Cambridge: Cambridge University Press, 1996), 3.

[5] See *Sacrosanctum Concilium* 11, 14, 19, 21, 27, 30, 41, 48, 50, 113, 121, 124.

[6] Martin Stuflesser, "*Actuosa Participatio*: Between Hectic Actionism and New Interiority: Reflections on 'Active Participation' in the Worship of the Church as Both Right and Obligation of the Faithful," trans. Robert J. Daly, *Studia Liturgica* 41, no. 1 (2011): 94.

"active participation" better indicates that the goal is harmony of interior and exterior *activity*.[7]

*Sacrosanctum Concilium* borrows the metaphor from chapter 19 of the Rule of Benedict to describe how the laity's participation in the liturgy becomes *real*, in the sense of possessing performative authenticity. "In order that the liturgy may be able to produce its full effects it is necessary that the faithful come to it with proper dispositions, that their minds be attuned to their voices, and that they cooperate with heavenly grace lest they receive it in vain" (SC 11). The people's participation in the liturgical action becomes real when their interior activity harmonizes with their exterior activity. When minds and voices are in tune, the people become completely "imbued with the spirit of the liturgy."[8] That phrase, repeated throughout *Sacrosanctum Concilium*, evokes the title of Romano Guardini's most famous book and, with it, the highest aspiration of the modern liturgical movement.

The Second Vatican Council's initiation of a broad reform of the liturgy has its roots in the liturgical movement of the nineteenth and twentieth centuries. The meaning, the implications, and even the origins of the liturgical movement continue to be discussed and debated. My limited purpose here is not to argue for a normative description of the movement's overall trajectory, but simply to show that authenticity was a central concern of the modern liturgical movement long before Vatican II. This can be proven by referring to leading representatives of the movement, though I will suggest in subsequent sections of this chapter that the concern for authenticity can also be discerned in the thought of lay Catholics like Charles Péguy, *ressourcement* theologians like Yves Congar, and the papal magisterium leading up to the council. I will argue that these sources—and finally *Sacrosanctum Concilium* itself—refuse to pit the genealogical and performative meanings of authenticity against one another. Instead, the work of reforming the liturgy so that the faithful can "take part fully aware of what they are doing, actively engaged in the rite and enriched

[7] Stuflesser, "*Actuosa Participatio*," 109–113, 118–19. Stuflesser suggests that the German translation, *tätige Teilnahme*, is a more "successful" rendering than the English "active participation" because the German captures the Latin's sense of "being internally filled with something; in this case, with activity." On the other hand, he thinks that the church in the United States has been more successful than the German church, on the whole, in making this infusion of consciousness by liturgical activity a practical reality.

[8] See *Sacrosanctum Concilium* 14, 17, 29, 127.

by it," advances by creating new liturgical forms that "in some way grow organically from forms already existing" (SC 11, 23).

## Authenticity and the Mystical Body

Although the Rule of Benedict is far from unique in calling for liturgical participants to attune their minds and voices, it's significant that the twentieth-century liturgical movement received its initial impetus from Benedictine monks who understood the authenticity of liturgical prayer in just such terms. Even in the nineteenth century, as Prosper Guéranger was reestablishing European monasticism at Solesmes, his broader concern was to revitalize authentic participation in the church's liturgical prayer by the lay faithful in ordinary parishes.[9] In the general preface to his pioneering exposition of the liturgical year, he remarks that "liturgical prayer would soon become powerless were the faithful not to take a real share in it"—to "associate themselves to it in heart" and more frequently "unite themselves exteriorly with the prayer of the Church." Repeatedly, he exhorts the faithful to harmonious and magnanimous participation: "Obtain that largeness of heart which will make you pray the prayer of your mother. Come, and by your share in it fill up that harmony which is so sweet to the ear of God." Guéranger's well-known obsession with the purity of the Roman Rite—and his belief that its forms alone could blend "the most perfect harmony of thought and sentiment with the most marked diversity of genius and expression"—suggest that he was primarily concerned with the genealogical authenticity of the liturgy.[10] Still, Guéranger deserves credit for insisting that liturgy is the central activity of the church and that it is authentic only when it encompasses both exterior and interior activity, in harmony with one another. As R. W. Franklin points out, Guéranger encouraged "active and intelligent participation in the liturgy" at a time when his fellow Catholics saw that as a quixotic quest to turn laypeople into monks.[11]

[9] See R. W. Franklin, "Guéranger and Pastoral Liturgy: A Nineteenth Century Context," *Worship* 50, no. 2 (March 1976): 146–62.

[10] Prosper Guéranger, *The Liturgical Year*, ed. Lucien Fromage, trans. James Laurence Shepherd (Westminster, MD: Newman Press, 1948), vol. 1, 3–6, 18.

[11] R. W. Franklin, "The Nineteenth Century Liturgical Movement," *Worship* 53, no. 1 (January 1979): 16–17.

Most histories of the liturgical movement jump from Guéranger to giants of the twentieth century with little comment on intervening figures, but Joris Geldhof has recently drawn attention to the foundational contribution of Columba Marmion, OSB (1858–1923). The Pauline image of the church as the Body of Christ left earlier imprints on modern theology,[12] but Geldhof credits Marmion with ensuring that "the powerful idea of the Body of Christ was taken over by many a representative of the liturgical movement."[13] The image of the Mystical Body of Christ would supply the nascent liturgical movement with extraordinary theological depth, and its practical implications for the church and for society would be sought in every imaginable sphere. Above all, it implied the *corporate* nature of liturgy as the priestly work in which the members of the Body participate with their Head in glorifying God and sanctifying humans. Marmion similarly deserves credit for reasserting the Augustinian doctrine of the *totus Christus* and showing it to be "most intimately connected with the soteriological core of the faith and its sacramental liturgy."[14]

The beginning of a sustained movement for liturgical renewal in Europe is usually said to coincide with the Belgian National Congress of Catholic Works at Malines in 1909. There, Marmion's pupil Lambert Beauduin, OSB (1873–1960) delivered a report on "The True Prayer of the Church," in which he identifies liturgical participation as the authentic form of Christian piety because of its corporate character.[15] Beauduin stakes his claim for the liturgy's superiority to all other prayer on the 1903 *motu proprio* of Pope Pius X on sacred music, in which the pontiff supplied the famous words taken as a mandate for liturgical renewal:

[12] For instance, Johann Adam Möhler (1796–1838) made the Mystical Body of Christ central to his ecclesiology. See R. W. Franklin, "Response: Humanism and Transcendence in the 19th Century Liturgical Movement," *Worship* 59, no. 4 (July 1985): 347–48; John F. Baldovin, "The Development of the Liturgy: Theological and Historical Roots of *Sacrosanctum Concilium*," *Worship* 87, no. 6 (November 2013): 520–21.

[13] Joris Geldhof, *Liturgy and Secularism: Beyond the Divide* (Collegeville, MN: Liturgical Press, 2018), 105.

[14] Geldhof, *Liturgy and Secularism*, 104. See Columba Marmion, *Christ in His Mysteries* (St. Louis, MO: Herder, 1939); Marmion, *Christ, the Life of the Soul* (Bethesda, MD: Zaccheus Press, 2005).

[15] Lambert Beauduin, "La vraie prière de l'Église," *Questions Liturgiques/Studies in Liturgy* 91, no. 1–2 (2010): 37–41. My translation.

It being our ardent desire to see the true Christian spirit restored in every respect and be preserved by all the faithful, we deem it necessary to provide before everything else for the sanctity and dignity of the temple, in which the faithful assemble for the object of acquiring this spirit from its foremost and indispensable fount, which is the active participation in the holy mysteries and in the public and solemn prayer of the Church.[16]

Beauduin's paraphrase emphasizes that the pope's desire for a comprehensive renewal of Christian life must begin by restoring the participation of the whole Body of Christ in the enactment of the liturgy. "The primary and indispensable source of the true Christian spirit is found in the active participation of the faithful in the liturgy of the church." The need for liturgical renewal is evident, Beauduin thinks, in that "the Christian people," despite their attendance at worship, "no longer draw from the liturgy the authentic expression of their adoration and prayer and the substantial element of their spiritual life."[17]

In his report, Beauduin establishes the liturgical movement's fundamental outlook, in which the image of the Mystical Body of Christ shows that active participation by the faithful is the key to authentic liturgical renewal. He argues that *active* participation is a harmony of interior and exterior participation, in which the minds and voices of the Body's members are in tune individually and corporately. God's purpose is to realize the church's unity "not only by the internal bond of mind, but by a visible bond of external communion." If the church is one, and if its unity is visible, "it follows that the Christian is by definition the member of a body, and that his point of contact with the latter must be sensible." Liturgical prayer is "social and exterior" because only such prayer responds "to the requirements of our spiritual organism" and "will fully realize the desire for unity that Our Lord so emphatically expressed in his priestly prayer" (see John 17:20-24).[18]

---

[16] Pius X, *Tra le sollecitudini, Motu Proprio* on the Restoration of Church Music, November 22, 1903, trans. in *The Liturgy Documents, Volume Three: Foundational Documents on the Origins and Implementation of Sacrosanctum Concilium* (Chicago: Liturgy Training Publications, 2013), 25–32.

[17] Beauduin, "La vraie prière de l'Église," 38.

[18] Beauduin, "La vraie prière de l'Église," 39.

Since authentic liturgical prayer requires two kinds of participation, internal and external, "modern piety suffers from two opposing evils." On the one hand, "our Christian assemblies are losing more and more this collective soul" as many of the faithful "go to God on their own and leave the priest to celebrate mutely." This "religious individualism"—with its preference for "silence and inner prayer" and indifference to "silent rites and misunderstood readings"—debilitates the spiritual lives of the laity. "Weighed down by things of the earth," they cannot "worship God in spirit and in truth" without the "stimulant" and "attraction" of external prayer that "captivates the soul of the masses and holds their attention." According to Beauduin, "[I]t is easy to perceive" from the constrained and listless appearance of most people at church that "their bodies are present" but "their soul is elsewhere." And "if the people do not understand our prayers," there is a temptation for the church's pastors to look elsewhere for "supplementary nourishment." They may keep their people outwardly busy with a variety of pious and pedagogic activities, but the people's "very life is jeopardized" by the "scarcity of bread."[19]

Given the dire situation that Beauduin describes, his proposals for liturgical renewal seem rather modest. He recommends providing the laity with translations of the texts for Sunday Mass and Vespers, so they may participate with understanding instead of saying private prayers during the liturgy.[20] He takes the external forms of the liturgy as given and urges the faithful to attune their minds to the words of the church's official prayer. In a later booklet, for example, he quotes a report of Idesbald Ryelandt, OSB, delivered at one of the Liturgical Weeks hosted at Maredsous Abbey while Columba Marmion was abbot there. Ryelandt suggests that the liturgy forms "the attitudes of the sincere soul" from the outside in:

> In placing the formulas of her own prayer on our lips, the Church tends to put the holy dispositions of mind, which these formulas express, directly into our souls: interior acts of humility, of contrition, affections and acts of love, of praise, of acknowledgment,

[19] Beauduin, "La vraie prière de l'Église," 39–40.
[20] Beauduin, "La vraie prière de l'Église," 41.

of union of our will with God, etc. *Quod os dicit, cor sapit*: What
the mouth speaks, the heart feels.[21]

Other early advocates of liturgical renewal were similarly confident
in the formative power of the external words and rites of the Roman
Catholic liturgy. Their confidence goes hand in hand with belief in
the suitability of the same exterior forms to express the interior
thoughts and emotions of the whole assembly. Guardini, for example,
maintains that the liturgy allows participants to individually worship
God in the secret of their hearts even as the whole Body expresses its
corporate prayer. "The liturgy has perfected a masterly instrument
which has made it possible for us to express our inner life in all its
fullness and depth, without divulging our secrets—'*secretum meum
mihi.*' We can pour out our hearts, and still feel that nothing has been
dragged to light that should remain hidden." For Guardini, tuning
this liturgical "instrument" is mainly a matter of participants adjusting their spontaneous interior prayer to harmonize with the demands
and discretion of the liturgy's exterior forms—without erasing the
distinction between internal and external participation. "To the
Catholic who rightly understands it," the liturgy then becomes both
"a tremendously compelling form of expression" and "a school of
religious training and development."[22]

## Participation, symbolic and real

In the same influential book published during the last year of the
First World War, Guardini carefully delineates internal and external
participation as the two necessary elements of authentic *symbolic*
action. "A genuine symbol is occasioned by the spontaneous expression of an actual and particular spiritual condition. But at the same
time, like works of art, it must rise above the purely individual plane."
Most important, "the spiritual and physical elements must be united
in perfect harmony." Participation in the liturgy implies participation
in corporate, symbolic action. The authenticity of liturgical participation depends, therefore, on harmoniously "welding certain spiri-

[21] Idesbald Ryelandt, quoted in Lambert Beauduin, *Liturgy the Life of the Church*,
trans. Virgil Michel (Collegeville, MN: Liturgical Press, 1929), 92.
[22] Romano Guardini, *The Spirit of the Liturgy*, trans. Ada Lane, Milestones in Catholic
Theology (New York: Crossroad, 1998), 27–28, 47.

tual contents to certain external forms." This means approaching internal and external participation with both "the sense of cohesion and the power of discrimination."[23] To people who sense no symbolic *cohesion*, the external forms of the liturgy appear artificially formal and impersonal. To people who make no *distinction* between interior and exterior prayer, public worship becomes endlessly malleable, to the point of favoring the idiosyncratic expressions of individuals or groups. Guardini admits that both misunderstandings make an integrated liturgical act difficult for modern people to perform authentically:

> Great difficulties lie in the question of the adaptability of the liturgy to every individual, and more especially to the modern man. The latter wants to find in prayer—particularly if he is of an independent turn of mind—the direct expression of his spiritual condition. Yet in the liturgy he is expected to accept, as the mouthpiece of his inner life, a system of ideas, prayer and action, which is too highly generalized, and, as it were, unsuited to him. . . . He easily tends to consider the idiom of the liturgy as artificial, and its ritual as purely formal. Consequently he will often take refuge in forms of prayer and devotional practices whose spiritual value is far inferior to that of the liturgy, but which seem to have one advantage over the latter—that of contemporary, or, at any rate, of congenial origin.[24]

For Odo Casel, OSB (1886–1948), the symbolic cohesion of external and internal participation is expressed by the interchangeability of the words "liturgy" and "mystery." Both words associate worship with "the redeeming work of the risen Lord," but "*mystery* means the heart of the action" while *liturgy* "means rather the action of the church in conjunction with this saving action of Christ's." Still, the action of Christ and the action of the church are not two separate acts but one integral act of the Mystical Body of Christ. "For when the church performs her exterior rites, Christ is inwardly at work in them; thus what the church does is truly mystery."[25] As members of one body, the faithful participate in both the inward and the outward

[23] Guardini, *Spirit of the Liturgy*, 57–58.
[24] Guardini, *Spirit of the Liturgy*, 47–48.
[25] Odo Casel, *The Mystery of Christian Worship* (New York: Crossroad, 1999), 40.

activity. The "necessity of the mystery of worship," as Casel puts it, is a consequence of the mysterious unity of human and divine action in the liturgy—a unity that requires the *harmony* of internal and external activity to perform the liturgy's symbolic action. "A visible community can only express its inward oneness and its harmonious action in God's service through a common ritual act. An act common to God and his human community can only be properly carried out in a symbolic action."[26]

Like Beauduin and Guardini, Casel identifies the "active participation" desired by Pius X as neither internal nor external participation alone, but as the harmonious integration of both. Because these authors are at such pains to show that liturgy is not merely an external act of religion, they place more emphasis on internal participation. "With the liturgy," says Casel, "the decisive thing is inward participation, which does not require unconditionally to be made external." In other words, lay members of the assembly might not express their participation outwardly, but each one would remain "a necessary and real sharer in the liturgical membership" by his or her "objective membership in Christ's body." To say that interior participation is "decisive" is to affirm that one's share in the objective offering made by Christ in his church "should be made real and brought up to its highest pitch by a personal sharing of life."[27] In this, authentic liturgy is no different from authentic private prayer. Both require a personal, subjective decision to conform my life to my prayer, if I want to offer God more than empty words and gestures.

The liturgy, however, is not an individual offering, but a corporate offering. "Healthy members share in the action of a body," so *all* members who remain joined to Christ receive "a living, active sharing in the redeeming deed of Christ." And since "this special sharing in the life of Christ" is "both symbolic and real," *each* member participates in the *whole* offering of the Body of Christ, which is both interior and exterior. "As Christ, not by inward devotion alone, but by his own blood, became minister of the Sanctuary . . . so, too, his people must make true, outwardly recognizable liturgical sacrifice."[28] Thus, the inward devotion of a member of Christ's body is "decisive" *only*

---

[26] Casel, *Mystery of Christian Worship*, 22.
[27] Casel, *Mystery of Christian Worship*, 48.
[28] Casel, *Mystery of Christian Worship*, 14, 16, 22.

if it is a decision to internalize the outward sacrifice that no individual member can perform for himself or herself, since Christ alone makes the decisive offering of his own blood. But this means that the exterior, symbolic action of the liturgy is just as indispensable as the interior act of conforming one's life to what one celebrates. "For without this exterior act we could not recognize God's act."[29] We would forget that we are saved through the participation we have been given in Christ's sacrifice and not through any internal or external perfection of our own.

For Casel, the decisiveness of internal participation implies that the external forms of the liturgy can and should change as much as necessary to make the action of God "outwardly recognizable" in every time and place in which the mystery of redemption is celebrated. He is unusually clear in explaining how the church can adjust the ritual forms of the liturgy without unintentionally making the action of God *un*recognizable to the faithful.

> The content, and so the essential form of the mysteries have been instituted and commanded by our Lord himself; he has entrusted their performance to the church, but not laid down to the last detail what is necessary or desirable for a communal celebration. By leaving the Spirit to his church, he has given her the ability as well, to mint inexhaustible treasure from the mystery entrusted to her, to develop it and to display it to her children in ever new words and gestures.[30]

The gift of the Holy Spirit enables the church to adjust the rites and prayers of the liturgy from the inside out. The same gift allows the church to mint new treasures of liturgical prayer at every level of its hierarchical corporate order. *All* members of the Body of Christ collaborate in the creative enrichment of the liturgy because by baptism they "were all made to drink of one Spirit" (1 Cor 12:13). If Christ has entrusted the performance of the mysteries to his church without specifying every detail, then his ordained ministers should imitate the faith of their Lord. When led by the Spirit, authority in the church insists only on the external forms necessary for communal celebration and excludes only those that hinder communal celebration.

---

[29] Casel, *Mystery of Christian Worship*, 41.
[30] Casel, *Mystery of Christian Worship*, 41.

Although not all have fully internalized what they are given in the celebration of the mysteries, all have some share in the gifts of the Spirit, and all may use their spiritual gifts in a variety of ways to enrich the rites and prayers of the liturgy. Indeed, the catholicity of the church *requires* that a diversity of gifts be employed in worship. "Despite all unity in faith and moral teaching," the church "can and must express itself in a variety of ways." For Casel, unity in variety doesn't require use of the vernacular, and it doesn't imply that decisions about the external forms of the liturgy should be made democratically. Still, authentic hierarchy is not autocracy but "true common life," in which "every order shares what belongs to it with another." Although the clergy have taken a leading part in enriching the liturgy, "laymen, too, have contributed with poetry, music, and the other arts." The same Spirit that unites the church inspires these new outward expressions of worship because it dwells within each member of the Body of Christ. "The whole church, therefore, and all conditions of men in her have worked together, and shaped the liturgical ornaments of the mystery, each man in his way, each according to his *charisma*, all on the ground of their inner sharing in the mysteries."[31]

What is the principle for discerning which new expressions are desirable for communal worship? According to Casel, that principle is *mutual love*. "Common life does not mean everyone having the same, but each giving from his riches to the other to fill up that other's lack. Love is founded on mutual giving." St. Paul's teaching about the Body of Christ is fulfilled, Casel says, when different gifts build up "the whole ecclesia" in the *agape* of God. "Speaking the truth in love, we must grow up in every way into him who is the head, into Christ, from whom the whole body, joined and knit together by every ligament with which it is equipped, as each part is working properly, promotes the body's growth in building itself up in love" (Eph 4:15-16).[32] Authentic liturgy results from all members of the Body speaking the truth in love about the gifts that each member offers.

While he clarified the theological basis for development and change in the outward forms of the liturgy, Casel did not propose any revisions to the Mass or other Catholic rites. Calls for ritual reform on a large scale were rare even among representatives of the

[31] Casel, *Mystery of Christian Worship*, 47–49.
[32] Casel, *Mystery of Christian Worship*, 49.

liturgical movement before the Second World War. There were official reforms of the breviary and sacred chant, and there were experiments with dialogue Masses, freestanding altars, and the vernacular. But the movement primarily emphasized a renewal of liturgical piety from the outside in. In Beauduin's words, the movement sought the "active participation of the Christian people . . . by means of understanding and following the liturgical rites and texts."[33] This meant familiarizing the faithful with the Latin prayers of the Tridentine Mass, for example, so they could tune their minds to what they, the choir, or the priest was saying. Leaders of the movement didn't necessarily advocate revising the rites or celebrating them in the vernacular to facilitate the understanding and active participation of the people.[34]

## Internal and external participation

Calls for reform of the liturgy's exterior were in the air, however, following World War II. The experiences of German and French Catholics during the war coalesced with the wishes of overseas missionaries to form "an ever-broader consensus" regarding the liturgical changes that would bring about more active lay participation.[35] Pope Pius XII responded with a restoration of the ancient liturgical order for Holy Week, a partial relaxation of the eucharistic fast, and expanded permission to sing vernacular hymns and play instruments other than the organ at Mass. However, *Mediator Dei*, the pope's 1947 encyclical directly addressing the liturgical movement, conspicuously

---

[33] Beauduin, *Liturgy the Life of the Church*, 58.

[34] Roland Millare summarizes the initial aims of the liturgical movement well: "The goal of the liturgical movement was not initially or principally ritual reform. In continuity with Pius, the focus of the movement was promoting active participation. In its later years, members of the liturgical movement would concentrate on ritual reforms. Initially, however, the primary concentration was the formation and education of the faithful so they could fully and actively worship God during the liturgy." Roland Millare, "The Spirit of the Liturgical Movement: A Benedictine Renewal of Culture," *Logos* 17, no. 4 (September 2014): 134.

[35] André Haquin, "The Liturgical Movement and Catholic Ritual Revision," in *The Oxford History of Christian Worship* (Oxford: Oxford University Press, 2006), 696–720, at 703–4. See also Siegfried Schmitt, *Die internationalen liturgischen Studientreffen, 1951–1960: Zur Vorgeschichte der Liturgiekonstitution* (Trier: Paulinus-Verlag, 1992).

avoids the word "reform."[36] While affirming the hierarchy's authority "to modify what it deemed not altogether fitting, and to add what appeared more likely to increase the honor paid to Jesus Christ and the august Trinity" (49), the pope doesn't say there is any *current* need for changes to the external rites.

Despite this decisive difference from *Sacrosanctum Concilium*, Pius XII's encyclical anticipates the constitution in many other ways, especially in its rich theology of the liturgy. Above all, *Mediator Dei* continues to urge active participation in the liturgy by all members of the Mystical Body (78, 192, 199), and it defines this desired participation as a harmony of interior and exterior prayer. David Fagerberg says the pope's "main assertion" about participation "is that worship must be both interior and exterior, because people are a composite of soul and body."[37] An equally important reason divine worship must be "manifested outwardly" is that it is "the concern not merely of individuals but of the whole community of mankind." By its "social" character, "exterior worship reveals and emphasizes the unity of the mystical Body" (MD 23). The pope cites St. Augustine and St. Robert Bellarmine to reinforce the mysterious relationship between the church's invisible unity in Christ and the visible celebration of the Eucharist. Through the liturgy of the Mass, "the Church is made to see that in what she offers she herself is offered" (103).[38]

Concerning the participation of the people, *Mediator Dei* holds that "the chief element of divine worship must be interior" (24). "God cannot be honored worthily unless the mind and heart turn to Him in quest of the perfect life" (26). By this, Pius XII indicates that the

---

[36] Pius XII, *Mediator Dei*, Encyclical on the Sacred Liturgy, November 20, 1947, trans. in *The Liturgy Documents, Volume Three: Foundational Documents on the Origins and Implementation of* Sacrosanctum Concilium (Chicago: Liturgy Training Publications, 2013), 107–56 (hereafter cited in the text as MD). The verb *reformare* appears twice in *Mediator Dei*'s 210 paragraphs: once to recall Christ's teaching that "we must be born again and undergo a complete reformation" (156), and once to condemn anyone "who would dare to take on himself to reform" or eradicate popular devotions that do not belong to the liturgy (184). By contrast, forms of the verb *instaurare*, meaning either "to restore" or "to reform," appear twenty times in *Sacrosanctum Concilium*. *Instaurare* does not appear in *Mediator Dei*, nor *reformare* in *Sacrosanctum Concilium*.

[37] David W. Fagerberg, "An Overview of *Mediator Dei*," in *The Liturgy Documents, Volume Three: Foundational Documents on the Origins and Implementation of* Sacrosanctum Concilium (Chicago: Liturgy Training Publications, 2013), 103.

[38] See Augustine, *Sermo* 272; Robert Bellarmine, *De missa*, 2, ch. 8.

most pressing task of liturgical renewal will always be for the faithful to internalize the spirit of the liturgy and make their worship a complete offering of their lives in imitation of Christ's sacrifice. "Whatever pertains to the external worship has assuredly its importance; however, the most pressing duty of Christians is to live the liturgical life, and increase and cherish its supernatural spirit" (197). Although performing "a visible liturgical rite" is the "privilege only of the minister who has been divinely appointed" to represent Christ as Head of the Body, the laity should "consider to what a high dignity they are raised by the sacrament of baptism" (93, 104). By baptism, all Christians "are appointed to give worship to God" and "participate, according to their condition, in the priesthood of Christ" (88). The laity accept their participation in Christ's act of worship "by virtue of their intention" (86),[39] and they make their participation more complete by conforming their hearts to the self-sacrifice of Christ. The interior participation of a layperson is equal in dignity to that of a priest, and it demands no less. "While we stand before the altar, then, it is our duty to transform our hearts, that every trace of sin may be completely blotted out, while whatever promotes supernatural life through Christ may be zealously fostered and strengthened even to the extent that, in union with the immaculate Victim, we become a victim acceptable to the eternal Father" (100).

Provided that representatives of the liturgical movement don't denigrate the high dignity of internal participation, they deserve to be commended when they "strive to make the liturgy even in an external way a sacred act in which all who are present may share." Pius XII doesn't propose new ways of encouraging exterior participation, but he does explicitly approve dialogue Masses, congregational chant, and hymn-singing (105). The "chief aim" of all external participation is "to arouse those internal sentiments and dispositions which should make our hearts become like to that of the High Priest of the New Testament" (106). The greatest distortion that the exterior forms of the liturgy can suffer is to be performed without a corresponding interior act. After affirming the superiority of internal participation, therefore, the pope immediately says that "the sacred liturgy requires" the internal and external elements of participation to be "intimately linked with each other":

---

[39] Pius XII quotes Pope Innocent III, *De Sacro Altaris Mysterio*, 3.6.

This recommendation the liturgy itself is careful to repeat, as often as it prescribes an exterior act of worship. Thus we are urged, when there is question of fasting, for example, "to give interior effect to our outward observance."[40] Otherwise religion clearly amounts to mere formalism, without meaning and without content. You recall, Venerable Brethren, how the divine Master expels from the sacred temple, as unworthy to worship there, people who pretend to honor God with nothing but neat and well-turned phrases, like actors in a theater, and think themselves perfectly capable of working out their eternal salvation without plucking their inveterate vices from their hearts (24).[41]

Elsewhere in *Mediator Dei*, Pius XII denounces the "mistake" of treating the liturgy as "an ornamental ceremonial," and he stresses the "danger of liturgical prayers becoming an empty ritual" (25, 175). He warns that the performance of the rites and prayers can become inauthentic. The exterior acts of the liturgy can lack "genuine and real piety"—"piety of the authentic sort" by which the participants "freely and spontaneously give themselves to the worship of God in its fullest sense" (32).[42] The pope is eager to correct inauthentic celebration that is "inert and negligent," that gives way "to distractions and day-dreaming," or that treats the laity "as if they were outsiders or mute onlookers" rather than real participants (80, 192). Although he prioritizes active participation in the Eucharist, Pius XII also discusses the Divine Office in *Mediator Dei*. In this context, the exhortation from chapter 19 of the Rule of Benedict makes its way into the papal magisterium:

To this lofty dignity of the Church's prayer, there should correspond earnest devotion in our souls. For when in prayer the voice repeats those hymns written under the inspiration of the Holy Ghost and extols God's infinite perfections, it is necessary that the interior sentiment of our souls should accompany the

[40] Pius XII quotes the *secreta* (Prayer over the Offerings) for Thursday after the Second Sunday of Lent, which has been maintained in the post-Vatican II Missal of Paul VI.

[41] Pius XII refers here to the examples of the hypocritical Pharisees in Mark 7:6 and the "lip service" described in Isaiah 29:13.

[42] Pius XII notes that this "authentic" piety corresponds to the "principal act of the virtue of religion," which Thomas Aquinas calls "devotion." See *Summa Theologiae* II–II, q. 82, a. 1.

voice so as to make those sentiments our own in which we are elevated to heaven, adoring and giving due praise and thanks to the Blessed Trinity; "so let us chant in choir that mind and voice may accord together." It is not merely a question of recitation or of singing which, however perfect according to norms of music and the sacred rites, only reaches the ear, but it is especially a question of the ascent of the mind and heart to God so that, united with Christ, we may completely dedicate ourselves and all our actions to Him. (MD 145)

Harmony of mind and voice is essential to an authentic offering of prayer, in which the sacrifice of the High Priest "comes to life again" in all the members of the Body who imitate their Head in total "dedication and even immolation" of themselves, "promptly, generously and earnestly." Christians imitate the life of Jesus Christ, which the liturgy "proposes" for them to make their own, "since it is fitting that the mind believes what the lips sing, and that what the mind believes should be practiced in public and private life" (152–53).

The integrity of each member's life and the authenticity of each member's participation in the liturgy ultimately serve the harmony of the whole Body of Christ. This communion of mind and spirit within the whole church is much more important, says the pope, than any external uniformity in the liturgical participation of the faithful:

> However much variety and disparity there may be in the exterior manner and circumstances in which the Christian laity participate in the Mass and other liturgical functions, constant and earnest effort must be made to unite the congregation in spirit as much as possible with the divine Redeemer, so that their lives may be daily enriched with more abundant sanctity, and greater glory be given to the heavenly Father (111).

Pius XII is anxious that the clergy and laity cooperate in the celebration of the liturgy without resentment or disregard for each other's proper external role. He exhorts his fellow bishops to foster a communion like that of the apostolic church:

> Try in every way . . . that the clergy and people become one in mind and heart, and that the Christian people take such an active part in the liturgy that it becomes a truly sacred action of due worship to the eternal Lord in which the priest . . . and the ordinary faithful are united together (199).

The pope's closing prayer in *Mediator Dei* is a petition for harmony that evokes Acts 4:32 as a model of ecclesial unity. Looking forward to the final consummation of the church's communion in Christ, the prayer also acknowledges Mary, the "ordinary" woman whose life of extraordinary integrity sets the standard for authentic worship of her son:

> May God, whom we worship, and who is "not the God of dissension but of peace" (1 Cor 14:33), graciously grant to us all that during our earthly exile we may with one mind and one heart participate in the sacred liturgy which is, as it were, a preparation and a token of that heavenly liturgy in which we hope one day to sing together with the most glorious Mother of God and our most loving Mother, "To Him that sitteth on the throne, and to the Lamb, benediction and honor, and glory and power for ever and ever" (Rev 5:13).

## Liturgy and contemplation

Twelve years later, as shock over Pope John XXIII's decision to convoke an ecumenical council was giving way to preparatory work, a fascinating and important exchange about "liturgy and contemplation" took place in the pages of two Catholic journals in the United States. *Spiritual Life*, a relatively new publication of the Discalced Carmelites, published a lengthy essay by Jacques and Raïssa Maritain.[43] The review's editor prefaced the essay with an article entitled "A Re-examination of the Liturgical Movement in the United States,"[44] signaling the Maritains' critical view of the supposed excesses of the liturgical movement on both sides of the Atlantic. The couple's stated purpose in writing was to refute "certain opinions" that "can only hurt the liturgical movement, because they go counter to the spirit of the liturgy."[45] The critique from these two famous Catholic philosophers elicited two immediate responses in *Worship*, the liturgical

---

[43] Jacques Maritain and Raïssa Maritain, "Liturgy and Contemplation," *Spiritual Life* 5 (1959): 94–131, republished as Jacques Maritain and Raïssa Maritain, *Liturgy and Contemplation*, trans. Joseph W. Evans (New York: P.J. Kenedy, 1960). All of the following references are to the book version.

[44] Fr. William, OCD, "A Re-examination of the Liturgical Movement in the United States," *Spiritual Life* 5 (1959): 82–93.

[45] Maritain and Maritain, *Liturgy and Contemplation*, 12.

movement's primary organ in the United States, which Virgil Michel, OSB (1888–1938), had founded as *Orate Fratres* thirty-three years earlier at St. John's Abbey in Collegeville, Minnesota. A short piece in the journal's regular book review section offered gentle correctives but was generally appreciative of the Maritains' essay.[46] Two issues later, however, *Worship* published a much longer reaction written by Cipriano Vagaggini, OSB (1909–99),[47] an Italian theologian just named to the preparatory commission on the liturgy for the upcoming ecumenical council. Vagaggini would soon have "the major role in drafting the Constitution on the Liturgy, in which his perspectives on the liturgy, already articulated in his *Theological Dimensions* came to be normatively articulated."[48] His "eirenical" yet forceful demonstration of the "deficiency" of the Maritains' arguments illuminates the perspective that *Sacrosanctum Concilium* would take on the relationship between internal and external participation in the liturgy.[49]

The Maritains' starting point is the stress that *Mediator Dei* repeatedly places on the priority of interior participation. The public worship of the church is necessarily social and exterior, but if it isn't "principally interior," then it becomes "empty formalism."[50] This point is unlikely to draw any objection from supporters of the liturgical movement. The Maritains rightly see that the authenticity of the liturgy is at stake in the question of *how* the faithful participate in its celebration. "Catholic liturgy requires—in order that the public worship rendered to God be authentic and real, and really *dignum et justum*—that the theological virtues be at work in those who participate in it; Catholic liturgy lives on faith, hope and charity."[51] The Maritains' argument rests on the conviction that the three theological virtues, which pertain directly to the love of God, are superior to the

[46] Robert F. Lechner, "Liturgy and Contemplation," *Worship* 34, no. 7 (June 1960): 418–19.

[47] Cipriano Vagaggini, "Liturgy and Contemplation," *Worship* 34, no. 9 (October 1960): 507–23.

[48] Ernest Skublics, "Vagaggini Remembered," *Worship* 93 (January 2019): 32–36. See Cipriano Vagaggini, *Theological Dimensions of the Liturgy: A General Treatise on the Theology of the Liturgy*, trans. Leonard J. Doyle (Collegeville, MN: Liturgical Press, 1959).

[49] Vagaggini, "Liturgy and Contemplation," 519, 523.

[50] Maritain and Maritain, *Liturgy and Contemplation*, 13. See *Mediator Dei* 24, 26, 31–33, 93–106.

[51] Maritain and Maritain, *Liturgy and Contemplation*, 15.

moral virtues, which have as their object subordinate duties to God
and neighbor. Religion appears among the moral virtues in Thomas
Aquinas's account,[52] and in the Maritains' view, "worship and the
liturgy depend essentially on the virtue of religion," but "infused
contemplation depends essentially on the theological virtues." While
"liturgical worship is in itself an end of very great dignity," there is
yet "a higher end" that "liturgical worship implies" and toward which
"it must normally dispose souls." That higher end is the interior
exercise of faith, hope, and charity through contemplative prayer.[53]

Despite what the Maritains say about liturgy implying the direct
exercise of the theological virtues, they seem intent on viewing liturgical participation in opposition to contemplation. In their view, it is
a "great error to conclude that simple participation in the liturgy
would establish our spiritual life at a more elevated degree than the
one to which it is drawn by union with God in contemplation."[54]
What they denigrate as "simple participation" is never explicitly
defined, but they apparently mean a merely external participation
that makes no interior effort to attain perfect love of God and neighbor. They can't identify any representative of the liturgical movement
who actually advocates such empty formalism. Rather, they praise
"one of the most remarkable liturgical parishes in the United States,"
whose pastor continually stresses that "the aim of worship—through
Mass and the sacraments—is love."[55]

Still, they reproach a certain "pseudo-liturgical systematization"
for confusing mere gregariousness in prayer with the true spiritual
fellowship of the Mystical Body. They lament that "the expression
'active participation' has in actual fact taken the sense of participation
externally manifested." As evidence of this misunderstanding, the
Maritains mention "friends in Europe" who "complain that in entering into the church to meditate they are deafened by the noise." One
source of the cacophony is a dialogue Mass whose participants have
forgotten to keep their voices "discreet and prayerful, not screeching."
Another example of "pseudo-liturgical" excess is an overemphasis

---

[52] ST II-II, q.81, a. 5.

[53] Maritain and Maritain, *Liturgy and Contemplation*, 24–28.

[54] Maritain and Maritain, *Liturgy and Contemplation*, 28.

[55] Maritain and Maritain, 77. The Maritains quote Fr. Alfred C. Longley of St.
Richard's in Minneapolis.

on solemn High Mass, to the point of holding Low Mass in contempt. And the Maritains hint that some "arbitrary" experimentation with forms of lay participation is to blame for introducing both "novelty" and "archaism" into the liturgy.[56]

The Maritains' main complaint, however, is that "pseudo-liturgical" enthusiasts are minimizing the importance of individual contemplation, especially that which takes place outside of the church's official liturgy:

> In holding as valid one single form of piety, that in which each one acts in common with the others, and in demanding of all that by word and gesture they obey the liturgical forms with a military precision; in challenging or putting in question private devotions, nay even the adoration of the Blessed Sacrament outside of Mass, those who confuse liturgy and pseudo-liturgy impose on souls rigid frameworks and burden them with external obligations which are of the same type as the observances of the Old Law.[57]

Although the Maritains again cite no examples, a charitable consideration of their concerns would grant that condemnation of solitary contemplation and private devotion has sometimes infiltrated the liturgical movement, risking a rigid collectivism. They grant no such charity, however, to anyone who suggests that contemplative prayer is susceptible to opposite excesses of individualism. "It is absurd to reproach mental prayer and interior recollection with what is their counterfeit," they insist. True contemplatives "are the first to denounce the illusions" caused by "psychological fixation on oneself," so it is "pure nonsense" to suggest that introspection might lead to egoism rather than single-minded devotion to God.[58]

Vagaggini correctly perceives that the Maritains haven't defended the priority of internal participation over external participation so much as they have defined a double standard that tries to curb liturgical excesses while giving free rein to mental prayer. "Every liturgist as well as every contemplative who enjoys the experience of the liturgical life lived in its profound dimensions is justly alarmed"

---

[56] Maritain and Maritain, *Liturgy and Contemplation*, 77–87.
[57] Maritain and Maritain, *Liturgy and Contemplation*, 89–90.
[58] Maritain and Maritain, *Liturgy and Contemplation*, 67.

by the famous couple's accusations. While directed at "abuses," their attacks risk injuring the "authentic values and achievements of the more genuine liturgical movement," for they fail to make "a clear distinction between intra-liturgical contemplation (liturgical-contemplative worship) and extra-liturgical contemplation of a purely private character." Equally unsettling are the absence of any caution about interiority and the near-absence of regard for the visible communion of the liturgical assembly.[59] Vagaggini suspects that the Maritains understand the priority of internal participation "in the sense of private prayer's superiority to liturgical prayer and private contemplation's superiority to liturgical contemplation."[60]

Pius XII teaches the opposite in *Mediator Dei*. "Unquestionably, liturgical prayer, being the public supplication of the illustrious Spouse of Jesus Christ, is superior in excellence to private prayers." Far from lowering the value of interior contemplation, the promotion of liturgical participation raises personal prayer to its highest dignity. *Mediator Dei* holds that the laity's participation integrates their individual prayers into the corporate "action of the church," the *opus operantis Ecclesiae*, whose effectiveness in "achieving sanctity" is as certain as the *ex opere operato* effectiveness of the sacraments (MD 37). "It is in virtue of this doctrine that the [personal] acts of charity, performed in internal and corresponding conformity with the liturgical action, are not purely private acts but become part of the liturgy and share in its special efficacy."[61]

It's obvious, says Vagaggini, that "worship without charity" can exist, "although this would be very imperfect worship."[62] In such inauthentic worship, the exterior offering isn't joined to an interior offering of love, but only to the impulses of a "dead" faith. Whatever motivates lip service can't animate works of love, and this will demonstrate that faith is dead "just as the body without the spirit is dead"

---

[59] Vagaggini, "Liturgy and Contemplation," 519. The most positive thing that the Maritains have to say regarding the visibility of the assembly is that "Jesus likes that we be several—even if only two or three—gathered together in his name." They apparently do not think that what "Jesus likes" has much prescriptive force in this case, since "what counts" is always the individual's "wholly unique presence before God." Maritain and Maritain, *Liturgy and Contemplation*, 83.

[60] Vagaggini, "Liturgy and Contemplation," 519.

[61] Vagaggini, "Liturgy and Contemplation," 521.

[62] Vagaggini, "Liturgy and Contemplation," 511.

(Jas 2:26). But "the more worship includes this actual exercise of charity to a degree as high as possible and together with its offering to God in homage, the more perfect it is." When minds and voices are in tune, "worship cannot help being the perfect and actual exercise of charity." Vagaggini explains:

> What St. Augustine said about the singing of the psalms, per-
> formed with a true, internal and corresponding conformity of
> mind, is true of the whole liturgy for the person in the state of
> grace, and the more perfect the worship the more true it is: "He
> who sings praise not only sings but also loves Him who he
> hymns. In praise there is the speaking forth of the one who
> praises; in song there is the affection of the lover."[63]

To put it another way, the charity of one's liturgical offering increases in direct proportion to the authenticity of one's liturgical participation. As correspondence between mind and voice approaches perfection, one's song of praise becomes a more complete offering of love to God.

All agree that outward worship without interior charity is deeply imperfect. It is a "sophism," Vagaggini argues, to rank liturgy below contemplation simply because liturgical participation satisfies an external duty of religion. If both kinds of prayer depend on the theological virtue of charity for their perfection, then liturgical prayer is not somehow demoted because it also involves the moral virtue of religion while purely interior contemplative prayer doesn't. "That which is offered remains formally an act of charity and not of some other inferior virtue," even though the liturgical "offering as such" is "formally an act of religion."[64]

If one insists that liturgical participation must be weighed in the balance against extra-liturgical contemplation, then the greatest weight must be ascribed to that which is indubitably offered in the liturgy. What is offered is the charity of Christ: the love by which he sacrifices himself for his church and makes them to drink of his Holy Spirit. By the same Spirit, the same charity animates the Mystical

---

[63] Vagaggini, "Liturgy and Contemplation," 511. Vagaggini quotes Augustine, *Enarratio in Ps.* 72, 1.

[64] Vagaggini, "Liturgy and Contemplation," 511–12.

Body as its bond of communion and as the source of salvation for each of its members. Liturgical participation in Christ's offering of love is at once the most intimately personal and the most profoundly communal act. It's true, Vagaggini admits, that every act of charity offered to God is the act of an individual seeking "Person to person contact":

> But when this act, however intimate and personal, is none other than the mind's internal and connaturally corresponding conformity (at least in its general and profound sense) to the performance of and participation in the liturgical act (e.g. Mass, recitation or singing of psalms), it is not at all the purely private act of the person who performs it; it is also an act of the Church as such which, in intimate union with her divine Head, performs the act and offers it to God in and through this person. And as such this act of prayer, though internal and personal, possesses a dignity and efficacy superior to any other act of prayer which, though it be similar in all other respects, is purely private.[65]

The superiority of internal participation over external participation must be understood alongside the superiority of liturgical prayer over private contemplation. Vagaggini rightly emphasizes that *Mediator Dei* insists on *both* points, and it does so for a single reason. The inward offering of love is performed more perfectly by members of Christ's body when they join themselves more closely to the perfect offering of their Head. The liturgy *is* that perfect offering of Christ because it is the *corporate* act of the church, the Body of Christ, Head and members. Although the liturgy isn't corporate in its exterior forms alone, it's through external participation in those forms of worship that the minds of the members attain closer harmony with one another and greater conformity with the mind of Christ. Voices mediate the attunement of minds and therefore the internalization of the "true Christian spirit," acquired from its "foremost and indispensable fount, which is the active participation in the holy mysteries and in the public and solemn prayer of the Church."[66] If "the chief element of divine worship must be interior," then "the sacred liturgy requires" that internal and external participation "be intimately

---

[65] Vagaggini, "Liturgy and Contemplation," 514.
[66] Pius X, *Tra le sollecitudini*.

linked with each other" (MD 24). Harmony of minds *and* voices is the indispensable condition of becoming imbued with the authentic spirit of the liturgy.

About one month after the publication of Vagaggini's reply to the Maritains' essay, he attended the first meeting of the preparatory commission on the liturgy for the Second Vatican Ecumenical Council. He was appointed secretary of the subcommission tasked with drafting "a theological-ascetical chapter on the mystery of the liturgy in the life of the church," to introduce the council's prospective document on the liturgy. According to the commission's overall secretary, Annibale Bugnini, "The chapter grew more substantial and became the most important part of the entire Constitution." The contribution of Vagaggini's group thus became the first part of the first chapter of the Constitution on the Sacred Liturgy (SC 5–13). Vagaggini was joined on that subcommission by one other Benedictine, Giovanni Bruno Cannizzaro, OSB, abbot of Sant'Andrea in Genoa, who also served as relator for the subcommission on participation of the faithful in the sacred liturgy. After laboring for two days straight with Pierre Jounel to meet the deadline for drafting the text that would become *Sacrosanctum Concilium* 14–20, Abbot Cannizzaro died suddenly at age fifty-eight, a "martyr" to the work of the preparatory commission.[67]

Paragraph 11 is the hinge that connects these two opening sections of *Sacrosanctum Concilium* by introducing the goal of having the faithful "take part fully aware of what they are doing, actively engaged in the rite and enriched by it." At this critical juncture, the influence of the Rule of Benedict—and, doubtless, of the Benedictines on the commission—is heard in the words that express how the faithful may authentically participate in the liturgy: "Their minds should be attuned to their voices (*mentem suam voci accommodent*)."

## Real liturgy and true reform

After trying out a few different titles, the drafters named the first chapter of the constitution "General Principles for the Restoration

---

[67] Annibale Bugnini, *The Reform of the Liturgy, 1948–1975*, trans. Matthew J. O'Connell (Collegeville, MN: Liturgical Press, 1990), 15–17, 27–28.

and Promotion of the Sacred Liturgy."[68] The ideal of performative authenticity articulated in *Sacrosanctum Concilium* 11 is one guiding principle, but in what sense is it a principle of *reform* that justifies changes aimed at renewing and invigorating the liturgical participation of the faithful? The paragraph appears to address only interior change: tuning adjustments that proceed inward from the received external forms of the liturgy. The faithful are asked to come to the liturgy "with proper dispositions." And in the traditional formula that follows, *mentem suam voci accommodent* more closely resembles the Benedictine wording (*ut mens concordet voci*) than the Franciscan variant (*ut vox concordet menti*). We shouldn't conclude from this, however, that the constitution excludes adjustments to the traditional external rites and prayers of the liturgy. It should be obvious from the thoroughness and vast scope of the mandated ritual revision that the council deemed exterior changes necessary, if speech, song, and gesture are to accord with the "spirit of the liturgy" so frequently mentioned in *Sacrosanctum Concilium*.[69] The constitution also declares that the church is ready to admit new external elements drawn from "the qualities and talents of the various races and nations . . . into the liturgy itself, provided they harmonize with its true and authentic spirit" (SC 37).

Representatives of the liturgical movement had emphasized the need for modern worshippers to attune their interior prayer more closely to the liturgical prayer of the church. While the council was debating the schema for the liturgy constitution, Guardini reiterated that the faithful, "in co-celebrating the liturgy, will do so the more purely and correctly, the more sincerely they disregard their own private wishes" and "entrust themselves" to the "slow movements" of the Holy Spirit at work "in the heart of the Church."[70] Yet he also recognized that the external forms of the liturgy sometimes failed to resonate with the liturgy's authentic spirit. "People are driven from the church by having outmoded forms of worship forced upon them."

[68] Bugnini, *The Reform of the Liturgy*, 17 n. 2.

[69] The "spirit of the liturgy" is mentioned in these or similar words seven times (SC 14, 17, 29, 37, 116, 127). Additionally, the "true Christian spirit," which the faithful are to derive from their participation in the liturgy, is mentioned twice (SC 14, 121).

[70] Romano Guardini, "Personal Prayer and the Prayers of the Church," in *Unto the Altar: The Practice of Catholic Worship*, ed. Alfons Kirchgaessner, trans. Rosaleen Brennan (New York: Herder and Herder, 1963), 32–43, at 37.

Critics who balk "as soon as someone does something other than what has always been done" should take care that what they are trying to preserve is "the true liturgy of the Church" and not one of the "popular and private devotions, sometimes of very doubtful value" that dominate even "the celebration of Holy Mass itself."[71]

Yves Congar discussed the need to adjust the external forms of the liturgy in an essay published some fifteen years before the council. He claims that he is simply following traditional sacramental theology in granting the place of first importance to the faithful's internalization of what they participate in externally.[72] In the analysis suggested by Augustine and systematized by Aquinas, the union of Christian believers with God and with each other is the *res* of every sacrament. Communion is the inward *reality* that constitutes the ultimate fruit of sacramental signs.[73] Without this real fruition in the souls of the faithful, manifest "not in the offering of anything external but rather in believers' offering their very selves," the rules for valid and licit administration of the sacraments have no real purpose and no true meaning:

> Conversion to the deepest Reality is a movement of conversion from the outside to the inside, from sense experience to spiritual reality, from signs to the Truth itself. . . .
>
> Every "sacrament" exists for the sake of its *res*, which is a spiritual reality *in the believer*. Therefore liturgy, rituals, and the church, which is itself the Great Sacrament, have to find their fulfillment and their verification *in the persons who live out their meaning*. So to be "real," then, means to arrive at this reality, to become one's true self—a reality and a truth which have become a spiritual fruition in believers themselves. Put another way, for sacraments to be "real" means for them to achieve their *res*, the fulfillment of their spiritual reality, which is light and grace in the consciousness of a spiritual person.[74]

[71] Romano Guardini, "Some Dangers of the Liturgical Revival," in *Unto the Altar: The Practice of Catholic Worship*, ed. Alfons Kirchgaessner, trans. Rosaleen Brennan (New York: Herder and Herder, 1963), 13–22, at 18–20.

[72] Yves Congar, " 'Real' Liturgy, 'Real' Preaching," in *At the Heart of Christian Worship: Liturgical Essays of Yves Congar*, trans. Paul Philibert (Collegeville, MN: Liturgical Press, 2010), 4–5. See also Congar, *True and False Reform*, 128–29.

[73] See ST III, q. 66, a. 1.

[74] Congar, " 'Real' Liturgy, 'Real' Preaching," 4–6. Italics in original.

Congar believes that the external forms of sacramental celebration must change if they are not bearing "real" fruit in the lives of Christians. "A 'real' liturgy is one adapted to being internalized, to producing its *res*—its spiritual effect—in the souls of the faithful, to being received and personalized in people's awareness. As long as what occurs is merely *something special happening* that remains exterior to the hearts of the faithful, what we still have are sacrifices of the kind criticized by the prophets."[75] Congar is specifically concerned that the rites and prayers of the Mass, unchanged since the Council of Trent, are not well adapted to being internalized in the souls of the faithful. Language is the first obstacle, since none of the laity understand prayers and readings spoken in Latin "and almost nobody wants to be bothered to try to follow them." Similarly, "ritual gestures that require a complicated historical explanation in order to make sense are not adapted to the spiritual needs of our contemporaries." In Congar's view, "[A] ceremony that is artificial and uses language that is uncommon" becomes "nothing more than a ritual" that "adds nothing and changes nothing even in the lives of those who still practice it."[76]

Although Congar is more willing than others to criticize the exterior forms of the Roman liturgy as outmoded, he bases his assessment on the same belief in the superiority of interior participation taught by *Mediator Dei* and expressed by representatives of the liturgical movement. He agrees about the need for the faithful to tune their minds to their voices and internalize what they participate in externally. Yet he sees that such internalization of the liturgy's "reality" also requires adjustments to its external forms. These adjustments proceed from an understanding of the liturgy's true spirit—a spirit of communion and cooperation in prayer—already internalized in the minds and hearts of the faithful. Though incomplete and realized to varying degrees in different members of the Mystical Body, their understanding of the liturgy's true nature can nevertheless serve as the basis for adjusting the exterior forms of worship from the inside out.

Congar went further than many of his contemporaries in arguing that these necessary external adjustments should include significant

[75] Congar, " 'Real' Liturgy, 'Real' Preaching," 6. Italics in original.
[76] Congar, " 'Real' Liturgy, 'Real' Preaching," 7–8, 10–11.

revision of the liturgy's rites and prayers. He didn't propose specific changes to the rites like Vagaggini did. But he showed that such reforms, far from threatening the genealogical authenticity of the liturgy, are essential to the preservation of the church's liturgical tradition. His main role in liturgical renewal was to demonstrate that authentic *ecclesial* reform should begin by adjusting liturgical forms to allow for a more authentic celebration by all members of the Body of Christ. This was no small contribution, coming from one of the most influential theologians of Vatican II.[77] It's not surprising that Congar would give pride of place to liturgical reform. In the 1950 introduction to *True and False Reform in the Church*, he acknowledges that "the first of all modern reform movements is the liturgical movement," which "was interested in a more communal and more intelligent celebration of liturgical rites but was also linked to the movement of retrieving the theological sources—the Bible and the Fathers—and to the renewal of preaching and catechetics."[78] From its beginnings, the liturgical movement showed that the performative authenticity of the liturgy goes hand in hand with its genealogical authenticity.

In *True and False Reform*, Congar identifies "a passion for authenticity" as both a "current attitude" of contemporary people and a theological orientation of permanent value. Throughout the book, he uses "sincerity" and "authenticity" interchangeably to speak of correspondence between interior and exterior. He distinguishes "authenticity" from "truth," however. "Objective truth" has a right to reason's obedience, but it "does not say everything about the authenticity of the

---

[77] Innocent Smith analyzes the contributions of Vagaggini and Congar together, noting that it is limiting to think of the former only as a liturgist and the latter only as an ecclesiologist. "Although known today principally as a liturgist, Vagaggini made important contributions in the fields of patristic studies and theological criteriology. Likewise, Congar, although known today especially for his work on ecclesiology and ecumenism, was an influential figure in the French Liturgical Movement and was immersed in the life of the liturgy as well as in the research of his liturgist colleagues." Smith argues that the Second Vatican Council's "extensive liturgical documentation" and overall "appeal to the liturgy as a monument of Tradition" are "indebted to the renewed theological interest in liturgical sources that is represented by scholars such as Congar and Vagaggini." Innocent Smith, "Vagaggini and Congar on the Liturgy and Theology," *Questions Liturgiques* 96, no. 3–4 (2015): 192, 220.

[78] Congar, *True and False Reform*, 26.

gesture *of some particular person."*[79] The authenticity of a person's gesture is precisely subjective, though it is objectively demanded by "the very reality of being Christian—the truth about the religious relation of the human person with God." One might be tempted to dismiss such a modern turn to the subject as a superficial "itch to call into question received customs," but Congar argues that "the taste for authentic gestures is also a taste for the authenticity of Christian reality."[80] And the liturgy is the place where the church can least afford to ignore this taste for authenticity:

> The wish for authentic self-expression means just what it sounds like. This has always been a requirement of genuine Christian character, but it is now an irrepressible need in the light of modern sincerity—especially with respect to worship, which is our relation to God. . . .
>
> People want a Mass that is genuinely the praise and the self-offering of a community united in faith, not just a ritual that goes its own way page after page as people, who may or may not follow the Mass, watch. Here's the point: too many things have become "rituals" for us, "things" that exist in themselves, ready-made. We are preoccupied to carry out the ceremony, meet the conditions for validity, but without being concerned whether these rituals are the actions of real living persons.[81]

The difference between an authentic expression of the tradition and "just a ritual" is the difference between life and death. In Congar's account, authentic worship must maintain fidelity to the "living principle of tradition" even if that "requires letting go of the forms that [the principle] has taken at times." Fidelity that "exists only at the level of articulated forms and formulas" is condemned to deteriorate into "mere routine" as forms that no longer express the principle grind on (though only for a time) by mere force of "habit."[82] For Congar, "habit" is mainly an obstacle to authenticity. He admits the danger of changing practices that have become habitual.[83] But he believes that the greater threat is habitual conformity masquerading as fidelity

[79] Congar, *True and False Reform*, 40–42. Italics in original.
[80] Congar, *True and False Reform*, 47.
[81] Congar, *True and False Reform*, 45–46.
[82] Congar, *True and False Reform*, 155–56.
[83] Congar, *True and False Reform*, 151.

to tradition. "Most people don't live Christianity at the level of principles but at the level of habits. Such habits are less personal choices than the custom of a sociological group, behaviors belonging to a cultural milieu. Practically speaking, they confuse received ideas with tradition. Imagining that they are maintaining fidelity to principle, in fact people cling to a simple translation of said principle into the language of a cultural period."[84]

Congar's frequent references to Charles Péguy (1873–1914), the French poet and polemicist, are the key to his critique of "habitual" Christianity in *True and False Reform*.[85] Charles Taylor recounts Péguy's distinctly modern "itinerary to the Faith":

> A crucial distinction for Péguy lay between a life dominated by fixed habits, and one in which one could creatively renew oneself, even against the force of acquired and rigidified forms. The habit-dominated life was indeed one in which one was determined by one's past, repeating the established forms which had been stamped into one. Creative renewal was only possible in action which by its very nature had to have a certain temporal depth. This kind of action had to draw on the forms which had been shaped in a deeper past, but not by a simple mechanical reproduction, as with "habit," rather by a creative re-application of the spirit of the tradition.[86]

As Taylor observes, it is "not hard to recognize in Péguy some of the themes which became central to the reforms of Vatican II" because "much of the crucial theological writing that laid the groundwork for the Council . . . emerged from a milieu of Catholic thought and sensibility which had been marked by Péguy." Péguy influenced Congar, Henri de Lubac, Jean Daniélou, and Hans Urs von Balthasar, among other Catholic theologians.[87] The broad twentieth-century

---

[84] Congar, *True and False Reform*, 154.

[85] There are as many references to Péguy by name, for example, as there are to Thomas Aquinas. See Congar, *True and False Reform*, 374–75.

[86] Taylor, *A Secular Age*, 747.

[87] Taylor, *A Secular Age*, 752. Note that Péguy's influence is not limited to theologians who, like Congar, became associated with the journal *Concilium* and with a more "progressive" interpretation of Vatican II. The bulk of Péguy's postconciliar admirers seem to be among the theologians who aligned themselves with the "rival" journal, *Communio*, including de Lubac, Daniélou, and especially Hans Urs von Balthasar. See Hans Urs von Balthasar, "Péguy," in *The Glory of the Lord: A Theological*

theological movement to "return to the sources" even borrowed its name, "*ressourcement*," from Péguy.[88]

Following Vatican II, *ressourcement* remained a guiding principle of liturgical, patristic, biblical, and ecumenical renewal.[89] In its deepest sense, though, liturgical *ressourcement* is more than a movement to rediscover the authentic sources of the liturgy; it is a movement to rediscover the liturgy as the authentic source of the church's life. As Andrea Grillo says, the liturgical movement aimed to ameliorate the "experience of troubling inauthenticity in ritual worship," so that the "liturgy's essential role" as "source and summit" of the church's activity could become more apparent. "The late modern age approached the 'liturgical question' on two levels: that of an *initiation into the rite* and *the reform of the rites themselves*."[90] The classical liturgical movement understood that ritual reform without inward spiritual renewal would be fruitless *and* that efforts to initiate the people into more active participation would have little impact without faithful, creative renewal of the liturgy's external ritual forms. The movement for authentic liturgical renewal has to proceed in both directions simultaneously. The exterior rites initiate the faithful *into* a more liturgical consciousness, while the church reforms the exterior ritual *out of* fidelity to the people's living and growing awareness of their communion in Christ.

---

*Aesthetics, Vol. 3: Studies in Theological Style: Lay Styles*, trans. Andrew Louth et al. (San Francisco: Ignatius Press, 1986), 400–517; John Saward, "The Pedagogy of Péguy," *The Chesterton Review* 19, no. 3 (August 1993): 357–79; Michelle K. Borras, "Péguy, Expositor of Christian Hope," *Communio* 35, no. 2 (Summer 2008): 221–54.

[88] Congar precisely locates the first appearance of the word "ressourcement" in Péguy's essay, *L'Argent* (in *Oeuvres complètes*, vol. 14 [Paris: Ed. de la Nouvelle revue française, 1932], 218). See Yves Congar, "Le prophète Péguy," *Témoignage Chrétien* 26 (August 1949), 1; Congar, *True and False Reform*, 39; Gabriel Flynn and Paul D. Murray, eds., *Ressourcement: A Movement for Renewal in Twentieth-Century Catholic Theology* (Oxford: Oxford University Press, 2012), 4.

[89] For an overview of how *ressourcement* was understood within the liturgical movement, see Keith F. Pecklers, "Ressourcement and the Renewal of Catholic Liturgy: On Celebrating the New Rite," in *Ressourcement: A Movement for Renewal in Twentieth-Century Catholic Theology*, ed. Gabriel Flynn and Paul D. Murray (Oxford: Oxford University Press, 2012), 318–32.

[90] Andrea Grillo, *Beyond Pius V: Conflicting Interpretations of the Liturgical Reform*, trans. Barry Hudock (Collegeville, MN: Liturgical Press, 2013), 55–56, 34. Italics in original.

The final decision to echo chapter 19 of the Rule of Benedict in *Sacrosanctum Concilium* 11—and to quote it in paragraph 90, where *"mens concordet voci"* appears word for word in a section on the Divine Office—must be attributed to the bishops of the council. The reference is no surprise, given the pioneering role of Benedictines in the liturgical movement, the influence of *Mediator Dei* on *Sacrosanctum Concilium*, and the direct contribution of Vagaggini and other monks to drafting the Constitution on the Sacred Liturgy. Above all, however, the exhortation to attune minds with voices reflects the council's conviction that authentic liturgical participation is the overarching goal of authentic liturgical reform. "In the restoration and development of the sacred liturgy, the full and active participation by all the people is the paramount concern, for it is the primary, indeed the indispensable source from which the faithful are to derive the true Christian spirit" (SC 14). *Sacrosanctum Concilium* 14 is undoubtedly the most frequently quoted paragraph of the constitution—rightly so, since it names the chief aim of the reform by recalling the famous words of Pius X. But paragraph 11, which first calls the faithful to participate "actively" in the rite, shows that the "full and active" participation prescribed in paragraph 14 is a *harmony* of interior and exterior participation. According to Stuflesser, this harmony is "tension-laden." The authenticity of the liturgical action dissolves if the people's participation becomes only external or only internal. Authentic liturgy must not allow the participation of the faithful to collapse into the unreality of either "mindless actionism" or "abstract interiority."[91] To put it in Congar's terms, "true reform" aims to restore authenticity to liturgy that has become "unreal" due to disharmony between interior and exterior participation. The council embraced just such a reform, which prioritizes performative authenticity above all else.

## Active participation and organic development

To commemorate the twentieth anniversary of *Sacrosanctum Concilium* and honor one of its major architects, the Catholic Institute of Toulouse published a massive collection of essays by Monsignor

---

[91] Stuflesser, *"Actuosa Participatio,"* 109–13.

Aimé-Georges Martimort and his colleagues.[92] Though Martimort wasn't a monk, his admirers took the collection's title from the Rule of Benedict: *Mens concordet voci*.[93] Bishop René Boudon, president of the Francophone commission for liturgical translations and one of the council fathers, added his appreciation for Martimort's contributions:

> The title that you have chosen, inspired by the Rule of Saint Benedict and taken up again by the conciliar Constitution, expresses well the efforts he has spent without counting for an *authentic participation of the faithful* in the liturgy: *Mens concordet voci*: "May the soul harmonize with the voice."[94]

Most essays in the collection are historical studies, reflecting the belief of Martimort and his fellow liturgical scholars that organic development and active participation—genealogical authenticity and performative authenticity—can and should be pursued together.

Regrettably, as M. Francis Mannion observes, the liturgical movement has splintered into competing "agendas" since Vatican II. The dissipation of the liturgical movement's unity and energy is manifest in the tendency for each agenda to favor "a particular reading of the Constitution" that emphasizes one of the document's aims while criticizing the overemphasis or misunderstanding of another. Most detrimental to the work of liturgical renewal is the acrimony between agendas that see active participation as the "overriding concern" of liturgical reform and agendas whose "guiding prescription" is *Sacrosanctum Concilium* 23, which requires that "any new forms adopted

[92] Martimort was one of ten consultors who participated in an extra meeting of the subcommission charged with drafting the first chapter of the Constitution on the Sacred Liturgy. The meeting was held in October 1961 to complete a "more careful development of the text" of the chapter. The preparatory commission's secretary, Annibale Bugnini, later felt compelled to deny that the group had "gathered secretly to interfere with the work of the other groups and revise it along 'progressive' lines." Cipriano Vagaggini also participated in the meeting and revision of the chapter. See Bugnini, *Reform of the Liturgy*, 19–20.

[93] *Mens concordet voci pour Mgr A.G. Martimort: à l'occasion de ses quarante années d'enseignement et des vingt ans de la Constitution* Sacrosanctum Concilium (Paris: Desclée, 1983). A few years earlier, a similar *festschrift* with an almost identical title honored Eugène Cardine, OSB, probably the most important contributor to the restoration of Gregorian chant since the refounding of the Abbey of Solesmes. Eugène Cardine and Johannes Berchmans Göschl, *Ut mens concordet voci: Festschr. Eugene Cardine zum 75. Geburtstag* (S[ank]t Ottilien: Eos-Verlag, 1980).

[94] *Mens concordet voci*, 7. My translation. Emphasis added.

should in some way grow organically from forms already existing."[95] Neither camp admits that its concerns are one-sided. Instead, the defenders of organic development claim they are also upholding the "authentic" meaning of *participatio actuosa*.[96] Those who emphasize that the active participation of the people is the "paramount concern" of liturgical renewal (SC 14) claim they are honoring the "authentic" meaning of tradition. In this family quarrel over authentic reform, authentic renewal, the authentic heritage of the liturgical movement, and the authentic interpretation of *Sacrosanctum Concilium*, the word "authentic" is thrown around in ways that do nothing to advance our understanding of what makes the liturgical act authentic. A professor of liturgy at a Roman pontifical university warns that the church must "protect the authentic intentions of *Sacrosanctum Concilium*" from traditionalists who promote wider use of the preconciliar rite of Mass, since the council fathers unambiguously ordered the revision of that rite (see SC 50).[97] Meanwhile, the prefect of the Congregation for Divine Worship and Discipline of the Sacraments recommends forming seminarians in the preconciliar rite as a means to "a more authentic implementation of *Sacrosanctum Concilium*," since the previous rite had formed the liturgical sensibility of the council fathers themselves.[98]

In their efforts to prevail, the competing agendas seeking "authentic liturgical reform" too often speak of authentic liturgy as something produced by ecclesiastical authority. But authenticity, in both its performative and genealogical meanings, is properly the fruit of obedience to the Holy Spirit. The role of legitimate authority is to discern and acknowledge authentic participation in the liturgy and authentic

---

[95] M. Francis Mannion, "The Catholicity of the Liturgy: Shaping a New Agenda," in *Beyond the Prosaic: Renewing the Liturgical Movement*, ed. Stratford Caldecott (Edinburgh: T&T Clark, 1998), 11–48. Though Mannion's essay is over twenty years old, the church bureaucracies, lay organizations, academic societies, and individuals that he identifies with different liturgical "agendas" remain committed to essentially the same positions today.

[96] See Alcuin Reid, "*Ut Mens Nostra Concordet Voci Nostrae:* Sacred Music and Actual Participation in the Liturgy," *Sacred Music* 139, no. 1 (2012): 9–10; Reid, "The New Liturgical Movement after the Pontificate of Benedict XVI," *Sacred Music* 141, no. 1 (2014): 24–25.

[97] Grillo, *Beyond Pius V*, 33.

[98] Robert Cardinal Sarah, "Towards an Authentic Implementation of *Sacrosanctum Concilium*," in *Authentic Liturgical Renewal in Contemporary Perspective*, ed. Uwe Michael Lang (London: Bloomsbury T&T Clark, 2017), 3–19, at 13–14.

development of the liturgy wherever both flourish in response to the prompting of the Spirit. "Ecclesiastical authorities should take steps against arbitrary innovations," Guardini says, but they should also maintain confidence in "those who have been working on these matters for so long with seriousness and feelings of responsibility."[99] Guardini's point isn't that established experts have earned the privilege of a freer hand, but that longtime laborers in the field of liturgical renewal have cultivated in themselves the authentic spirit of the liturgy. Their ability to perform an integrated liturgical act and call forth authentic participation from all the faithful rests on their own "good understanding" of the "sacred action" (SC 48).[100] The seriousness, responsibility, and performative authenticity with which they approach the liturgy promotes its organic development in a way that the sheer exercise of authority cannot.

The modern movement for performative authenticity in the liturgy has always been a movement for genealogical authenticity too. If the liturgical movement's vision remains unfulfilled, it isn't because organic development has been sacrificed on the altar of active participation. The temptation to dichotomize the two meanings of authenticity hinders progress in liturgical renewal. The more troubling dichotomy, however, is a split in the quest for performative authenticity. The next chapter will argue that to fulfill the council's goal of "minds in tune with voices," the heirs of the liturgical movement must harmonize two broad approaches to authentic liturgy: those that prioritize tuning voices to minds, from the inside out, and those that privilege tuning minds to voices, from the outside in.

---

[99] Guardini, "Some Dangers," 13–22, at 21.

[100] Here and in the next chapter, I render *bene intellegentes* as "good understanding," following the translation prepared by the International Commission on English in the Liturgy (ICEL). The translation in the collection edited by Austin Flannery renders *bene intellegentes* more idiomatically, but less precisely, as "good grasp." Apart from the word "understanding," the translations throughout this book follow Flannery. For the full ICEL translation of *Sacrosanctum Concilium* 48, see *Documents on the Liturgy, 1963–1979: Conciliar, Papal, and Curial Texts* (Collegeville, MN: Liturgical Press, 1982), 14.

*Chapter Six*

# Tuning Adjustments

Romano Guardini's call to "relearn a forgotten way of doing things" echoes with urgency down the years because he issued it while expressing deep satisfaction with the "foundations for the future" that the Second Vatican Council had just laid. As one of the liturgical movement's most respected veterans, he could speak with authority about the "important juncture" that modern liturgical renewal had reached. And anyone who observed the "intensity" of the council's debates over the liturgy could see that the cause of "such fierce arguments" must be "a matter of fundamental importance" for the life of the church. The council had shown with "inescapable" finality that "the religious act underlying the liturgy was something singular and important" and that its singular importance lay in its *corporate* character. "The way this came to pass and truth became manifest will remain a classical example of the way the Holy Spirit guides the Church," Guardini wrote. "But now the question arises how we are to set about our task, so that truth may become reality."[1]

Many metaphors have been used to describe the postconciliar work of liturgical renewal: restoring a time-ravaged cathedral, pruning an unruly garden, or repairing the crumbling infrastructure of an ancient city, among others. A recurring theme is that the building, the seedbed, or the aqueducts have been made ready for use by the revisers of

---

[1] Romano Guardini, "A Letter from Romano Guardini," *Herder Correspondence* 1, no. 8 (August 1964): 237–39.

liturgical books. It remains to learn how to use the renewed rites in the right way and to the proper end. As Jean Corbon says, "The channels have been repaired, indeed, but what about the fountain?"[2]

Adopting the musical metaphor of *Sacrosanctum Concilium* 11, we could compare the postconciliar situation to an orchestra embarking on a new season. The instruments, the musicians, and the scores have been carefully chosen, prepared, and put in place. But none of this guarantees a harmonious performance; adjustments will have to be made during rehearsals and concerts. An orchestra only achieves harmony when all the players are closely attuned to one another, and this requires two things of the individual musicians. First, the players must be attuned to *all* the sounds and vibrations entering their minds through their senses—not only those made by their individual instruments. Less obvious, but no less important, is the requirement that each player be attuned to the whole work of music, which the orchestra makes corporately even though each musician plays only a part. This understanding of the whole doesn't reside in the score or in the gestures of the conductor, but in the minds of the musicians. As the orchestra rehearses its exterior performance, the musicians adjust not only the sounds made by their instruments but also the thought and feeling with which they play those sounds. Through these *outside-in tuning adjustments*, the musicians grow in their ability to perform the music with full understanding of the whole piece. But because the musical offering, like the liturgical offering, is a *corporate* act, the whole orchestra becomes imbued with the spirit of the music only when the players also make *inside-out tuning adjustments* to the exterior performance. Though no single musician—not even the conductor—possesses a perfect interior understanding of the music, the growing harmony of thought and feeling among the players is the essential basis of any growth in the perfection of their external harmony.

In liturgy, the necessity of both kinds of tuning adjustments, *inside-out* and *outside-in*, is more than a postulate about authentic performance. The unity of the church is at stake in its members' ability to worship with one mind and voice. Christians believe that the same Holy Spirit guides the whole church and comes to dwell within each

---

[2] Jean Corbon, *The Wellspring of Worship*, trans. Matthew J. O'Connell, 2nd ed. (San Francisco: Ignatius Press, 2005), 24.

member of Christ's body.[3] Praying with one accord requires discernment of the Spirit's will through bold speech and obedient listening, ordered by mutual submission "out of reverence for Christ" (Eph 5:21).

### The aim of attunement: "a good understanding"

In the immediate aftermath of Vatican II, advocates of liturgical renewal wrote with great expectation and almost equal trepidation about the new work set for them by the council. "The Constitution *Sacrosanctum Concilium* is a seed sown in the soil of the Church," wrote *peritus* William Baraúna in 1966. "This is a fertile soil, but it is productive only when it is watered by the waters of the Holy Spirit which 'springs up into life everlasting' (Jn 4:14)."[4] The experts charged with revising the liturgical books would need to rely on the Spirit's guidance. Guardini knew, however, that even the most inspired revisions wouldn't "impart an ever-increasing vigor to the Christian lives of the faithful" unless the people and their pastors learned how to become "imbued with the spirit and power of the liturgy" (SC 1, 14). "If the intentions of the Council are to be realized, proper instruction will be needed, but real education will be needed too; practice will be necessary in order to learn the act. . . . Our problem is to rise above reading and writing and learn really to look with understanding."[5]

Learning "to look with understanding" evokes the vision of the Eucharist articulated in *Sacrosanctum Concilium* 48: "When present at this mystery of faith, Christian believers should not be there as strangers or silent spectators. On the contrary, having a good understanding of it through the rites and prayers (*per ritus et preces bene intellegentes*), they should take part in the sacred action, actively, fully aware, and

---

[3] See, for example, Matt 10:20; Mark 13:11; Luke 11:13; 12:12; John 3:34; 14:15-17, 26; 16:7-15; 20:22; Acts 1:8; 2:4, 38; 4:31; 5:32; 8:17; 10:44-47; 11:15-18; 13:52; 19:1-7; Rom 5:5; 8:9-17, 26-27; 1 Cor 2:9-16; 3:16; 6:19; 12:1-13; 2 Cor 1:21-22; 3:2-3, 17-18; 5:4-6; Gal 3:2-5, 13-14; 4:6-7; 6:1; Eph 1:13; 2:18; 3:16-19; 4:1-6; 5:18-20; 6:18; Phil 2:1-2; 3:3; 1 Thess 1:6; 4:8; 2 Tim 14; Titus 3:5-7; Heb 6:4-6; Jas 4:5; 1 Pet 4:14; 1 John 4:12-13; Jude 1:20; Rev 22:17.

[4] William Baraúna and Jovian Lang, eds., *The Liturgy of Vatican II: A Symposium*, English ed., vol. 1 (Chicago: Franciscan Herald Press, 1966), xi.

[5] Guardini, "Letter from Romano Guardini," 238.

devoutly (*conscie, pie et actuose*)."[6] This famous passage, which "has lost none of its force," appears in Pope Benedict XVI's 2007 apostolic exhortation on the Eucharist, *Sacramentum Caritatis*, as the definitive ideal of "authentic participation (*participatio authentica*)" by the faithful in the liturgy. In his exhortation, the pope wants to correct misunderstandings of the "precise meaning" of the constitution's call to "active participation (*participatio actuosa*)," which "does not refer to mere external activity," but "must be understood . . . on the basis of a greater awareness of the mystery being celebrated and its relationship to daily life" (52).[7]

We have seen that the desire for the faithful to pray with a "good understanding" is by no means an invention of modern liturgical reformers. The demand for this kind of authenticity in worship could hardly be more ancient or more common. God's basic complaint to Isaiah is that his people "do not understand" (Isa 1:3), despite their persistence in offering external sacrifices. Jesus asks his own disciples whether they "also fail to understand" what sort of devotion God desires (Mark 7:18). Paul tells Christians to imitate him in praying "with the spirit" but "with the understanding also" (1 Cor 14:15).[8] Origen could be speaking for the whole early church when he says, "If nothing else should accrue to us in praying, we have nonetheless received the best of gains by praying with understanding."[9] Simply put, the greatest commandment is to worship God with understanding. " 'To love him with all the heart, and with all the understanding, and with all the strength,' and 'to love one's neighbor as oneself,'—this is much more important than all whole burnt offerings and sacrifices" (Mark 12:33).

Although the precedent for requiring "a good understanding" reaches back beyond the foundation of the church, a persistent stream

---

[6] The translation of *Sacrosanctum Concilium* in the collection edited by Austin Flannery renders *bene intellegentes* as "good grasp." The earlier translation prepared by the International Commission on English in the Liturgy (ICEL) renders this key word less idiomatically, but more precisely, as "good understanding." Apart from the word "understanding," the translation here follows Flannery. For the full ICEL translation, see *Documents on the Liturgy, 1963–1979: Conciliar, Papal, and Curial Texts* (Collegeville, MN: Liturgical Press, 1982), 14.

[7] Benedict XVI, *Sacramentum Caritatis*: Post-Synodal Apostolic Exhortation on the Eucharist as the Source and Summit of the Church's Life and Mission, February 22, 2007 (Washington, DC: United States Conference of Catholic Bishops, 2007).

[8] NRSV translates *nous* as "with the mind also."

[9] Origen, *Peri euchēs* 10.1, in Tertullian, Cyprian, and Origen, *On the Lord's Prayer*, trans. Alistair Stewart–Sykes (Crestwood, NY: St. Vladimir's Seminary Press, 2004).

of criticism directed against *Sacrosanctum Concilium* and its subsequent implementation has been that the changes to the liturgy are excessively preoccupied with making the rites and prayers immediately intelligible to the people. In this critique, the modern desire for authenticity is disparaged as "anti-ritualism." The argument, in its most basic form, is that the Catholic Church "Protestantized" its liturgy following Vatican II by eliminating external rites and prayers that were challenging to perform or difficult to understand. The most charitable forms of this critique blame the revisers for trying to engage the *minds* of participants too directly, without attending to the mediating role of the *body* and its senses. These critics doubt the wisdom of revising liturgical rites so that the faithful can "understand them easily" (SC 21). According to them, the council's insistence that "both texts and rites should be ordered so as to express more clearly the holy things which they signify" betrays an ignorance of how ritual works. The liturgy's texts and rites are deeply embodied symbols that allow the people to encounter holy things through sight, sound, taste, touch, and smell. Even some staunch defenders of the liturgical reform believe that the council's focus on intelligibility has led to "a neglect of gesture," "over-verbalization of the rite," "a certain flatness and didactic emphasis in liturgical celebrations," and "anti-ritual bias" in a liturgy "once known for its excessive rubricism."[10]

I wish to push back against this line of critique for two reasons. First, its supposed basis in anthropology, sociology, and phenomenology of religion is not as sound as the critics or the supporters of the liturgical reform believe. Second, and more important, it undermines one way Christian worshippers, from the beginning, have sought to bring their minds and voices into tune. Drawing individually and corporately upon their "good understanding" of "the sacred action" (SC 48), Christ's faithful are not only permitted but *expected* to adjust the exterior rites and prayers of the liturgy. Such changes are required to restore authenticity to rites and prayers "if they have suffered from the intrusion of anything out of harmony with the inner nature of

---

[10] John F. Baldovin, *Reforming the Liturgy: A Response to the Critics* (Collegeville, MN: Liturgical Press, 2008), 97, 104; Kevin W. Irwin, *What We Have Done, What We Have Failed to Do: Assessing the Liturgical Reforms of Vatican II* (New York: Paulist Press, 2013), 60; M. Francis Mannion, "The Catholicity of the Liturgy: Shaping a New Agenda," in *Beyond the Prosaic: Renewing the Liturgical Movement*, ed. Stratford Caldecott (Edinburgh: T&T Clark, 1998), 28.

the liturgy" (SC 21). Changes to the liturgy's externals also allow the church to "cultivate and foster the qualities and talents of the various races and nations" by admitting "into the liturgy itself" those things in their way of life that "harmonize with its true and authentic spirit" (SC 37). Therefore, any good understanding of the liturgy expects that the "good of the church" will require ongoing adjustment of external forms. These "innovations" can only "grow organically from forms already existing" if the church recognizes the legitimacy of authentic creativity exercised by individuals, congregations, and local churches who share the Spirit of God and the mind of Christ (SC 23; see 1 Cor 2:9-16).

I claim there is nothing "anti-ritual" about subjecting the external forms of the liturgy to scrutiny and adjustment in response to intellectual reflection on the "authentic spirit" of the liturgy and the "good of the church," both locally and universally. The church entrusts this intellectual work in a particular way to pastors, poets, artists, and scholars, but these experts aren't the only members of Christ's faithful with an interest in rites and prayers that can be readily grasped by the intellect. The aim of adjusting externals to be in greater harmony with the inner spirit of the liturgy is to help *all* participants internalize a good understanding of what they are doing. To say that the faithful know more about the liturgy in their bones than the experts do in their minds scores a few worthy points against intellectual elitism, and it reminds us that the church's liturgical theology is always embodied in external rites and prayers. But this image of understanding residing in the bones does no justice to the liturgical tradition's high regard for the mind, and it misrepresents what studies of ritual teach us about how liturgical participation works.

The argument that modern liturgical reforms have emphasized intellectual understanding at the expense of ritual know-how depends heavily on theories of religion with roots in the Romantic turn to inner experience.[11] In the twentieth century, these theories are exemplified by two texts that remain foundational for modern religious studies: Émile Durkheim's *Elementary Forms of Religious Life* (1912)

---

[11] Martin Riesebrodt adds that in these theories of religion, the inner experience of "the holy" is understood ethnocentrically. "It is always a variant of Romantic 'experience' [*Erfahrung*] that has been smuggled in and claims universality." Martin Riesebrodt, *The Promise of Salvation: A Theory of Religion* (Chicago: University of Chicago Press, 2010), 53.

and Rudolf Otto's *Idea of the Holy* (1917). Both theories define authentic religiosity in relation to some inward experience of sacred power whose origins are nevertheless felt to come from outside oneself.[12] The two authors take "radically different approaches" to identifying and accounting for this supposedly innate sense of the sacred. Durkheim attributes a shared yet individually felt experience of collective "effervescence" to the influence of society, while Otto believes that a "numinous" experience of the "wholly other" reflects the ontological structure of the cosmos.[13] Otto's phenomenological approach is favored by historians of religion like Gerardus Van der Leeuw and Mircea Eliade, while Durkheim's heirs are generally found in sociology and anthropology. Mary Douglas and Victor Turner both maintain links to Durkheim's account of religious experience, though Douglas professes her loyalty to Durkheim while Turner insists that the central idea of his theory of ritual is "strikingly different."[14] Still, Turner's concept of "*communitas*"—the group solidarity generated in the ritual process—is essentially an inner experience of self-transcendence.[15]

Defining authentic religion in relation to an inner experience of sacredness puts the external practices of religion "beyond the reach of criticism" and so beyond the reach of reform. Critics who associate the postconciliar liturgical reform with "desacralization" and antiritualism believe that the comparative unintelligibility of the preconciliar Latin liturgy is a feature, not a bug. Kieran Flanagan, for instance, argues that "the liturgical instructions of Vatican II were conceived in a climate of imperfect sociological understanding" that favored "intelligibility, clarity, 'a noble simplicity' and the need to make manifest the sacred properties of rite." To Flanagan, the council's assertion that intelligibility can heighten interior participation "makes an odd sociological argument," for he is convinced sociology

[12] Émile Durkheim, *The Elementary Forms of Religious Life*, trans. Karen E. Fields (New York: Free Press, 1995); Rudolf Otto, *The Idea of the Holy: An Inquiry into the Non-Rational Factor in the Idea of the Divine and Its Relation to the Rational*, trans. John W. Harvey (New York: Oxford University Press, 1958).

[13] Gordon Lynch, *The Sacred in the Modern World: A Cultural Sociological Approach* (Oxford: Oxford University Press, 2012), 9–29.

[14] Mary Douglas, *Natural Symbols: Explorations in Cosmology*, 2nd ed. (London: Routledge, 1996), xvii; Victor W. Turner, *The Ritual Process: Structure and Anti-Structure* (Chicago: Aldine, 1969), 132.

[15] See Lynch, *Sacred in the Modern World*, 20.

proves that people inwardly experience "opaque" external rituals as more sacred than those that are easily understood.[16]

In fact, neither opacity nor intelligibility provides a straightforward index of whether a rite will be experienced as sacred. There is also no sociological justification for associating authentic religious experience exclusively with formalism or with spontaneity, as Douglas acknowledges: "The Catholic rituals I know are not conducive to the arousing of emotion which Durkheim seemed to think is the function of ritual. . . . But the Sacred can be engraved in the hearts and minds of worshippers in more ways than one: there are several kinds of religion. Some ritualists plan to achieve spontaneity, others aim at coordination."[17] Admittedly, Douglas sees little potential benefit to having theologians draw up new rites or revise old ones "so as to express more clearly the holy things which they signify" (SC 21). "This could be a total waste of effort," she argues, because "people at different historic periods are more or less sensitive to signs as such." However we define modernization, it has involved massive changes to the material and symbolic organization of social life, and "the perception of symbols in general, as well as their interpretation, is socially determined."[18]

But it doesn't follow that adjusting the external texts and rites of the liturgy to the understanding of its modern participants is a wasted, anti-ritual effort. The anthropological assumption that ritual is *symbolic* behavior is little older than the liturgical reform itself. Jan Bremmer conclusively demonstrates that scholarly interest "turned away from beliefs and mythology to ritual" only "in the late 1880s and 1890s." Even after this "ritual turn" in the late nineteenth century, the emerging disciplines of social science didn't associate ritual with meaningful symbolism but with the "'irrational rules' of religion which could not be explained by the more rationalistic theories of the time." Social scientific interest in ritual as symbolic behavior "started to take off" *only* in the 1960s, just as the liturgical reform was getting underway.[19] Douglas, Turner, and other anthropologists

---

[16] Kieran Flanagan, *Sociology and Liturgy: Re-Presentations of the Holy* (New York: St. Martin's Press, 1991), 52, 179. See *Sacrosanctum Concilium* 21, 34.

[17] Douglas, *Natural Symbols*, xvii.

[18] Douglas, *Natural Symbols*, 9.

[19] Jan N. Bremmer, "'Religion,' 'Ritual' and the Opposition 'Sacred vs. Profane': Notes Towards a Terminological 'Genealogy,'" in *Ansichten Griechischer Rituale:*

Tuning Adjustments 197

whose influential work appeared around the same time are rightly seen as pioneers in the study of ritual. But when their theories are applied uncritically to modern liturgical reform, the resulting analysis suffers from two assumptions that have become widespread in anthropological studies of ritual.

First, as Catherine Bell shows, these theories assume that ritual is a communicative activity in which "cultural meaning" is enacted.[20] Through their ritual performance, the "native" actors symbolically affirm the community's values and mediate social contradictions that an anthropologist can identify and resolve through rational thought. Often, as in Clifford Geertz's influential theory of cultural interpretation, religious ritual is understood as the "symbolic fusion" of conceptual thought and emotional or volitional dispositions. Ritual brings together "under the agency of a single set of symbolic forms" the "world as lived and the world as imagined."[21] Talal Asad shows, however, that "the distinction between 'feelings' as private and ineffable and 'ritual' as public and legible" is an invention of modern anthropology that displaced a much older and less differentiated understanding of ritual as part of an overall program for "teaching the body to develop 'virtues' through material means."[22]

Second, while appearing to vindicate ritual, such theories retain an attenuated prejudice against ritual as behavior that isn't fully rational. The assumption is disguised by the tendency for social scientists to "cast ritual as good and healthy, somehow humanizing in its shared symbols and communal affirmations." This scholarly romanticizing of ritual has become prevalent at a historical moment when many communities are abandoning or transforming the traditional rituals that had been the anthropologist's key to interpreting their religious cultures.[23] Despite claims to the contrary, scholarly theories of ritual presume that the anthropologist, as a "ritual expert," has greater

Geburtstags-Symposium Für Walter Burkert, Castelen Bei Basel 15. Bis 18. März 1996, ed. Franz Graf (Stuttgart: Teubner, 1998), 9–32.

[20] Catherine M. Bell, *Ritual Theory, Ritual Practice* (New York: Oxford University Press, 1992).

[21] Clifford Geertz, *The Interpretation of Cultures* (New York: Basic Books, 1973), 112–13.

[22] Talal Asad, *Genealogies of Religion: Discipline and Reasons of Power in Christianity and Islam* (Baltimore: Johns Hopkins University Press, 1993), 72.

[23] Catherine M. Bell, "The Authority of Ritual Experts," *Studia Liturgica* 23, no. 1 (1993): 112.

insight into the meaning and importance of a ritual's symbolism than the ritual practitioners do themselves. When experts like Turner and Douglas have intervened in the debate over liturgical reform, their scholarship has sounded like a warning to the unsuspecting faithful. The "liturgical signal boxes" are being "manned by color-blind signalmen."[24] Clumsy efforts to encourage the faithful to participate with understanding are replacing the treasured symbols of Catholicism with "a hackwork of contemporaneous improvisation."[25] Such scholarly idealization of traditional ritual has "contributed to the popularity of oversimplified ethnographic models of ritual and the critical attitude of some social scientists to modern examples of ritual change at home."[26] Regrettably, it has also fueled the narrative that the pastors and experts responsible for the liturgical reform have failed the ordinary faithful, whose attachment to the common symbols of the faith is presumed to be unsophisticated, unreflective, and socially determined from without.

The "good understanding" that allows the Christian faithful to "take part in the sacred action" is neither a set of intellectual propositions believed inwardly nor an inner experience of sacredness, transcendence, effervescence, or the numinous. Participating with a good understanding means harmonizing one's interior and exterior participation, so what one does inwardly *and* outwardly is done "actively, fully aware, and devoutly" (SC 48). Such participation might coincide with some exciting or calming inner experience, but it isn't the role of ritual's external forms to produce these feelings. To avoid halting the work of attunement before it reaches the goal of participation with understanding, modern worshippers must guard against confusing awareness and devotion with a particular emotional or intel-

---

[24] Douglas, *Natural Symbols*, 44.

[25] Victor W. Turner, "Ritual, Tribal and Catholic," *Worship* 50, no. 6 (1976): 524. Douglas and Turner write as practicing Catholics in addition to claiming anthropological expertise in ritual. Their dual identity as ritual experts and ritual practitioners has undoubtedly facilitated the reception of their theories by Catholic critics of the liturgical reform. In their own theories, however, being a practitioner is irrelevant to the anthropologist's claim to expertise, and both authors write more often about the rituals of communities that they observe as cultural outsiders.

[26] Bell, "Authority of Ritual Experts," 113. Bell states that she is referring to the critiques of Douglas, Turner, and David Martin. The latter can be found in David Martin and Peter Mullen, eds., *No Alternative: The Prayer Book Controversy* (Oxford: Basil Blackwell, 1981).

lectual experience. *Sacrosanctum Concilium* 11 asks the faithful to come to the liturgy with "proper dispositions" that make them ready to tune their minds to their voices, if their interior participation requires adjustment. They must also be properly disposed to tune their voices to their minds, if their exterior participation requires adjustment. The inner experience and the external ritual are not separate ends; tuning aims at an *integrated* liturgical act.

## Tuning from the inside out

The idea that modern liturgical reform is congenitally opposed to ritual, scornful of the body, and cavalier about symbols has taken root even among liturgical scholars who support the goal of more intelligible and participatory worship. Ironically, concern about anti-ritualism is especially strong among scholars who seek a contemporary renewal of Protestant worship. Brent Peterson, an ordained elder in the Church of the Nazarene, confesses that his denomination's need to "worship in ways that would not hinder the Holy Spirit . . . has often been naively embodied by our disdain for rituals and liturgy."[27] In describing "what's wrong with evangelical theology," Peter Leithart opines that evangelicals' "instinctive anti-ritualism leaves them bereft of the theological tools required for understanding how rites mold, sustain, and nourish the Church."[28]

The existence of a robust ecumenical conversation about ritual and authentic worship "challenges any simplistic one-dimensional ritual-sincerity analytical axis that contrasts Orthodox and Catholic worship on one end of a spectrum with Quakers and Pentecostal worship on the other." John Witvliet gives evidence of this conversation, and he suggests several ways he and his students might draw on the wisdom of other Christian traditions to correct "common astigmatisms" in their "more-or-less free-church Protestant way of viewing the world." Among these "corrective lenses," he first proposes "a lens of *outside-in sincerity*" to "correct the temptation to treat as normative an expressivist approach to liturgical experience, which posits that the concordance of internal experience and external actions happens

---

[27] Brent Peterson, "The Science of the Sacraments: The Being and Becoming of Persons in Community," *Wesleyan Theological Journal* 44, no. 1 (2009): 180.

[28] Peter J. Leithart, "What's Wrong with Evangelical Theology," *First Things* 65 (August 1996): 20.

'inside out' when we pray out of the overflow of what we already think or feel."[29] One tradition's astigmatism, however, might be another tradition's corrective lens. If "humility borne of catholicity" has led Witvliet to learn from "critiques of earnest sincerity," then magnanimity borne of the same catholicity ought to allow adherents of "liturgical" traditions to learn from the *inside-out* approach to authentic worship that Witvliet rightly honors as an "evangelical charism."[30]

To see what *tuning from the inside out* looks like, I will refer to firsthand accounts of contemporary evangelical worship in the free church tradition—much as I will offer my own observations of the worship of contemporary Latin Mass Catholics in the next section to illustrate *tuning from the outside in*. Melanie Ross supplies two case studies of evangelical worship that help to illuminate a "promising new paradigm for understanding evangelicalism's relationship to liturgical Christianity today," in which "the two traditions are more symbiotic than contradictory."[31] She recognizes that there is already vigorous interchange among various evangelical and liturgical churches, but her paradigm goes beyond musical styles, preaching methods, and models of prayer.

Ross focuses on a theological symbiosis that is akin to the relationship between the Synoptic Gospels and the Gospel according to John. The free church tradition contributes a Johannine ecclesiology that emphasizes personal faith, de-emphasizes hierarchical office, and—while not opposing sacramental signs—focuses more on the signified savior than on the ritual signifiers that point to him.[32] The Fourth Gospel also addresses authentic worship with somewhat different images than the bodily metaphors typical of the Synoptics and Paul.[33] Ross points out that John's images of the church as "flock" and as

---

[29] John D. Witvliet, "The Mysteries of Liturgical Sincerity: The Amen Corner," *Worship* 92 (May 2018): 199, 201. See also Witvliet, " 'Planting and Harvesting' Godly Sincerity: Pastoral Wisdom in the Practice of Public Worship," *Evangelical Quarterly* 87, no. 4 (October 2015): 297.

[30] Witvliet, " 'Planting and Harvesting' Godly Sincerity," 296.

[31] Melanie C. Ross, *Evangelical Versus Liturgical? Defying a Dichotomy* (Grand Rapids, MI: Eerdmans, 2014), 8.

[32] Ross, *Evangelical Versus Liturgical?*, 92–98.

[33] For this reason, I included very little Johannine literature in chapter 2 of this book. As I argue here, however, the correspondence of interior and exterior worship is at least as important to John as it is to Paul and the Synoptics.

"vine and branches" are less corporate and more attentive to the "ir-replaceable decision of the individual," even though "the Johannine sense of community and *koinonia . . .* is stronger than that of any New Testament writer except for Paul."[34] Jesus's encounter with the Samaritan woman in chapter 4 of John's gospel similarly emphasizes the individual response of faith as that which forms a community of "true worshippers" who "worship the Father in spirit and truth" (4:23). Christ offers the "living water" of his own Spirit to the woman and to each believer personally (4:10-15; see also 7:37-39). Far from replacing corporate worship with individualistic faith, however, the personal gift of the Spirit allows the disciples of Jesus to *collaborate* with one another in "gathering fruit for eternal life" and offering that "harvest" to the Father (4:35-38). Strikingly, the Samaritan woman's testimony to Jesus's intimate knowledge of her own mind—"He told me everything I have ever done"—convinces her community to re-quest his presence so they can hear the voice of the Messiah for them-selves (4:28-30, 39-42). "For John, what is truly essential is the living presence of Jesus *in the Christian* through the Paraclete: no institution or structure can substitute for that." According to Ross, "Herein lies the evangelical concern": not the avoidance of structured rituals and instituted symbols, but the sovereignty of Christ and the freedom of the Holy Spirit.[35]

In Ross's case studies, the evangelical congregations prioritize the indwelling of the Holy Spirit as the key to authentic worship. At West Shore Evangelical Free Church in Mechanicsburg, Pennsylvania, the senior pastor's extemporaneous opening prayer asks Jesus to send his Spirit to free his people from visions of false glory that imprison their minds and keep them from being true to who they are:

> Forgive us for not even holding you in our minds and hearts, for being distracted and drawn by such lesser glories. Lord Jesus, don't just forgive us. Send your Spirit. Send your Spirit in power to set us free from the things that draw us away from you; set us free from the things that cloud our minds and that cloud our minds' eyes. Set us free to see who you are, and what you have done, and what you have called us to be.

---

[34] Ross, *Evangelical Versus Liturgical?*, 93–94.
[35] Ross, *Evangelical Versus Liturgical?*, 98. Emphasis added.

In the sermon that follows, the pastor challenges the congregation to receive Christ's Spirit within themselves, using unmistakably sacramental language: "Do you realize that God has called you to be the body of Christ—the visible manifestation of Christ's invisible presence in the world—his hands, feet, eyes, and voice, if you will? God has called you to be the place where his Holy Spirit dwells. He has given us the opportunity to join his mission to transform created reality through the person of his Son."[36] The direction of the transformation described here is *inside-out*. The Holy Spirit liberates the Christian's mind and resides there so the Christian's voice can become the powerful, creative voice of Christ.

The evangelical focus on the Holy Spirit provides a Christian ecclesiology, not an individualist psychology. The pastor from West Shore claims that a person in whom the Spirit dwells becomes a member of Christ's body and a participant in his mission, not the solitary mouthpiece of God. The senior pastor at Eastbrook Church in Milwaukee, Wisconsin, also describes the indwelling of the Spirit as the source of the church's unity. It's a recurring theme in his sermons, and he expresses it with a variety of metaphors:

> "In [Christ] the whole building is joined together and rises to become a holy temple in the Lord. And in him you too are being built together to become a dwelling in which God lives by his Spirit" (Eph 2:21-22). . . . The temple Paul talks about in Ephesians is not a Catholic temple. It's not a Lutheran temple, or a Protestant temple, or a nondenominational evangelical temple. No. The Spirit's power is immense. He not only holds the universe together physically; he also holds the church of Jesus Christ together with all its members and makes us one. . . .
>
> In order to be a Christian, you have to be indwelt by the Spirit of God. And the Spirit indwelling a Catholic is the same Spirit indwelling a Baptist, is the same Spirit indwelling someone from Eastbrook. . . . If you put your trust in Christ, you're stuck with all the rest of us. There's nothing you can do about it. Everyone who has a genuine relationship with Christ is your brother or sister. This is the unity the Spirit gives. . . .
>
> We're held together by the Holy Spirit. He's not a gas. He's not a ghost. Think of him as steel. He's eternal. He's all-powerful. And he's living in every single believer on the surface of the

---

[36] Quoted in Ross, *Evangelical Versus Liturgical?*, 106–8.

planet, and every single person in heaven. He's gathering a group of people, growing larger by the minute, and every one of them is indwelt by the Spirit of God. We're already united. The problem is that it's not very visible.[37]

Catholic, Orthodox, and mainline Protestant Christians maintain the importance of an ecumenical liturgical *ordo* as an outwardly *visible* sign of the church's unity. Ross argues that the evangelical insistence on the living presence of Jesus through the indwelling of the Holy Spirit is just as ecumenical and essential for authentic worship. "For churches like Eastbrook, it is less the practice of a particular liturgical 'shape' and more the theological content of the prayers, songs, and sermons offered *within* that shape that determines whether worship is faithful to the Christian tradition."[38] Many evangelicals worry that mindless adherence to an exterior shape of worship will stifle the Spirit that invisibly unites Christians. They can sound indifferent or hostile toward the "classic *ordo*" of "word next to table, scripture next to scripture next to preaching leading to communal prayer leading to the table leading to sending to the poor."[39] Yet they recognize the "formative power of corporate ecclesial practices" and are deeply committed to an ecclesiology that views the gathered community as the primary place of encounter with Christ.[40] The pastor at West Shore cites Matthew 18:20 to emphasize that authentic worship is always corporate. "The Spirit comes to dwell in the body first—it's as two or three are gathered together that I am in your midst. We can't worship, in its full and proper sense, individually. . . . We can't pray individually: the Lord's Prayer is 'we,' not 'I.'"[41]

"While there is wisdom in practice, habit, and ritual," Ross says, there is also something "profoundly right" about worship that prioritizes flexibility, creativity, and eclecticism over "inherited liturgical

---

[37] Quoted in Ross, *Evangelical Versus Liturgical?*, 36, 47.

[38] Ross, *Evangelical Versus Liturgical?*, 55. Emphasis in original.

[39] Gordon Lathrop, "New Pentecost or Joseph's Britches? Reflections on the History and Meaning of the Worship Ordo in the Megachurches," *Worship* 72, no. 6 (November 1998): 538. For a response to Lathrop's criticism of churches that ignore this "classic *ordo*," see Melanie C. Ross, "Joseph's Britches Revisited: Reflections on Method in Liturgical Theology," *Worship* 80, no. 6 (November 1, 2006): 528–50.

[40] Ross, *Evangelical Versus Liturgical?*, 120. See Miroslav Volf, *After Our Likeness: The Church as the Image of the Trinity* (Grand Rapids, MI: Eerdmans, 1998), 162.

[41] Quoted in Ross, *Evangelical Versus Liturgical?*, 120.

structure." Weekly rhythms of liturgical prayer offer "a healthy challenge to many evangelical theologies of worship," but free church
congregations "excel at the task of dissuading the church from pre-
mature closure" to the " 'limitless creativity of God.' "[42] Jesus inau-
gurates a new outpouring of God's creativity at his resurrection,
animating his church with the gift of his Spirit. One worship leader
and thirty-year member of West Shore explains that their worship is
"authentic" not because *they* invent it themselves, but because they
rely on *God's* creativity:

> Worship here is not formulaic. There is no "equation." But there
> has been historically, and continues to be, a desire to seek after
> God with an authentic and sincere heart of worship and depen-
> dence. We manage to bring some things that are pretty different
> together in a way that still makes sense and continues to point
> us to God. This eclecticism makes worship exciting, and authen-
> tic, and maybe just enough of a conundrum to help us think more
> deeply about who God is.[43]

While ritual formulas help establish Christians in the "grammar of
faith,"[44] they aren't equations that *solve* the conundrum of an integrated liturgical act. Liturgy shouldn't try to *dissolve* the endlessly
creative dialogue with God; it should invite the church to participate
with deeper understanding and greater harmony of minds and
voices.

   Free church evangelicals aren't the only Christians who emphasize
the creative indwelling of the Holy Spirit as the key to making their
worship more authentic. A 1997 study report for a synod of the Christian Reformed Church in North America, entitled *Authentic Worship
in a Changing Culture*, encourages congregations to allow changes to
worship to proceed "from the inside out." Recognizing that "in every
congregation people are already present who challenge the church
to think creatively about changes in worship," leaders should avoid
imposing changes "from the outside in," whether to make services

---

[42] Ross, *Evangelical Versus Liturgical?*, 121–23. Ross quotes John Webster, "The
Church as Theological Community," *Anglican Theological Review* 75, no. 1 (Winter
1993): 115.

   [43] Quoted in Ross, *Evangelical Versus Liturgical?*, 122.

   [44] David W. Fagerberg, *Theologia Prima: What Is Liturgical Theology?*, 2nd ed. (Mundelein, IL: Hillenbrand Books, 2004), 154.

more traditional or more "seeker friendly." Instead, by asking what will "enable all members who are already present to worship God more fully," congregations ensure that change will be "organic."[45]

Similarly, a 1990 statement of the US Catholic bishops argues that "spirituality must be the starting point of a distinctively African American Catholic liturgy." *Plenty Good Room* defends the ritual structures of Roman Catholic liturgy against efforts to "bring whole structures of African American Protestant worship into Catholic liturgy." But the bishops also affirm the "thirst for African American cultural expression" that has led Black Catholics to work "toward an authentic African American Catholic worship." Taking their lead from the African American members of their conference, the bishops describe a distinctive spirituality that "involves the whole person: intellect and emotion, spirit and body, action and contemplation, individual and community, secular and sacred." This wholeness in worship is a particular gift of African American spirituality to the church, in a society that often isolates mind from body in work, education, and public life. To follow the lead of this spirituality, one begins in "contemplative prayer" that moves from the inside out and "explodes in the joy of movement, song, rhythm, feeling, color, and sensation." African American liturgy values "improvisation and creativity," especially in song, and it "calls forth a greater sense of spontaneity" than other Catholic congregations may expect. This "spirit-filled" and spirit-led approach to authentic liturgy might seem marginal and out of favor in the Roman Catholic Church. Yet the US bishops reissued *Plenty Good Room* without changes after the 2011 promulgation of *The Roman Missal, Third Edition*, because its "central messages" about worship that is "authentically African American and truly Catholic" remain intact.[46]

## Tuning from the outside in

In over eighty hours of interviews, homilies, and events I recorded while studying four Latin Mass communities between 2010 and 2013,

[45] *Authentic Worship in a Changing Culture* (Grand Rapids, MI: CRC Publications, 1997), 73–74.
[46] *Plenty Good Room: The Spirit and Truth of African American Worship* (Washington, DC: United States Conference of Catholic Bishops, 1990), nos. 77–84, 101, 103, 123.

I fail to find a single reference to the indwelling of the Holy Spirit.[47] Most participants in my research, both lay and ordained, rarely mentioned the Holy Spirit outside of the formulas of the liturgy or the habitual invocation of the Trinity to begin a prayer.[48] The scarcity of talk about the Holy Spirit is made more conspicuous by the frequency with which these Catholics speak about "spirituality," the "spiritual life," and "spiritual direction." Many of them venerate saints who emphasized interior prayer and intense personal attachment to Christ: Francis de Sales, Thérèse of Lisieux, and Faustina Kowalska, for example. Latin Mass Catholics don't doubt the transformative power of the Holy Spirit, but their primary way of conceiving the movement of the Spirit is *outside-in*, not *inside-out*. They try to be "docile to the Holy Spirit," as one twenty-two-year-old seminarian put it, by internalizing the sacramental doctrine and liturgical regulations of the church. They believe the Holy Spirit ensures the transmission of the church's authentic liturgical tradition, and they also trust the Spirit to guide the pope and the bishops in authentically articulating and interpreting that tradition.

Most of the Latin Mass Catholics whom I interviewed were especially ready to listen to the then-reigning pontiff, Benedict XVI. After "invoking the Holy Spirit," Pope Benedict decreed in 2007 that the pre-Vatican II Mass should be recognized as an "extraordinary form of the Liturgy of the Church," and he instructed pastors to "willingly accept" requests for its celebration by any "stable group" of parish-

[47] This section of the chapter is based on interviews, participant-observation of liturgies, and other fieldwork conducted in four Latin Mass communities. The communities are located in two midwestern cities but differ significantly in size, demographic composition, leadership, and canonical structure, though all are recognized as fully legitimate communities within the Roman Catholic Church. The phrase "Latin Mass Catholic" doesn't refer here to members of the Society of St. Pius X or other groups whose canonical relationship with the Roman Catholic Church is irregular or not recognized. Also, some of the participants in my study regularly attend the post-Vatican II Mass (*Novus Ordo*/Ordinary Form) in Latin, not the pre-Vatican II Mass (Tridentine Mass/Extraordinary Form). See Nathaniel Marx, "Ritual in the Age of Authenticity: An Ethnography of Latin Mass Catholics" (PhD diss., University of Notre Dame, 2013).

[48] Some interviewees spoke more readily and directly of the Holy Spirit. One woman who said she had been "caught up in the charismatic [movement]" for several years before joining a Latin Mass parish described how she and other charismatic Catholics used to "fall in the Spirit." A fourth-generation African American Catholic agreed to sit for an interview because he discerned the "seal of the Holy Spirit" on the project.

ioners. A few years later, the first postconciliar pope to adopt the name of St. Benedict of Nursia used a general audience in St. Peter's square to call attention to *Sacrosanctum Concilium*'s citation of chapter 19 of the Rule of Benedict:

> St. Benedict, speaking in his Rule of prayer in the Psalms, pointed out to his monks: *mens concordet voci*, "the mind must be in accord with the voice." The Saint teaches that in the prayers of the Psalms words must precede our thought. It does not usually happen like this because we have to think and then what we have thought is converted into words. Here, instead, in the liturgy, the opposite is true, words come first. God has given us the word and the sacred liturgy offers us words; we must enter into the words, into their meaning and receive them within us, we must attune ourselves to these words; in this way we become children of God, we become like God. As *Sacrosanctum Concilium* recalls, "in order that the liturgy may be able to produce its full effects it is necessary that the faithful come to it with proper dispositions, that their minds be attuned to their voices, and that they cooperate with heavenly grace lest they receive it in vain." A fundamental, primary element of the dialogue with God in the liturgy is the agreement between what we say with our lips and what we carry in our hearts. By entering into the words of the great history of prayer, we ourselves are conformed to the spirit of these words and are enabled to speak to God.[49]

Before his election, Joseph Ratzinger had written about the liturgy much more extensively than any of his recent predecessors. In 2000, while cardinal-prefect of the Congregation for the Doctrine of the Faith, he published *The Spirit of the Liturgy*, evoking the title of Guardini's pioneering book, which Ratzinger had read at the beginning of his theological studies.[50] In the preface, he expresses his desire to "assist" Guardini in promoting a "renewal of understanding" that would lead to authentic celebration of the liturgy as an integrated act of the Body of Christ: "If this book were to encourage, in a new way, something like a 'liturgical movement,' a movement toward the

---

[49] Benedict XVI, General Audience, September 26, 2012, http://w2.vatican.va/content/benedict-xvi/en/audiences/2012/documents/hf_ben-xvi_aud_20120926.html.

[50] Joseph Ratzinger, *The Spirit of the Liturgy*, trans. John Saward (San Francisco: Ignatius Press, 2000).

liturgy and toward the right way of celebrating the liturgy, *inwardly and outwardly*, then the intention that inspired its writing would be richly fulfilled."[51] Additionally, Ratzinger wants to demonstrate that the right approach to the ideal of authentic, integral liturgy is from the outside in. *The Spirit of the Liturgy* anticipates his later interpretation of chapter 19 of Benedict's Rule, especially in the book's repeated insistence on the liturgy's "unspontaneity" (*Unbeliebigkeit*).[52] The same approach characterizes the pope's exhortation to "interior participation" in *Sacramentum Caritatis*. While liturgies should be "carefully planned and executed," they "risk falling into a certain ritualism" unless the faithful are "helped to make their interior dispositions correspond to their gestures and words."[53]

Latin Mass Catholics similarly claim that authentic liturgy has nothing to do with spontaneous expression of emotion. Instead, liturgical ritual is an ensemble of external practices that inculcate interior dispositions. In describing the right dispositions, they speak most frequently of "reverence." The importance of cultivating reverence is why Barbara, the catechesis director at one Latin Mass parish, insists that liturgical vestments are not "costumes" but exterior aids to an interior disposition:

> The vestments aren't about who you are at all; it's about what you're trying to become. At this wedding, this kid shows up— he's in high school—and he's got sandals on and shorts. And I'm like, "Um, do you have dress pants and shoes in your car?" . . . And he looked at me like I'm crazy. And his mother came up and she said, "Well, he's going to put on his costume. It'll cover it all up." . . . Even the mother of this boy—who was good enough to influence him to be an altar boy and to want to do all these things—still didn't have the understanding of what all of this means, that it's all part of a whole, and when you take off part of a whole, you're missing a piece.

[51] Ratzinger, *Spirit of the Liturgy*, 9. Emphasis added.

[52] Ratzinger, *Spirit of the Liturgy*, 164–70. *Unbeliebigkeit* could also be translated as "non-arbitrariness," in the sense of not being subject to the whim of the individual or community enacting the rite. "Unspontaneity" seems to me a misleading translation of what Ratzinger has in mind. Although he defends the given and scripted character of traditional liturgical forms, he also rejects any automatic or mechanical attitude in their performance.

[53] Benedict XVI, *Sacramentum Caritatis*, 64.

In a *performative* sense, the vestments make the priest or the altar boy. But there is also a *formative* sense in which Barbara believes this to be true, and this is the sense she and other Latin Mass Catholics emphasize. The practice of prayerfully donning vestments day after day and week after week leaves a mark on the wearer's conscience. Though the alb covers everything underneath, one feels "improperly dressed" in sweatpants and gym shoes. More important, one perceives the greatness of the "Holy Sacrifice" and senses one's inability to offer fitting worship without the assistance of divine grace.

In this understanding of liturgy, one becomes a more authentic participant from the outside in. This applies to laypeople in the pews as much as to the priest and ministers in the sanctuary. When a young woman named Bridget started attending the Latin Mass at a Catholic college, she found many things "awkward," but receiving Communion on her tongue while kneeling was especially difficult to do without worrying about how she looked. Back home, such behavior always seemed "really ostentatious and kind of weird." She agreed to "experiment" with receiving only on the tongue for a period of time. By the end of the "experiment"—she doesn't recall exactly how long it took—Bridget had reversed her opinion. Now, receiving Communion in the hand feels "awkward" and "looks weird." She has even become "paranoid" about dropping a crumb when the host is placed in her hand, but she doesn't mind her changed attitude. "It helps me have a lot of respect for the Eucharist," she says.

Many of the specific points that Latin Mass Catholics emphasize when describing a "reverent" Mass are not unique to the Tridentine Mass. Kneeling for Communion, celebration *ad orientem*, and using Latin are possibilities to which the post-Vatican II Mass is open. For most Latin Mass Catholics, the opposite of reverence is not deliberate "sacrilege," even if they tell stories of "desecration" and "abuse" observed at vernacular Masses. Rather, what they find most inimical to the cultivation of authentic interior participation is a compulsory informality and exaggerated spontaneity that comes across to them as predictable, banal, and theatrical in its own way.[54] In their view,

---

[54] Bruce Ellis Benson says that members of "less liturgical churches" can also feel ambivalent about spontaneity in worship. "Those in the evangelical tradition know how 'spontaneous' prayers can become rather predictable. . . . Many seemingly nonliturgical churches fall into rhythms that might as well be scripted simply because

this insincere prayer results from *avoiding* the rote training and formal conventions that allow one to act out of long habit.

Josh, a post-Vatican II child of an interreligious marriage, says that the fear of "stuffy" or "fuddy-duddy liturgy" led his parents and other Catholics of their generation to rely on their personal creativity to make the ritual come alive. "My mom was enthralled by ritual, my dad had grown up with ritual as a Jew, so they liked it. But if it wasn't done with panache and verve, they read it as kind of rote, insincere, mechanical. . . . [My mom] likes solemnity, but she didn't want it to be rote. It had to have a personal stamp." For Josh, however, the emphasis on local, on-the-spot adaptation led to liturgy that seemed "contrived," that "felt like it wasn't real." When writing new prayers, inventing liturgical dances, or substituting alternative translations of readings, his parents and the other worship leaders at his childhood parish would explain, "This is how we make a joyful noise," or "This is how we experience God's presence in our lives." Josh found it hard to agree:

> I was willing to accept that in a lot of other things. Like I did transcendental meditation after receiving Communion. . . . So, I was willing to accept that in other respects, but somehow the liturgy, the ritual itself, it didn't make sense to me to invent things. I liked the idea that the liturgy used to be bad and boring, and then the council came. . . . But I didn't like it when Joanie Miller's worship team—Lector Team A—would come up with some alternative text. When I was a lector and I would turn the page for the reading and I'd see somebody had taped something in, it just felt kind of hokey to me. It felt like being in a play. And being in a play and being in a liturgy just seemed like they ought to be different.

Latin Mass Catholics fear the inauthenticity of "stuffy" liturgy less than the inauthenticity of "hokey" or "cheesy" liturgy. I borrow the latter term from Jennifer, who is the same age as Josh. Unlike him, she grew up with little exposure to Catholic liturgy, but she shares his judgment that many contemporary parishes try so hard to avoid

---

they vary so little." Bruce Ellis Benson, *Liturgy as a Way of Life: Embodying the Arts in Christian Worship* (Grand Rapids, MI: Baker Academic, 2013), 140.

conformism that their rituals come across as made-up instead. Her Latin Mass parish avoids all such invention, she says:

> There's nothing schmaltzy about this place at all. You know what I mean? There's no guitar Mass; there's no "Let's turn to the left and share Jesus's handshake" or something totally made up and bizarre. Like [at] almost any suburban church, I just have this moment of, "Ughh," like it's so cheesy. You don't have to make things cheesy to make people come to church. . . . You just have to be real.

According to Jennifer, using Latin also contributes to the sense that the Mass is "real." For her, the foreign language actually emphasizes the importance of participating with a good understanding. Translating the prayers and simplifying the rites would cause her to miss an opportunity to increase her understanding from the outside in, and it would eliminate evidence of the congregation's authenticity:

> I think that having the Latin Mass, it was like, "They're so serious that I have to read this manual to figure out what's going on." And Latin seemed terribly intellectual, you know. And the fact that they were doing Latin seemed terribly earnest. And you can just tell from people's postures and attitudes here that they're not—they might be faking it; I don't know. They could be or couldn't be; I'm not sure. But they're not doing things that just seem so of our day and age, I guess—like trying to bend what should be kind of a timeless thing. . . .
>
> Maybe I didn't know at first, because it took me a really long time to like commit. And at least part of that might have been trying to detect a level of authenticity, I guess. And eventually I could not detect any inauthenticity here.

Jennifer's comments also show how Latin Mass Catholics integrate their assessments of performative authenticity with assessments of genealogical authenticity. She associates "faking it" with doing things "of our day and age" and "authenticity" with postures and attitudes that seem "timeless." Her judgment isn't based on comparative liturgiology or another historical science, but on the imaginative projection of a lineage of belief and practice. That sense of continuity is verified in a manner of performance—a "way of doing things"—

characterized by deference and submission to what has been done before, however vaguely understood.

The deference with which a ritual action is performed verifies the present performance's connection to the chain of memory more immediately and more strongly than a historical analysis of the performance's content does.[55] This is true even for participants who know the history of the Latin Mass too well to imagine that its external forms have been passed down unchanged since the days of Gregory the Great. Bernard, a professor of medieval history and former free church Protestant, was attracted to the Latin Mass by the "connection with the tradition" and the "knowledge that this is the way Catholics worshipped for centuries." He contrasts the intentional cultivation of continuity with the approach to worship taken by churches he attended while teaching at a Mennonite seminary in the late 1980s:

> The whole Mennonite subculture was breaking up and changing because of moving off of the farm and the mechanization of agriculture after the Second World War. So they were no longer doing the things the way they had always done them. And they were now having a different form of worship every Sunday depending on what the worship committee planned. And some-times they'd do something several times in a row. . . . But I could see that with the Mennonites losing their—just the way they'd always done things which was in effect an unwritten liturgical pattern—losing that, there was something missing.

Before giving up on his Mennonite church, Bernard even "wrote them a liturgy" by excerpting texts from the Roman Catholic Missal, but he realized that it was unlikely to be used more than once or twice before the pastor and worship committee moved on to something else.

Now that Bernard teaches at a Catholic university, he occasionally sends students to attend a Latin Mass and report their impressions.

---

[55] See Danièle Hervieu-Léger, *Religion as a Chain of Memory* (New Brunswick, NJ: Rutgers University Press, 2000); Maurice Bloch, "Ritual and Deference," in *Ritual and Memory: Toward a Comparative Anthropology of Religion*, ed. Harvey Whitehouse and James Laidlaw (Walnut Creek, CA: AltaMira Press, 2004), 65–78. Stephan Feuchtwang, "Ritual and Memory," in *Memory: History, Theories, Debates*, ed. Susannah Radstone and Bill Schwarz (New York: Fordham University Press, 2010), 281–98.

Although his Catholic students usually have no previous familiarity with the Latin Mass, the "single most common refrain" he hears from them speaks to their ability to project a lineage of belief from the participants' way of doing things. "Again and again, people would say, 'It was very important to me to sense that I was worshipping in the same way that my Catholic ancestors did.' " Among the Latin Mass Catholics I met, this refrain and others expressing a desire to connect with one's spiritual ancestors are very common. This is the case even among adherents whose recent biological ancestors were not Catholic. Critics correctly argue that Latin Mass Catholics aren't "getting the history right" when they claim the church never made major changes to the liturgy's external forms before Vatican II.[56] But Latin Mass Catholics aren't out to get the history right. They are trying to "relearn a forgotten way of doing things" from the outside in—even as many of their fellow Christians seek the same goal, an "integrated liturgical act," from the inside out.

### Harmonizing a dichotomy

Christian worship today is characterized by "dichotomy," to borrow Ross's description. A dichotomy is a cutting apart of two things that should be united as one. One dichotomy "pits evangelical churches against the liturgical renewal movement and allows for little ground in between."[57] Another dichotomy pits Latin Mass adherents against their fellow Catholics, with little enthusiasm on either side for the Ordinary and Extraordinary Forms of the Roman Rite to be "mutually enriching."[58] In these and other disagreements about worship, one can detect an underlying dichotomy between the *inside-out* and *outside-in* approaches to authentic liturgy. How do we coordinate the tuning adjustments that aim to harmonize minds and voices? How do we integrate creativity and repetition, spontaneity and stability, inhabiting the rite and habituating oneself to the rite?

[56] Bernard P. Prusak, "Getting the History Right," *Commonweal* 134, no. 14 (August 17, 2007): 16.

[57] Ross, *Evangelical Versus Liturgical?*, 2.

[58] See "Letter of Pope Benedict XVI Accompanying the Apostolic Letter *Summorum Pontificum*," *Newsletter of the United States Conference of Catholic Bishops Committee on the Liturgy* 43 (June 2007): 22.

How do we discern the Spirit that guides the church and the same Spirit that dwells within each believer?

Ross suggests that the "link between worship and ethics is a potentially rich site of connection between evangelical and liturgical traditions."[59] It's also an area in which *inside-out* and *outside-in* approaches to authentic liturgy are ripe for symbiosis instead of dichotomy. Both traditions and both approaches are tempted to dichotomize worship and ethics, separating what goes on inside the liturgy or worship service from what goes on outside the walls of the church. Both face the danger of seeing corporate worship only as the "summit" of the church's activity, forgetting that it is also the "source" of the church's mission to the world. Simultaneously, both are tempted to view outreach and evangelism as ends in themselves, forgetting that "the goal of apostolic endeavor is that all who are made children of God by faith and Baptism should come together to praise God in the midst of his church" (SC 10).

Each tradition also has a special charism for making the link between worship and ethics apparent. For those who seek authentic participation from the inside out, the indwelling Spirit that empowers them to inhabit corporate worship also calls them to refashion the rest of their lives. A member of one congregation in Ross's study explains:

> The worship that goes on here [in the sanctuary] puts a fire in us that carries us on to the other worship experience, which is what happens at work, or what happens at home, or what happens in any place you find yourself. How you do your job, or how you handle unemployment, or how you raise your kids at home, or how you plant lilies in the backyard. *All of it* is worship.[60]

A member of a Latin Mass parish whom I interviewed similarly connects liturgical participation to ethics, but he emphasizes his community's charism for docility to the formative power of the Spirit, working through ritual to inculcate a habit of "reverence" that carries over into everyday life:

[59] Ross, *Evangelical Versus Liturgical?*, 44.
[60] Quoted in Ross, *Evangelical Versus Liturgical?*, 44.

What's the old saying? What we pray is what we believe. *Lex orandi, lex credendi.* I guess that's part of our faith life, but it seems to me that it would also translate into our actions too. The way we pray is the way we act. At least it should be. . . . If you're concerned about the way that you pray and that you pray properly, that's going to carry over. . . .

If you're starting from the Mass, praying the Mass reverently, that's going to be the source of the grace in your soul that you're getting. And then from there, that's going to flow out into your actions. . . . If you're praying the right way, reverently, then you're going to think reverently; you're going to act reverently.

In worship and in ethics, acting with reverence and acting with the fire of the Holy Spirit should go together. Authentic liturgy harmonizes docility and creativity, respect for God's law and zeal for justice, stewardship of creation and love of neighbor. Authentic liturgy supports authentic ethics by overcoming the dichotomy between outside-in and inside-out approaches to discerning the movement of the Holy Spirit. The *freedom* to act in accord with the will of the Holy Spirit depends on integrating reverent and bold responses to the Spirit's prompting. As I will argue in the next chapter, an integrated liturgical act exercises the virtues of *humility* and *magnanimity*, which are also paired in authentic ethical praxis.

On the side of humility, Guardini says:

The freedom which is in the liturgy is exercised not by the will of the individual but by the will of the Church, governed by the Holy Spirit. This freedom finds its expression in broad slow movements which are worked out over the centuries and over the whole face of the earth. It finds its expression in the fact that the liturgy has no set goal, that it does not wish to "achieve" anything, but only to stand before God, to breathe and to develop, to love him and praise him.[61]

The humility that discerns the "broad slow movements" of the Holy Spirit in the received external forms of the liturgy is the same humility that prevents authentic action for justice from degenerating into

---

[61] Romano Guardini, "Personal Prayer and the Prayers of the Church," in *Unto the Altar: The Practice of Catholic Worship*, ed. Alfons Kirchgaessner, trans. Rosaleen Brennan (New York: Herder and Herder, 1963), 32–43, at 36–37.

mere "actionism."[62] Ethical praxis always faces the temptation to neglect "fruitful, penetrating and, above all, lasting activity," preferring instead "quick, immediate, even numerically tangible results." Humility ensures that people, not projects, are the end of ethical action, and the same virtue keeps worship from being reduced to a tool for "achieving moral or other stimulating effects."[63]

In both worship and ethics, however, humility must be paired with a magnanimous response to new promptings of the Spirit, as the Second Vatican Council teaches most clearly in *Gaudium et Spes* (4).[64] The church's free cooperation with the Holy Spirit isn't *only* worked out over centuries. The same freedom finds its expression "in every age," as the people of God "try to discern the true signs of God's presence and purpose in the events, the needs and the desires which it shares with the rest of humanity today." Faith that the church is "led by the Spirit of the Lord who fills the whole world . . . casts a new light on everything and makes known the full ideal which God has set for humanity, thus guiding the mind toward solutions that are fully human" (*Gaudium et Spes* 4, 11). The Holy Spirit, dwelling in the minds of God's people, guides the church toward more authentic solutions to the social concerns of the day. Even now, the same Spirit inspires adjustments to the outward celebration of the liturgy, so that in worship and in witness the church may become a more authentic "sign under which the scattered children of God may be gathered together" (SC 2).

[62] I borrow the word "actionism" from Martin Stuflesser, "*Actuosa Participatio*: Between Hectic Actionism and New Interiority: Reflections on 'Active Participation' in the Worship of the Church as Both Right and Obligation of the Faithful," trans. Robert J. Daly, *Studia Liturgica* 41, no. 1 (2011): 92–126. Although a neologism, it is a better word for inauthentic ethical praxis than "activism," which often enough implies deep and lasting engagement. See also Romano Guardini, "Some Dangers of the Liturgical Revival," in *Unto the Altar: The Practice of Catholic Worship*, ed. Alfons Kirchgaessner, trans. Rosaleen Brennan (New York: Herder and Herder, 1963), 13–22, at 14–16.

[63] Guardini, "Some Dangers," 15–16.

[64] Second Vatican Council, Pastoral Constitution on the Church in the Modern World (*Gaudium et Spes*), December 7, 1965, in *Vatican Council II: Constitutions, Decrees, Declarations; The Basic Sixteen Documents*, ed. Austin Flannery (Collegeville, MN: Liturgical Press, 2014).

As Vatican II moved modern liturgical renewal into a new phase, the danger of dichotomizing worship and ethics was readily apparent to Guardini. Such a split in the church's consciousness is multiplied by the danger of dichotomizing interior and exterior participation. If ecclesial renewal is not pursued in an integral way, then the whole work is endangered by four extremes. "Rubricists" ignore the "difficulties and duties of real life," so that their liturgical endeavors are "forced and exaggerated." "Activists" intent on social reform regard public worship as "a waste of time" unless it can be manipulated to produce immediate practical results. "Dilettantes" risk "confusion and arbitrary action" in their eagerness for innovative rituals. And "conservatives" focus so exclusively on "the inner basic religious life" that they reject any new external aids to participation. Guardini warned that various combinations of these temptations threatened to spoil the authentic fruit of the liturgical movement at the very moment when its long labors had made a "sudden leap into the awareness of the general public." Still, he believed that restrictions, "which would hinder a work, already several decades old, from yielding matured fruits, would be far worse than any temporary uncertainty."[65]

Several additional decades have now passed, and although the dangers to authentic liturgical renewal have not abated, it is more apparent than ever that the work must go on in ways that seek harmony, not dichotomy. Ethical witness must accompany liturgical participation, and interior transformation must accompany exterior reforms. This imperative applies equally to Roman Catholic, evangelical, mainline Protestant, and Orthodox churches. In every ecclesial tradition, authentic renewal of Christian worship requires both kinds of tuning adjustments. Tuning from the outside in brings minds into greater harmony with the broad movement of the Holy Spirit in the centuries-old rhythms of the liturgy. Tuning from the inside out brings voices into greater harmony with new movements of the Spirit in the minds and hearts of the faithful today.

Undoubtedly, efforts to habituate ourselves to the liturgy will mean that Christian worship often looks repetitive. Meanwhile, efforts to inhabit the liturgy will make some exterior elements appear unprecedented. But as David Fagerberg says, "Being liturgical decidedly

---

[65] Guardini, "Some Dangers," 14–18, 21.

218 of Authentic Liturgy

does *not* mean possessing repetitive protocol," and mere "precedence" is "a thin understanding of tradition."[66] An act of worship is
said to be "liturgical" because "the Holy Spirit makes possible our
participation in the Son's participation in the Father." If the participants cooperate with the Holy Spirit, then their liturgical performance
"could be said to be traditional the first time it was done."[67] And
because cooperation with the Holy Spirit is possible only when minds
and voices are in tune, such liturgy alone deserves to be called
*authentic*.

[66] David W. Fagerberg, *Theologia Prima: What Is Liturgical Theology?*, 2nd ed. (Mundelein, IL: Hillenbrand Books, 2004), 222, 224. Emphasis in original.
[67] David W. Fagerberg, "Traditional Liturgy and Liturgical Tradition," *Worship* 72,
no. 6 (November 1998): 484–87.

*Chapter Seven*

# Authentic Liturgy and the Virtue of Authenticity

The argument so far can be summarized simply. For liturgy to be authentic, sometimes the liturgists have to adjust their interior activity to be in harmony with what the ritual gives them to do externally. And sometimes, for the liturgy to be authentic, the liturgists have to adjust the exterior ritual to be in harmony with what the Spirit of God is inspiring them to do internally. Liturgists who aim to worship with "minds and voices in tune" must approach harmony in both directions, *outside-in* and *inside-out*.

I am using the word "liturgist" here as David Fagerberg does, to refer to someone who "commits liturgy."[1] It would be inauthentic (in a genealogical sense) to apply this title only to "experts" and "professionals"—to liturgical scholars, liturgy planners, music directors, and presiders, for example. The taproot of *leitourgia* is God's saving work on behalf of all people, brought to fulfillment in Jesus Christ. The source of the church's participation in the liturgy of Christ is his Holy Spirit poured out upon all who receive the gospel in faith. Full, conscious, and active participation in the liturgy is not, therefore, the peculiar task of liturgical experts. The exhortation in *Sacrosanctum Concilium* 11 is rightly directed to *all* the Christian faithful: "In order that the liturgy may be able to produce its full effects it is necessary

---

[1] David W. Fagerberg, *Theologia Prima: What Is Liturgical Theology?*, 2nd ed. (Mundelein, IL: Hillenbrand Books, 2004), 8.

that the faithful come to it with proper dispositions, that their minds be attuned to their voices, and that they cooperate with heavenly grace lest they receive it in vain." The Christian people who make adjustments to bring their minds and voices into tune are engaged in liturgical theology, so they are also rightly called theologians.[2]

I have traced the genealogy of the call to authentic participation in the liturgy from its scriptural sources, through the writings of early and medieval Christians, and into modern movements for liturgical reform and renewal. Throughout this history, we have seen the persistent importance of *performative* authenticity. The repeated call to pray "in such a way that our mind is in harmony with our voice" is the best evidence that the *genealogical* authenticity of liturgy also depends on cultivating the harmony of interior and exterior prayer that yields an integrated liturgical act. I aimed in the last chapter to give some contemporary examples of Christians attempting to tune their minds to their voices and their voices to their minds. They approach harmony from different directions, but they are guided by the same principle of discernment: communion in love, which unites the whole Body of Christ.

This concluding chapter reflects more philosophically on authentic participation in the liturgy. What are worshippers doing, individually and corporately, when they enact the liturgy? What is it about their activity that is more or less authentic? And what do they cultivate when they seek to enact the liturgy authentically? Having surveyed historical and contemporary articulations of authentic liturgy, I am attempting to respond systematically to Guardini's questions about the liturgical act *as action*: "What is the nature of the genuine liturgical action . . .? How is the basic liturgical act constituted? What forms can it take? What might go wrong with it? How are its demands related to the make-up of modern man? What must be done so that he can really and truly learn it?"[3] What is necessary, in short, to *enact* authentic liturgy?

[2] Aidan Kavanagh, *On Liturgical Theology* (Collegeville, MN: Liturgical Press, 1992), 73–74.
[3] Romano Guardini, "A Letter from Romano Guardini," *Herder Correspondence* 1, no. 8 (August 1964): 239.

## Articulating the interior/exterior distinction

The answer to this last question, already hinted at by Guardini, is that authentic liturgy requires the human participants to participate in the liturgical act with performative authenticity. Up to this point, however, I have defined performative authenticity somewhat vaguely as harmony between "interior" and "exterior" when performing liturgical prayer. This imprecision was necessary to encompass a wide variety of metaphorical and philosophical articulations of performative authenticity within a genealogy that is coherent even though it flows through many branches. Terms that Christians have used to articulate the *interior* have included "heart," "mind," "soul," "spirit," "meaning," "disposition," "intention," "emotion," "feeling," and "sentiment," while terms used to articulate the *exterior* have included "lips," "voice," "speech," "breath," "expression," "display," "performance," "ritual," and "show." The most obvious commonality in this variety is the binary interior/exterior distinction itself. The second clear constant is the ideal of harmonizing the two terms.

The interior/exterior binary is widespread not only in Christianity, but in many cultures past and present, as anthropologists Marilyn Strathern and Saba Mahmood point out. "What is analytically interesting is not so much the binary nature of the inner/outer distinction when found in a particular cultural context, but the relation between these two terms, the particular form their articulation takes."[4] In the cultural and historical contexts that we surveyed in the preceding chapters, the relation between interior and exterior is articulated in ways that seem to be incompatible or at least difficult to reconcile. The apparent incompatibility of two such articulations is presently a significant obstacle to harmony among Christian worshippers. Let me review these competing articulations of the interior/exterior distinction before proposing a better alternative based on Guardini's concept of the integrated liturgical act.

Worshippers suspicious of the formality of liturgical prayer often contrast interior sentiment or emotion with exterior expression or performance. We have seen this suspicion become outright hostility

---

[4] Saba Mahmood, *Politics of Piety: The Islamic Revival and the Feminist Subject* (Princeton, NJ: Princeton University Press, 2005), 133–34. Mahmood credits this observation to Marilyn Strathern, *The Gender of the Gift: Problems with Women and Problems with Society in Melanesia* (Berkeley: University of California Press, 1988), 88.

to scripted prayer among seventeenth-century Puritans, eighteenth-century Romantics, and twenty-first-century consumers, to name just a few examples of worshippers for whom emotional intensity and spontaneity are the marks of authentic liturgy. This is essentially an *expressive* approach to being an authentic participant in worship, for one becomes an integrated subject of prayer from the inside out. In a more or less conscious rejection, other modern Christians instead distinguish externally given texts and rituals from interior attention and assent. Catholics who consider the Tridentine Mass more authentic than the post-Vatican II liturgy articulate the interior/exterior binary in this way, but they are not an isolated example. This approach to authentic liturgical participation is more *formative* than expressive. The external forms of worship are given from outside the individual worshipper, the particular congregation, and even the present generation of Christians. On this view, the key to becoming an integrated subject of liturgical prayer is to allow these "objective" words and rites to work on the worshipper from the outside in, gradually transforming distraction into attention and individual willfulness into joyful submission to the will of God.

I argue that we can't adequately articulate the interior/exterior distinction or the relationship between the two terms by simply aggregating the formative and expressive approaches to liturgical participation. Worship's primary, fundamental, and essential aim is neither the formation of dispositions nor the expression of sentiments. Liturgy's end is found within liturgy itself. In the very performance of the liturgy, Jesus Christ accomplishes the glorification of God "with maximum effectiveness" (SC 7, 10). The sanctification that participants in the liturgy experience is also accomplished *in the performance itself*, not as a secondary effect of the external ritual's formative power. Lest we forget what is primary and what follows as a secondary effect, *Sacrosanctum Concilium* prefaces its discussion of the "educative and pastoral nature of the liturgy" with a reminder that "the sacred liturgy is principally the worship of the divine majesty" (SC 33).

As divine worship, liturgy refuses to be the mere tool of anything else. It can neither be "reduced to a merely esthetic reality" nor "considered an instrument whose aims are mainly pedagogical."[5] This

---

[5] John Paul II, Address to the Congregation for Divine Worship and the Discipline of the Sacraments, September 21, 2001, reprinted as "Papal Address on the Liturgy," *Sacred Music* 129, no. 1 (2002): 22–24.

self-sufficiency of the liturgy requires an articulation of the interior/ exterior distinction that situates the authenticity of the liturgical act in its own performance. Formation and self-expression both have major roles to play in bringing minds and voices into tune. But if the goal of such harmony is an "integrated liturgical act," as Guardini says,[6] then our philosophical inquiry should first ask what that act is and how it is performed. In pursuing this line of questioning, I am following Nicholas Wolterstorff, whose terminology is similar to my own:

> A common distinction in discussions about liturgy by non-philosophers is between the *expressive* function of liturgy and the *formative* function: liturgical activity as expressive of the beliefs, commitments, habits, emotions, and so forth of the participants, and liturgical activity as formative of those. The focus of my discussion will not be on the expressive and formative functions of liturgical activity but on *what is done* in liturgical enactments. Call this the *performative* dimension of liturgy. Insofar as liturgical activity is expressive and formative, it's what is done that is expressive and formative. What is done is basic.[7]

Questions about what the liturgy expresses and how the liturgy forms participants are important, but secondary, if we want to understand and recover authentic liturgy as "a forgotten way of *doing* things."[8]

In an integrated liturgical act, "what is done" is done both internally and externally. The interior/exterior distinction is therefore best articulated as a distinction in the liturgical act itself. That act, while incorporating the activity of individual members of the assembly, is a *corporate* act—an act of the whole liturgical body. It is also a *cooperative* corporate act, in which each member participates in the activity of the whole body. Of itself, cooperation among the members does not make the liturgy an act of the whole Body of Christ. Rather, it is Christ who "always associates the church with himself," making the liturgy "an action of Christ the priest and of his body, which is the church" (SC 7). Christ does not force the members of his body to participate in the liturgical act but allows them freely to "cooperate

---

[6] Guardini, "Letter from Romano Guardini," 238.

[7] Nicholas Wolterstorff, *Acting Liturgically: Philosophical Reflections on Religious Practice* (Oxford: Oxford University Press, 2018), 5.

[8] Guardini, "Letter from Romano Guardini," 238. Emphasis added.

with heavenly grace" (SC 11). It is the grace-enabled cooperation of the Body with its Head, "through the power of the Holy Spirit," that allows the "action of Christ" to be rightly called the "action of the church" (SC 6–7).

## An authentic "way of doing things"

Still, where in this corporate, cooperative, participatory action of Christ and the church do we distinguish interior from exterior activity? Here, Wolterstorff's description of "what is done" in liturgy is helpful. To locate liturgical action "on the ontological map," he classifies liturgy as a "species of ritual" comprised of "liturgical enactments," which are a species of "scripted activity":

> An enactment of a liturgy consists of the participants together performing scripted verbal, gestural, and auditory actions, the prescribed purpose of their doing so being both to engage God directly in acts of learning and acknowledging the excellence of who God is and what God has done, and to be engaged by God. And the liturgy itself is that type of sequence of act-types that is enacted when the participants do what the script prescribes.[9]

In Wolterstorff's description, the exterior aspect of a liturgical enactment is easy to identify. It consists of the "scripted verbal, gestural, and auditory actions" that the participants perform "together" by each participant performing all and only such actions as the script assigns him or her (see SC 28). Some prescriptions aren't inscribed in words, musical notations, or diagrams. Enacting the Liturgy of St. John Chrysostom, for example, requires following not just the text of that liturgy, but the prescriptions "embedded in the Orthodox social practice of enacting their liturgies (plus any that may be specified orally on the spot)."[10]

Written and unwritten scripts prescribe more than the verbal, gestural, and auditory actions of the liturgy. These external actions "are mostly not prescribed for their own sake," but for the sake of "counting as" acts of *worship*, which Wolterstorff defines more precisely as

[9] Wolterstorff, *Acting Liturgically*, 29–30.
[10] Wolterstorff, *Acting Liturgically*, 18.

"acts of learning and acknowledging the excellence of who God is and what God has done." His distinction between "counting-as acts" and "counted-as acts" follows speech-act theory, which observes that there are many conventional situations in which an agent's "performance of some perceptible behavioral act" counts as "performance of an imperceptible non-behavioral act."[11] In J. L. Austin's well-known example, performing the "locutionary act" of uttering the name of a newly launched ship while smashing a bottle of champagne against its stem counts as performing the "illocutionary act" of christening the vessel.[12] Convention prescribes not only the perceptible verbal and gestural actions, but also that the performance of the prescribed actions *counts as* performance of the imperceptible illocutionary act. A traditional custom of several navies prescribes the "illocutionary force" (Austin) or "count-as significance" (Wolterstorff) of the sacrifice of champagne. Similarly, the Liturgy of St. John Chrysostom prescribes that the singing of the *Trisagion* shall count as offering God "due worship and praise."[13]

If the *exterior* aspect of a liturgical enactment consists of the perceptible, locutionary, "counting-as" actions of speech, song, and gesture, then what is the *interior* aspect of the total, integrated liturgical act? It is tempting to directly identify interior participation with the imperceptible, illocutionary acts of worship that are "counted as" enacted whenever the exterior actions are performed as prescribed. It is tempting to say that the assembly sings a hymn outwardly but praises God inwardly, recounts God's deeds outwardly but acknowledges God's excellence inwardly, voices their needs outwardly but seeks God's aid inwardly. But the *interior aspect* of a liturgical enactment differs from the *illocutionary force* of the liturgy's external rites. It would be a mistake to say that only exterior actions "count as" acts

---

[11] Wolterstorff, *Acting Liturgically*, 23–26.

[12] J. L. Austin, *How to Do Things with Words*, ed. J. O. Urmson and Marina Sbisà, 2nd ed. (Cambridge, MA: Harvard University Press, 1975), 5.

[13] That the *Trisagion* shall count as offering God "due worship and praise" is explicitly prescribed in the prayer that precedes it: "You have counted us, your humble and unworthy servants, worthy to stand at this time before the glory of your Holy Altar, and to offer you due worship and praise. Accept, Master, the Thrice-holy Hymn even from the mouth of us sinners, and visit us in your goodness." See *The Divine Liturgy of Our Father among the Saints John Chrysostom: The Greek Text Together with a Translation into English* (Oxford: Oxford University Press, 1995), 12–13.

of worship while interior actions are the "counted-as" acts of worship themselves. It would put us back on the path to regarding interior participation as the only "real thing"—the liturgical act whole and entire—and the only thing that really offers God "due worship and praise."

Interior participation is not *identical* with "what is done" in liturgical enactments. Rather, the interior activity is an essential part of the liturgical "way of doing things." The interior part of the liturgical act is no less prescribed than the exterior part is. These prescriptions are always embedded in the social practice of liturgy, and we have seen them explicitly articulated in Scripture, official doctrine, and the teaching of pastors and theologians. Often, prescriptions for interior participation are included in the written script for a liturgy, and sometimes these prescriptions are themselves spoken as part of the prescribed verbal utterances of the liturgy. Consider these instructions spoken aloud at various points in the Liturgy of St. John Chrysostom:

> In peace, let us pray to the Lord . . .
>
> With all our soul and with all our mind, let us say . . .
>
> Let us now lay aside every care of this life . . .
>
> Let us love one another, that with one mind we may confess . . .
>
> With wisdom let us attend . . .
>
> Let us stand with awe; let us stand with fear; let us attend, that we may offer the holy oblation in peace . . .
>
> Let our hearts be on high . . .
>
> With fear of God, with faith and love, draw near . . .
>
> Again and again in peace, let us pray to the Lord . . .
>
> Let us go forth in peace.[14]

Most of these instructions prescribe the enactment of "peace" (*eirēnē*) on multiple levels. Worshippers are asked to "lay aside" earthly cares and attain to "wisdom." Out of this inner peace or *apatheia*, they are to harmonize their minds and voices so what they "say" with their lips, they also say with "soul" and "mind." And they

---

[14] *Divine Liturgy of St. John Chrysostom*, 4, 7, 9, 17, 20, 21, 22, 29, 30, 31, 37, 45, 49.

should "love one another" so what they "confess" and "offer" may be confessed and offered "with one mind." Some instructions combine an interior prescription with a prescription of exterior action (e.g., "with faith and love, draw near"), while others prescribe something that can only be done inwardly (e.g., "let our hearts be on high").

In every case, though, what is prescribed is *action*. Worshippers are not instructed merely to feel at peace with themselves, with each other, and with God; nor are they told to imagine, wish, or pray for such peace. Rather, as Terence Cuneo proposes, we should "understand the liturgy's frequent directives that the assembled perform actions in peace as speech acts that direct the assembled to perform these actions in such a way that they enact and enhance shalom/eirene."[15] Included among the prescribed *things to do* in a liturgical performance are utterances that further prescribe a *way of doing things*—the correct way of performing all the other prescribed actions. Participants follow this prescribed *way of doing things* by *doing things* inwardly while outwardly performing the prescribed verbal, gestural, and auditory actions. They set aside cares, lift up their hearts, join their souls, think with one mind, love one another, and make of their unity in Christ an offering to God in peace. In a word, the participants *cooperate*. The prescribed way of doing things in the liturgy is for minds to cooperate with voices, for members of the assembly to cooperate with one another, and for the whole body of the faithful to "cooperate with heavenly grace lest they receive it in vain" (SC 11). The liturgy is fruitless for those who don't work together as members of one body. Without cooperation, there is no authentic participation and no real acceptance of grace; there is only a simulation of worship.

While completely inauthentic participation is rare, at least some participants in a liturgical assembly are usually not performing the prescribed interior and exterior actions as fully and cooperatively as they could. It's no easy task to "lay aside every care of this life" when those cares are burdensome, to lift up our hearts when they are heavy with grief, or to look upon our fellow worshippers with love when some among them have sinned against us. In performing these prescribed interior actions, participants will often fall short of what they

---

[15] Terence Cuneo, *Ritualized Faith: Essays on the Philosophy of Liturgy* (Oxford: Oxford University Press, 2016), 134.

intend. But the intention to participate inwardly and outwardly is no intention at all if it doesn't aim at performing the prescribed interior and exterior actions *more* completely. Worshippers must intend to become *more authentic* participants in the liturgy. They must intend to *increase* the fullness and the harmony with which they lift up their hearts and open their lips, or else they do not enact the liturgy at all. It remains possible for the assembly to authentically perform the liturgical act even though many members are distracted, doubtful, imperfectly contrite, or imperfectly forgiving. Yet the liturgy is more fully itself—more *authentic*—when participants overcome these barriers to full, conscious, and active participation.

## Liturgical know-how

It may seem that I have carelessly conflated the *identity* of action (*what is done*) and the *mode* of action (the *way of doing things*). I admit the necessity of the distinction if we wish to uphold the truth of statements like "The priest celebrated Mass sloppily, but it was still the Mass" or "The music was too difficult for the congregation to sing well, but it was still their offering of praise." Yet even in these cases there is a sense in which the liturgical act, while validly performed and therefore identifiable, is less fully itself than it could be. Intuition tells us that a merely valid celebration is not identical with a celebration in which all participate fully, consciously, and actively. We recognize that a *more fully realized* celebration of the liturgy is nascent in the participants' intention to do what the church does. Recognition of this unfulfilled potential requires us to speak about the authenticity of a liturgical act differently than we would speak about its validity. Like a sacrament, a liturgical action cannot be "more valid" or "less valid"—but it can be "more authentic" or "less authentic."

I take it that knowing whether a liturgical rite has been validly enacted is propositional knowledge. Propositional knowledge is "knowing that" something is the case. Such knowledge may be "upgraded" into certainty, given the right evidence.[16] So, participants aim to know with certainty whether or not a sacrament is valid, even though evidence of what was said or what was intended might be

---

[16] Cuneo, *Ritualized Faith*, 151.

lacking in some circumstances. By contrast, participants who desire *authentic* liturgy strive for *mastery* or *excellence* rather than certainty. "Knowing how" to enact the liturgy with excellence differs from the propositional knowledge of what constitutes a valid sacrament. This is because "knowing how to perform an action is a species of objectual knowledge, having as its object not a proposition but a way of act-ing." As Cuneo argues, "For an agent to know how to perform some action, that agent's *understanding* of it must satisfy some threshold of completeness and accuracy."[17] We need not specify the threshold for authentic participation in the liturgy more precisely than *Sacrosanctum Concilium* does when it calls the laity to "a good understanding" of "the sacred action" (48).[18] The point remains that those who desire to participate in the liturgy more authentically are seeking *know-how* that grows with understanding and tends toward excellence.

"The very nature of the liturgy" demands that the church aim at a specific excellence when performing liturgical celebrations: the "full, conscious, and active" participation in those celebrations by "all the faithful." The Christian people are chosen by God and "bound by reason of their Baptism" to make this aim their own (SC 14). Mem-bership in the communion of the baptized is essential because the know-how that leads to excellence in liturgical participation is learned and handed on in what Wolterstorff, following Alasdair MacIntyre, calls the "social practice" of the liturgy. "A social practice is a way of performing actions of a certain type"—a *way of doing things*—that embeds both individual and collective actions within a community.[19] Because every liturgy "has of itself a public and social character," it remains a social practice even when celebrated by an individual, "quasi-privately" (SC 27). Practitioners of a social practice "regard some performances as better than others," and "these standards of excellence and criteria for correctness are handed on as part of the know-how so that, in this respect too, the activity is social and the practice has a tradition."[20]

---

[17] Cuneo, *Ritualized Faith*, 151–53; emphasis added.

[18] Here, as in the previous chapter, I render *bene intellegentes* as "good under-standing." See the explanation above, p. 192 n. 6.

[19] Wolterstorff, *Acting Liturgically*, 21–22. See Alasdair MacIntyre, *After Virtue: A Study in Moral Theory*, 2nd ed. (Notre Dame, IN: University of Notre Dame Press, 1984), 187–96.

[20] Wolterstorff, *Acting Liturgically*, 22.

Aiming at excellence in a social practice implies progressive growth according to the community's traditional standards of excellence. As MacIntyre emphasizes, pursuing such excellence unifies past and present practitioners in a shared effort directed toward a common end. "To enter into a practice is to enter into a relationship not only with its contemporary practitioners, but also with those who have preceded us in the practice, particularly those whose achievements extended the reach of the practice to its present point."[21] Imitating the saints in their pursuit of authentic *performance* of the liturgy therefore also fulfills the *genealogical* meaning of authenticity. Handing on the liturgy as a way of doing things establishes a community of practice that worships with one mind and one voice, in tune not only with all who are presently gathered but also with all who have come before. "Liturgical know-how is a shared know-how, shared both with one's fellow participants, making it possible to participate together, and with those who preceded one in enactments of that liturgy and others like it."[22]

What is this shared liturgical know-how handed down from generation to generation? I argued above that knowing how to perform the liturgy includes more than knowing what the prescribed verbal, gestural, and auditory actions are. There is a way of performing these actions more authentically, with better understanding and greater harmony of minds and voices. That liturgical way of doing things is for participants to *cooperate* in performing the prescribed actions—to "cooperate with heavenly grace" above all (SC 11), but also to cooperate with one another because of their communion in grace. Such cooperation is itself a gift from God, as Wolterstorff points out with an example from the Liturgy of St. John Chrysostom:

> At one point the priest says, "Grant us with one mouth and one heart to glorify and praise thy sublime and wondrous name, of the Father, and of the Son, and of the Holy Ghost; now and forever: world without end." The people must be empowered by God to glorify and praise God with one mouth and one heart.[23]

---

[21] MacIntyre, *After Virtue*, 194.
[22] Wolterstorff, *Acting Liturgically*, 23.
[23] Wolterstorff, *Acting Liturgically*, 70.

Yet because grace builds upon nature, the know-how to pray with one mouth and one heart can be taught, learned, and rehearsed within the community of practice. Each participant can learn to harmonize his or her prayer with those of the other members of Christ's body. And because concord among *all* the members requires *each* member to harmonize interior and exterior activity, the know-how that participants learn is how to *attune* their minds and voices, both from the inside out and from the outside in. Excellence in harmonizing minds and voices is a gift from God that builds upon a human *virtue*. A "virtue," to borrow MacIntyre's definition of the core concept, is "an acquired human quality" necessary to achieve goods that are "internal" to a social practice—internal in the sense that "their achievement is a good for the whole community who participate in the practice."[24] The good internal to the practice of liturgy is authentic prayer: "an integrated liturgical act," as Guardini puts it—good for each member of Christ's body and for the whole corporate assembly. And the virtue required for authentic liturgy is *authenticity*.

## Magnanimity and authentic liturgy

In claiming authenticity as a virtue rather than a vice, I follow Charles Taylor and Daniel Dahlstrom. For many years and in multiple works, Taylor has argued that "authenticity should be taken seriously as a moral ideal." Although too often "the espousal of authenticity takes the form of a kind of soft relativism," Taylor disagrees with "critics of contemporary culture" who conflate the ethic of authenticity with subjectivism or with "a non-moral desire to do what one wants." We are dealing instead with "an ideal that has degraded but that is very worthwhile in itself, and indeed . . . unrepudiable by moderns." Though the modern configuration of the ethic of authenticity is "a child of the Romantic period," its basic impulse is "a continuation and intensification of the development inaugurated by Saint Augustine, who saw the road to God as passing through our own reflexive awareness of ourselves."[25]

---

[24] MacIntyre, *After Virtue*, 190–91.
[25] Charles Taylor, *The Ethics of Authenticity* (Cambridge, MA: Harvard University Press, 1992), 17, 21–27.

In calling authenticity "a new name for an old virtue,"[26] Dahlstrom takes a slightly different approach to the rehabilitation of authenticity. First, he is less interested than Taylor in identifying specifically modern contributions to the current culture of authenticity that are worth keeping. He questions the historical narrative of authenticity associated with Lionel Trilling and other interpreters of modernity. Dahlstrom prefers to point out the many ancient and medieval reflections on being true to oneself that precede the famous line in *Hamlet* and the rebellious literature of Rousseau. Additionally, Dahlstrom views authenticity ("being true to ourselves") and sincerity ("being true to others") as something more specific than moral ideals to which modern people aspire. They are *virtues* in the classical sense articulated by Aristotle, Aquinas, Al-Ghazali, and MacIntyre, among many others. As virtues, authenticity and sincerity are "more or less habituated processes directed at ideals." They are not "fully completed states," for they "embody settled but unfinished dispositions that can only be rendered intelligible and real by reference, not only to aspirations and ideals but to repeated tests of them." This is reflected in the way we apply the adjective "authentic" to a person differently than we would apply it to an artifact. "We say that someone is sincere or that she is authentic, not because she is so unfailingly, but because she behaves for the most part in ways that show a settled tendency of striving to be sincere and authentic."[27] Likewise, because people grow in authenticity instead of attaining it once and for all, it makes little sense to speak of *human actions* in binary terms, as either authentic or inauthentic. Our participation in the liturgy becomes *more authentic* through repeated practice or *less authentic* through neglect of the virtue of authenticity.

Seen as virtues, authenticity and sincerity "are not particularly novel to modernity," but Dahlstrom agrees with Taylor that the modern ideal of being true to oneself has increasingly separated itself from any reference to being true to others.[28] For Taylor, recovering from this "slide to subjectivism" and avoiding a "culture of narcissism" means defining authenticity in ways that recognize shared

---

[26] Daniel O. Dahlstrom, *Identity, Authenticity, and Humility* (Milwaukee, WI: Marquette University Press, 2017), 136.

[27] Dahlstrom, *Identity, Authenticity, and Humility*, 104, 133.

[28] Dahlstrom, *Identity, Authenticity, and Humility*, 103–5.

"horizons of significance" to which individuals might look even as they pursue those horizons by different paths. When such shared horizons are acknowledged, "authenticity is not the enemy of demands that emanate from beyond the self; it supposes such demands."[29] Dahlstrom would undoubtedly endorse this statement, but he would add that the demand to act sincerely toward others is already included in the virtue of being true to oneself, if the latter is rightly understood. "We can begin to understand" the virtue of authenticity, he says, "by returning to the wisdom of Aristotle and Aquinas."[30] We won't find the virtue of being true to ourselves described as "authenticity" by these philosophers. In both the *Nicomachean Ethics* and the *Summa Theologiae*, we will need to look under the virtue of *magnanimity*. With Aquinas, we will also need to examine the virtue of *humility* to get a complete understanding of authenticity that encompasses being true to oneself *and* being true to God and neighbor.

Unfortunately, only scholars like Dahlstrom use "magnanimous" in the broad sense that Aristotle and Aquinas mean when they describe a person who possesses a "great soul" or "greatness of mind" (*megalopsychos / magnanimus*). Although I can find no instance of a contemporary worshipper being described as "magnanimous," potential alternatives like "generous," "gracious," and "unselfish" are all inadequate, as are other names for the virtue itself, such as "self-esteem" and "nobility." Magnanimity (*megalopsychia / magnanimitas*) is classically defined as a habit of the mind that inclines a person to perform virtuous but difficult acts, while hoping to accomplish these honorable deeds despite the great challenge. "By its very name," says Aquinas, magnanimity "denotes stretching forth of the mind to great things."[31] This definition corresponds with Aristotle's description of a magnanimous person as one who "thinks himself worthy of great things and is truly worthy of them."[32] By "great things," both Aristotle and Aquinas mean great acts of virtue rather than the great

---

[29] Taylor, *Ethics of Authenticity*, 38–41. Taylor borrows the phrase "culture of narcissism" from Christopher Lasch, *The Culture of Narcissism: American Life in an Age of Diminishing Expectations*, revised (New York: W. W. Norton, 1991).

[30] Dahlstrom, *Identity, Authenticity, and Humility*, 136.

[31] ST II-II, q. 129 a. 1 co.

[32] Aristotle, *Nicomachean Ethics* 1123b1-2, quoted in Dahlstrom, *Identity, Authenticity, and Humility*, 105.

honors that such acts rightly win from other people. "A man is said to be magnanimous chiefly because he is minded to do some great act" and therefore "strives to do what is deserving of honor, yet not so as to think much of the honor accorded by man."[33]

"Magnanimity is, in short," Dahlstrom says, "the virtue concerned with being authentic, with being true to ourselves in the sense of our true worth, regardless of what others—or, more precisely, what some others—think of us."[34] Magnanimous people know that they have something worthy to offer. They are confident in their ability to perform a great good, so they dare to offer their best.[35] Thus, magnanimity aims not so much at specific virtuous acts as at a virtuous *way of doing things*. "Whereas each virtue respectively indicates something that is supposed to be done, magnanimity aims at doing it as well as possible and thereby perfecting the virtues as a whole."[36] In terms that comport with the modern ethic of authenticity, magnanimity is the virtue that enables us to act with maximum faithfulness to who we are and what we can offer.

How do we describe the virtue of magnanimous participants in the liturgy? Above all, magnanimous liturgists are of a mind to offer the greatest gifts they can bring, individually and corporately, to the celebration of the church's public prayer. They "care enough to send the very best." Dennis Smolarski, in his popular handbook for "all concerned about authentic worship," makes the point negatively but succinctly by exhorting liturgists to "never be comfortable with shoddy worship." Significantly, he believes that the authenticity of liturgy is at stake:

> The biblical story of Cain and Abel can be interpreted as a story about authentic versus shoddy worship. Abel presented the best to God—thus his sacrifice of praise was accepted. Cain was comfortable with second best—his sacrifice was not accepted. How often in our eucharistic gatherings are we comfortable with second best, or even worse?[37]

---

[33] ST II-II, q. 129, a. 1

[34] Dahlstrom, *Identity, Authenticity, and Humility*, 107.

[35] Aquinas argues that confidence ("strength of hope") and security ("freedom from fear") both belong to magnanimity. See ST II-II, q. 129 a. 6–7.

[36] Dahlstrom, *Identity, Authenticity, and Humility*, 115.

[37] Dennis C. Smolarski, *How Not to Say Mass: A Guidebook for All Concerned about Authentic Worship* (New York: Paulist Press, 1986), 26.

Avoiding "shoddiness" doesn't mean that the external offering must be expensive. The best gift is the total offering of all that we are and all that we have. " 'To love [God] with all the heart, and with all the understanding, and with all the strength,' and 'to love one's neighbor as oneself,'—this is much more important than all whole burnt offerings and sacrifices" (Mark 12:33).

More precisely, magnanimity is the virtue that enables liturgists to approach the total, integral, and authentic performance of the liturgical act *from the inside out*. Magnanimous liturgists are not afraid to *inhabit* the liturgy—to use the symbols, language, and art of their own diverse cultures and their own inventive minds to adapt and adorn the liturgy in ways that help their contemporaries recognize it as a living source of faith. Magnanimity is necessary for authentic inculturation and authentic creativity. Through this virtue, each individual Christian and each local church comes to recognize that all the baptized have been "made to drink of one Spirit." The same Spirit allots gifts "to each one individually just as the Spirit chooses," and these manifestations of the Spirit are "for the common good" (1 Cor 12:4-13). When the outward liturgical offering doesn't match what the Spirit is inwardly calling an individual, an assembly, or the universal church to manifest, then magnanimous liturgists adjust their external performance.

### Humility and authentic liturgy

The greatest danger that comes with conceiving the virtue of authenticity in terms of magnanimity is a temptation that Augustine long ago recognized as more perverse than any other because it feeds upon the praise that doing great things wins from other people:

> The words that fall from our lips, and the deeds that draw attention from other people, present an exceedingly dangerous temptation because of our love for praise, a love that begs for applause and treasures every bit of it to inflate one's sense of personal superiority. It is a temptation for me even when I condemn it in myself, precisely because I condemn it in myself—my contempt for empty pride becomes a source of pride that is emptier still.[38]

---

[38] Augustine, *Confessions*, X.38.63, in Augustine, *Confessions*, trans. Thomas Williams (Indianapolis, IN: Hackett, 2019), 197.

"Pride," says Dahlstrom, "presents the supreme threat to being authentic."[39] As my actions become more worthy of praise, the temptation increases to pursue not the virtuous deeds themselves but the honors they attract. Eventually, this can cause me to misrepresent my virtue to others. Even if I avoid the pitfall of insincerity, I can deceive myself into believing that the great things I do are my own accomplishments rather than undeserved gifts from God. Such pride upends authentic worship, for "the one who offers praise delights in God's gift, but the one who receives it has more delight in the praise he receives from human beings than in the gift he has from God."[40]

What is to prevent the presider, the assembly, the artist, the musician, or the committee of "experts" from falling victim to pride when adjusting the external forms of the liturgy? Dahlstrom points out that magnanimity, as described by Aristotle, already depends upon reason to present a person "with a true estimate of her worth, steering a path between overestimating herself (pride) and underestimating herself (pusillanimity)."[41] For a magnanimous Christian, a reasonable estimate of one's worth would also take account of one's total dependence on grace to do any worthy thing. But how to overcome the temptation to perform for well-earned human praise instead of for the love of God? Dahlstrom proposes that "Aquinas' astute pairing of magnanimity with humility . . . outlines the necessary means of contending with the love of others' praise as the primary challenge to being authentic."[42]

For Aquinas, humility is not self-contempt any more than magnanimity is self-esteem. Humility's role is to oppose the vice of pride, not by counterbalancing magnanimity, but by working in tandem with that virtue to bridle the passion for receiving human honors. Answering the objection that "humility is apparently opposed to the virtue of magnanimity," Aquinas argues that they form a "twofold virtue" that is necessary for those who aspire to do great but difficult things. A human with such lofty designs is tempted both to excessive self-confidence (presumption) and to insufficient hope (despair). It belongs to humility "to temper and restrain the mind, lest it tend to high things immoderately," while it belongs to magnanimity "to

[39] Dahlstrom, *Identity, Authenticity, and Humility*, 96.
[40] Augustine, *Confessions*, X.36.59, 195.
[41] Dahlstrom, *Identity, Authenticity, and Humility*, 107.
[42] Dahlstrom, *Identity, Authenticity, and Humility*, 104–5.

strengthen the mind against despair, and urge it on to the pursuit of great things according to right reason."[43] Although Aquinas treats magnanimity and humility as distinct virtues, their joint operation is so close that Dahlstrom describes them as "one moral virtue"—a "single virtue" of authenticity that allows us to form a true estimate of ourselves.[44] Far from being a cause of inner conflict, magnanimity and humility incline a person to harmonious and integral action. "For St. Thomas, the harmony of the two virtues is evident from the fact that both apply the same rule: right reason." As Gregory Pine explains, the "initial aspect of incongruity gives way to a symphonic harmony of human perfection" as the two sides of this duplex virtue "complement each other, introducing distinct rules and movements whereby the passions of hope and despair can oscillate between the creative tension of impulse and restraint."[45]

Seeing that humility is the condition of authentic creativity and not its enemy, humble liturgists can approach the harmonious performance of the liturgical act *from the outside in*. In part, this means deliberately doing things in the way they have been done before. Even liturgists who emphasize spontaneity and improvisation in worship must accept the necessity of repetition, as Bruce Ellis Benson argues. "Spontaneity is only possible when one is well prepared," that is, when repeated practice has internalized a *habitus* capable of regulating one's improvisations on a traditional theme, which is reverently received as the communal legacy of earlier improvisations.[46] If newness is essential to authentic repetition, repetition is the condition of authentic newness. Creative *ressourcement* is distinguished from sterile iteration in liturgical celebration by newness and repetition together, not one or the other in isolation.[47] Humble liturgists show reverence for the traditional external forms of the liturgy, accepting them as gifts handed down to them.

---

[43] ST II-II, q. 161 a. 1. See also ST II-II, q. 161 a. 2 ad. 3.

[44] Dahlstrom, *Identity, Authenticity, and Humility*, 120, 122.

[45] Gregory Pine, "Magnanimity and Humility According to St. Thomas Aquinas," *The Thomist* 82, no. 2 (2018): 285–86.

[46] Bruce Ellis Benson, *Liturgy as a Way of Life: Embodying the Arts in Christian Worship* (Grand Rapids, MI: Baker Academic, 2013), 76, 140.

[47] Charles Péguy, who coined the term "ressourcement," emphasized its crucial difference from mere "iteration." See Jean Onimus, "Péguy, la différence et la répétition," *Revue d'Histoire littéraire de la France* 73, no. 2/3 (March 1, 1973): 470–90.

Yet there is a deeper sense in which humility grounds both repetition *and* newness in the gift of God. The simultaneously magnanimous and humble liturgist considers that the perfection of human virtue is always an unearned gift from God. A human may aspire to become worthy of performing great acts, including previously unimagined acts that give God glory by their very newness. But as Thomas Cajetan explains in his commentary on Aquinas's *Summa*, humility joins the hope of perfecting one's virtue to the hope of receiving "that which is of God," namely, the grace that makes it possible to accomplish acts beyond one's own worthiness. "Thus the humble magnanimous man proceeds to great acts: nevertheless always believing, knowing, and professing himself to be unworthy in relation to his own defects."[48] There is remorse in this admission of faults and limitations, "but, by the same token, humility provides a powerful foundation for gratitude."[49] Paradoxically, humble people can be more magnanimous and pursue great acts with increased vigor because their failures, instead of breaking them, redirect them to the unshakeable foundation of true greatness. "From the theological perspective, the human person is indeed all the greater to the extent that he or she humbly accepts dependence on God."[50]

Since "no other action of the church equals" the liturgy in performing "complete and definitive public worship" (SC 7), liturgical scripts are understandably replete with humble acknowledgments of our unworthiness to participate in this supremely great act. But almost always, these are also expressions of thanksgiving and magnanimous confidence in what we can do by God's gift:

> You have counted us, your humble and unworthy servants, worthy to stand at this time before the glory of your Holy Altar, and to offer you due worship and praise. . . .

> We thank you also for this liturgy, which you have been pleased to accept from our hands, though there stand around you thousands of Archangels and tens of thousands of Angels. . . .

---

[48] Thomas Cajetan, *Commentaria in Summa Theologiae* II-II, q. 161, a. 1, 3, translated in Pine, "Magnanimity and Humility," 284.

[49] Dahlstrom, *Identity, Authenticity, and Humility*, 125.

[50] Tobias Hoffman, "Albert the Great and Thomas Aquinas on Magnanimity," in *Virtue Ethics in the Middle Ages: Commentaries on Aristotle's Nicomachean Ethics, 1200–1500*, ed. István Bejczy (Leiden: Brill, 2008), 101–29, at 128.

> Let our mouth be filled with your praise, O Lord, that we may
> sing of your glory, for you have counted us worthy to partake
> of your holy mysteries.[51]

The list could be multiplied easily. A final example from Eucharistic
Prayer II of the Roman Missal is worth citing because it shows how
magnanimity and humility together direct the assembly to the goal
of *unity*.

> [W]e offer you, Lord,
> the Bread of life and the Chalice of salvation,
> giving thanks that you have held us worthy
> to be in your presence and minister to you.
>
> Humbly we pray
> that, partaking of the Body and Blood of Christ,
> we may be gathered into one by the Holy Spirit.

The second sentence is often described as a *communion epiclesis* because it asks God to transform those who partake of the Eucharist
into the Mystical Body of Christ. Humility is a necessary disposition
for making such a bold prayer, but so is magnanimity born of gratitude for being chosen for God's service.

The virtue of the humble, magnanimous worshipper is well expressed in Pope Francis's motto, *Miserando atque eligendo*, taken from
a homily of St. Bede on the call of Matthew. Jesus chooses a tax collector for his service because, with his eyes of mercy, he looks through
the sinner's evident defects and sees the hidden greatness that is from
God. Authentic worship proceeds from awareness of having been
mercifully chosen.

### Mutual love and authentic liturgy

The virtue of humility is exercised through acts of obedience and
submission of one's own will to that of another. "Humility, considered
as a special virtue," Aquinas says, "regards chiefly the subjection of
man to God, for Whose sake he humbles himself by subjecting himself
to others."[52] Humble liturgists subject their speech, song, and gestures

---

[51] *Divine Liturgy of St. John Chrysostom*, 12, 31, 47.
[52] ST II-II, q. 161, a. 1, ad. 5.

to the rite of the church, and they submit their artistry, creativity, and discernment of the Spirit to the judgment of other members of the church. By making sure that their subjection to others is always and only for God, they ensure that their humility is authentic. The danger in framing authenticity in terms of humility alone, without reference to magnanimity, is that surrender to social power can be misconstrued as obedience to God. But obsequiousness is pride under a different guise. It is self-regard that seeks the praise of others by avoiding or suppressing what is best in oneself. To deny what is truly of God in myself is not humility, but pusillanimity.

As a virtue comprising magnanimity and humility, authenticity is best understood as (1) knowing what is of God in myself and what is of God in others and (2) subjecting myself to what is of God in each. Reverence for God requires such authenticity, for "we must not only revere God in Himself, but also that which is His in each one."[53] Aquinas claims that the requisite knowledge of one's own gifts is possible. As evidence, he cites Paul's account of spiritual discernment: "We have received not the spirit of the world, but the Spirit that is from God, so that we may understand the gifts bestowed on us by God" (1 Cor 2:12).

Discernment of one's own spiritual gifts is necessary to authentically obey the New Testament's exhortations to submission:

"In humility regard others as better than yourselves." (Phil 2:3)

"For the Lord's sake accept the authority of every human institution." (1 Pet 2:13)

"Be subject to one another out of reverence for Christ." (Eph 5:21)

Humility never requires Christians to deny or demote the gifts they have received from God. "Without prejudice to humility," Aquinas says, a Christian may discern that one's own gift, known with certainty to have come from God, is of greater value than "those that others [only] appear to have received from Him." Still, "if we set what our neighbor has of God's above that which we have of our own, we cannot incur falsehood."[54] Without prejudice to magnanimity, Christians can and should believe that their neighbors may pos-

---

[53] ST II-II, q. 161, a. 3, ad. 1.
[54] ST II-II, q. 161, a. 3.

sess hidden gifts greater than their own. In either case, the essential thing is to defer to that which is God's. Through mutual subjection to one another, Christians learn to rejoice in the greatness of the divine giver rather than the greatness of human recipients.

Humility and magnanimity both depend on having *others*—a community of practice for whom this duplex virtue supplies the know-how required for authentic performance of the liturgy and Christian life. Authentic humility requires others in whom I can recognize the gifts of the Holy Spirit and so subject myself to what is God's. Authentic magnanimity requires others who can recognize and subject themselves to what is God's in me. "Realizing our dependence on others is central to the virtue of humility, the virtue that, together with magnanimity, is the virtue of authenticity." Being true to ourselves, Dahlstrom concludes, is something that we can't do for ourselves without help.

> We also desperately need others to show us not only who we are and optimally can be but also the worthiness and, yes, the lovableness of being true to that reality and potential. Only with the help of others ("the communion of saints"), can we approach some measure of a true estimate of ourselves, an estimate that makes abundantly clear our neediness and dependence upon others as well as our genuine prospects for doing great things.[55]

Authentic discernment is mutual discernment. Only with help from the communion of saints can I understand who I am and how I may return a gift to God in thanksgiving for the gifts I have received. Only by learning to appreciate the gifts of others and harmonize my offering with theirs can I attune my own mind and voice.

Some of this mutual discernment is formal, and occasionally it requires official meetings, synods, or (rarely) an ecumenical council. More often, mutual discernment and mutual subjection out of reverence for Christ belong to what Cuneo calls "the unduly neglected category of *ordinary religious experience*."[56] Most tuning adjustments of minds and voices happen during ordinary daily, weekly, and annual celebrations of the liturgy. Participants adjust through ordinary

---

[55] Dahlstrom, *Identity, Authenticity, and Humility*, 129, 131.
[56] Cuneo, *Ritualized Faith*, 144. Emphasis in original.

acts of mutual tolerance, mutual empathy, and mutual responsiveness. Cuneo and Wolterstorff argue that these ordinary liturgical actions express, form, and—most important—*enact* love of God and love of neighbor. Regarding mutual tolerance, Wolterstorff says:

> Participating on a regular basis in the liturgical enactments of a community requires that one tolerate a good many things that one doesn't like: some of the hymns that are sung, the casual way some people dress, the fact that God is regularly referred to as "he," the minister's telling jokes in his sermons, and so forth, on and on. Tolerating what one doesn't like is a form of love.

It's also ordinary for liturgical scripts to have participants "rejoice with those who rejoice" through prayers of thanksgiving and "weep with those who weep" through prayers of intercession. We enact Christ's love when we turn away from resentment of others' happiness toward sharing in their joy. We enact Christ's compassion when we overcome indifference to others' pain and join them in grieving.[57] Just by adjusting our minds and voices to sing a psalm or hymn together, says Cuneo, we enact the harmony of the reign of God. "Shalom/eirene, after all, does not descend upon us from out of the blue; it is something that is achieved by doing such things as being attentive to the actions of the other, responding in appropriate ways to these actions, and acting together for the purpose of actualizing something commonly recognized to be of worth."[58]

These ordinary adjustments for the sake of harmony aren't secondary by-products of liturgical participation; they constitute the church's "faith in motion," its *theologia prima*. "The adjustment," Aidan Kavanagh says, makes participation in the liturgical act "theological."[59] Tuning adjustments enact the mutual love that binds and builds up the church. "One of the ultimate purposes of liturgy," says Kevin Irwin, "is to build up the body of Christ—to be and become 'one body, one spirit in Christ.' One way to support and build up the church is by a reverent listening and by having a profound respect for each other."[60] Working together to harmonize our minds and voices

---

[57] Wolterstorff, *Acting Liturgically*, 257, 263. See Rom 12:15.

[58] Cuneo, *Ritualized Faith*, 142.

[59] Kavanagh, *On Liturgical Theology*, 8, 74.

[60] Kevin W. Irwin, "Authentic Worship in Spirit and in Truth," *Pastoral Music* 33, no. 1 (October 2008): 53.

in prayer, we enact our communion in the Body of Christ. If this is a "forgotten way of doing things," then there is only one way for the members of Christ's body to relearn authentic liturgy: *together*.

## An examination of conscience for liturgists

Authentic liturgy requires authentic participants. The argument of this book, especially in this final chapter, has been that the liturgy itself calls worshippers to make their participation *more authentic* through practice, reflection on practice, and adjustment of practice based on reflection. Practice, reflection, and adjustment strengthen the virtue of authenticity, so liturgical participants, liturgical participation, and the liturgy become more authentic together.

Reading this book is obviously not equivalent to practicing the liturgical act, and I have tried to avoid recommending specific adjustments to any community's liturgical practice. The following examination of conscience is intended as an aid to reflection on liturgical practice that might help any worshipper or any community discern particular adjustments, interior and exterior, needed to bring minds and voices into tune. It is written for all members of the Body of Christ, with a view to more authentic participation in the liturgy and to cultivation of authenticity as a virtue.

### *Worship with humility:*
### *Tuning our minds to our voices*

Do we study and try to understand the external elements of the liturgy handed down to us, including rites, texts, music, artworks, and buildings used by worshippers who have come before us?

Do we listen to the Scriptures and the homily with eager anticipation, expecting to receive words of challenge and hope addressed to us in our situations? (Readers and preachers should ask themselves this question too.)

Do we seek stability in worship to become more rooted in faith, not just to feel more comfortable?

Do we respect attention as a holy offering by cultivating it in ourselves while cherishing and acknowledging the attention offered by fellow worshippers?

Do we say and do the prescribed prayers and gestures of the liturgy not by habit alone, but with understanding?

## Worship with magnanimity: Tuning our voices to our minds

Do we prepare to celebrate the liturgy by discerning the spirit within us through contemplation and personal prayer?

Do we carry out all the functions that pertain to us as liturgical ministers or as members of the congregation in a way worthy of honor and praise?

Do we refer whatever honor and praise we receive for our liturgical ministry and participation to God?

Do we call forth the creative gifts of artists, poets, and musicians in our community to increase the artistic quality of the worship we offer God?

Do we seek newness in worship to remain open to God's unlimited creativity, not just to experience novelty?

## Worship with mutual love: Harmony in the Body of Christ

Do we affirm our need for each member of the Body of Christ to join us in worship?

Do we have reverence for what is of God in other members of the Body of Christ?

Do we have reverence for what is of God in ourselves, as members of the Body of Christ?

Is our reverence for one another visible in liturgy and in everyday life?

# Bibliography

Anderson, Gary A. *Charity: The Place of the Poor in the Biblical Tradition*. New Haven: Yale University Press, 2013.

Aquinas, Thomas. *Summa Theologica*. Translated by Fathers of the English Dominican Province. Rev. ed., 1920.

Aristotle. *The Basic Works of Aristotle*. Edited by Richard McKeon. New York: Random House, 1941.

Asad, Talal. *Genealogies of Religion: Discipline and Reasons of Power in Christianity and Islam*. Baltimore: The Johns Hopkins University Press, 1993. See esp. ch. 4, "On Discipline and Humility in Medieval Christian Monasticism."

Auerbach, Erich. *Literary Language and Its Public in Late Latin Antiquity and in the Middle Ages*. Translated by Ralph Manheim. New York: Pantheon, 1965.

Augustine. *Letters 1–99*. Edited by John E. Rotelle. Translated by Roland Teske. The Works of Saint Augustine, pt. 2, vol. 1. Hyde Park, NY: New City Press, 2001.

———. *The Monastic Rules*. Translated by Gerald Bonner and Agatha Mary. Hyde Park, NY: New City Press, 2004.

———. *On Free Choice of the Will*. Translated by Thomas Williams. Indianapolis: Hackett, 1993.

———. *Sermons on the Liturgical Seasons*. Translated by Edmund Hill. The Works of Saint Augustine, pt. 3, vol. 7. Hyde Park, NY: New City Press, 1993.

Austin, J. L. *How to Do Things with Words*. Edited by J. O. Urmson and Marina Sbisà. 2nd ed. Cambridge, MA: Harvard University Press, 1975.

*Authentic Worship in a Changing Culture*. Grand Rapids, MI: CRC Publications, 1997.

Avvakumov, Yury P. "Sacramental Ritual in Middle and Later Byzantine Theology: Ninth–Fifteenth Centuries." In *The Oxford Handbook of Sacramental Theology*, edited by Hans Boersma and Matthew Levering, 249–66. Oxford: Oxford University Press, 2015.

Baker, Kimberly F. "Augustine's Doctrine of the Totus Christus: Reflecting on the Church as Sacrament of Unity." *Horizons* 37, no. 1 (March 2010): 7–24.

Baldovin, John F. "The Development of the Liturgy: Theological and Historical Roots of *Sacrosanctum Concilium*." *Worship* 87, no. 6 (November 2013): 517–32.

———. *Reforming the Liturgy: A Response to the Critics*. Collegeville, MN: Liturgical Press, 2008.

Balthasar, Hans Urs von. "Péguy." In *The Glory of the Lord: A Theological Aesthetics, Vol. 3: Studies in Theological Style: Lay Styles*, translated by Andrew Louth, John Saward, Martin Simon, and Rowan Williams, 400–517. San Francisco: Ignatius Press, 1986.

Banerjee, Neela. "Teenagers Mix Churches for Faith That Fits." *The New York Times*, December 30, 2005.

Baraúna, William, and Jovian Lang, eds. *The Liturgy of Vatican II: A Symposium*. English ed. 2 vols. Chicago: Franciscan Herald Press, 1966.

Barish, Jonas A. *The Antitheatrical Prejudice*. Berkeley: University of California Press, 1981.

Barnes, Andrew E. "Religious Reform and the War Against Ritual." *Journal of Ritual Studies* 4, no. 1 (1990): 127–33.

Barron, Jessica M., and Rhys H. Williams. *The Urban Church Imagined: Religion, Race, and Authenticity in the City*. New York: NYU Press, 2017.

Beauduin, Lambert. "La Vraie Prière de l'Église." *Questions Liturgiques/Studies in Liturgy* 91, no. 1–2 (2010): 37–41.

———. *Liturgy the Life of the Church*. Translated by Virgil Michel. Collegeville, MN: Liturgical Press, 1929.

Bell, Catherine M. *Ritual Theory, Ritual Practice*. New York: Oxford University Press, 1992.

———. "The Authority of Ritual Experts." *Studia Liturgica* 23, no. 1 (1993): 98–120.

Bell, Daniel. *The Cultural Contradictions of Capitalism*. New York: Basic Books, 1976.

Benedict XVI. General Audience. September 26, 2012. http://w2.vatican.va /content/benedict-xvi/en/audiences/2012/documents/hf_ben-xvi _aud_20120926.html.

―――. "Letter of Pope Benedict XVI Accompanying the Apostolic Letter *Summorum Pontificum.*" *Newsletter of the United States Conference of Catholic Bishops Committee on the Liturgy* 43 (June 2007): 20–23.

―――. *Sacramentum Caritatis*: Post-Synodal Apostolic Exhortation on the Eucharist as the Source and Summit of the Church's Life and Mission. Washington, DC: United States Conference of Catholic Bishops, 2007.

Benson, Bruce Ellis. *Liturgy as a Way of Life: Embodying the Arts in Christian Worship.* Grand Rapids, MI: Baker Academic, 2013.

Berlière, Ursmer, ed. *Documents inédits pour servir a l'histoire ecclésiastique de la Belgique.* Maredsous: Abbaye de Saint-Benoit, 1894.

Bloch, Maurice. "Ritual and Deference." In *Ritual and Memory: Toward a Comparative Anthropology of Religion*, edited by Harvey Whitehouse and James Laidlaw, 65–78. Walnut Creek, CA: AltaMira Press, 2004.

Bloom, Allan. *The Closing of the American Mind: How Higher Education Has Failed Democracy and Impoverished the Souls of Today's Students.* New York: Simon and Schuster, 1987.

Boer, Bertilo de. "La soi-disant opposition de saint François d'Assise à saint Benoît." *Études franciscaines* N.S. 8, N.S. 9 (1957, 1958): 181–94, 57–65.

Borras, Michelle K. "Péguy, Expositor of Christian Hope." *Communio* 35, no. 2 (Summer 2008): 221–54.

Bossy, John. *Christianity in the West, 1400–1700.* Oxford: Oxford University Press, 1985.

Bouley, Allan. *From Freedom to Formula: The Evolution of the Eucharistic Prayer from Oral Improvisation to Written Texts.* Washington, DC: Catholic University of America Press, 1981.

Bovon, François. *Luke 2: A Commentary on the Gospel of Luke 9:51–19:27.* Edited by Helmut Koester. Translated by Donald S. Deer. Hermeneia—A Critical and Historical Commentary on the Bible. Augsburg Fortress, 2013.

Bradshaw, Paul F. *Eucharistic Origins.* Oxford: Oxford University Press, 2004.

Braman, Brian J. *Meaning and Authenticity: Bernard Lonergan and Charles Taylor on the Drama of Authentic Human Existence.* Toronto: University of Toronto Press, 2008.

Branch, Lori. *Rituals of Spontaneity: Sentiment and Secularism from Free Prayer to Wordsworth.* Waco, TX: Baylor University Press, 2006.

Bremmer, Jan N. " 'Religion,' 'Ritual' and the Opposition 'Sacred vs. Profane': Notes Towards a Terminological 'Genealogy.' " In *Ansichten Griechischer Rituale: Geburtstags-Symposium Für Walter Burkert, Castelen Bei Basel 15. Bis 18. März 1996*, edited by Franz Graf, 9–32. Stuttgart: Teubner, 1998.

Bugnini, Annibale. *The Reform of the Liturgy, 1948–1975.* Translated by Matthew J. O'Connell. Collegeville, MN: Liturgical Press, 1990.

Bunyan, John. *I Will Pray with the Spirit, and I Will Pray with the Understanding Also: Or, A Discourse Touching Prayer, From I Cor. 14.15.* 2nd ed. London: Printed for the Author, 1663.

Burke, Peter. "The Repudiation of Ritual in Early Modern Europe." In *The Historical Anthropology of Early Modern Italy: Essays on Perception and Communication*, 223–38. Cambridge: Cambridge University Press, 1987.

Carpenter, Anne M. " 'Incline the Ear of Your Heart.' " *Questions Liturgiques* 95, no. 3 (2014): 159–182.

Casel, Odo. *The Mystery of Christian Worship.* Edited by Burkhard Neunheuser. Milestones in Catholic Theology. New York: Crossroad, 1999.

———. "Response to H. Dausend, 'Der Franziskanerorden und die Entwickelung der Liturgie,' Franzisk. Stud. 11 [1924] 165–178." *Jahrbuch für Liturgiewissenschaft* 4 (1924): 219–20.

Chauvet, Louis-Marie. *Symbol and Sacrament: A Sacramental Reinterpretation of Christian Existence.* Translated by Patrick Madigan. Collegeville, MN: Liturgical Press, 1995.

Christian, William A. *Local Religion in Sixteenth-Century Spain.* Princeton, NJ: Princeton University Press, 1981.

Cicero. *On the Nature of the Gods; Academics.* Translated by H. Rackham. Loeb Classical Library 268. London: Heinemann, 1933.

Congar, Yves. "Le prophète Péguy." *Témoignage Chrétien* 26 (August 1949).

———. " 'Real' Liturgy, 'Real' Preaching." In *At the Heart of Christian Worship: Liturgical Essays of Yves Congar*, translated by Paul Philibert, 1–12. Collegeville, MN: Liturgical Press, 2010.

———. *True and False Reform in the Church.* Translated by Paul Philibert. Rev. ed. Collegeville, MN: Liturgical Press, 2011.

Congregation for Divine Worship and Discipline of the Sacraments. *Liturgiam Authenticam.* Fifth Instruction on the Right Implementation of the Constitution on the Sacred Liturgy of the Second Vatican Council. March 28, 2001. Translated in *The Liturgy Documents, Volume Three: Foundational Documents on the Origins and Implementation of* Sacrosanctum Concilium, 527–62. Chicago: Liturgy Training Publications, 2013.

Consilium for Implementing the Constitution on the Sacred Liturgy. *Comme le prévoit.* Instruction on the Translation of Liturgical Texts for Celebration with a Congregation. January 25, 1969. In *The Liturgy Documents, Volume Three: Foundational Documents on the Origins and Implementation of* Sacrosanctum Concilium, 417-25. Chicago: Liturgy Training Publications, 2013.

Constable, Giles. "The Ceremonies and Symbolism of Entering Religious Life and Taking the Monastic Habit, from the Fourth to the Twelfth Century." In *Segni e Ritti Nella Chiesa Altomedievale Occidentale, Spoleto, 11–17 Aprile 1985*. Settimane Di Studio Del Centro Italiano Di Studi Sull'alto Medioevo 33. Spoleto, 1987.

―――. "The Concern for Sincerity and Understanding in Liturgical Prayer, Especially in the Twelfth Century." In *Classica Et Mediaevalia: Studies in Honor of Joseph Szövérffy*, edited by Helmut Buschhausen and Irene Vaslef, 17–30. Washington; Leyden: Classical Folia Editions, 1986.

―――. *The Reformation of the Twelfth Century*. Cambridge: Cambridge University Press, 1996.

Conzelmann, Hans. *1 Corinthians: A Commentary on the First Epistle to the Corinthians*. Edited by George W. MacRae. Translated by James W. Leitch. Hermeneia—A Critical and Historical Commentary on the Bible. Philadelphia: Fortress, 1975.

Corbon, Jean. *The Wellspring of Worship*. Translated by Matthew J. O'Connell. 2nd ed. San Francisco: Ignatius Press, 2005.

Cramer, Winfrid. "Mens Concordet Voci: Zum Fortleben Einer Stoischen Gebetsmaxime in Der Regula Benedicti." In *Pietas: Festschrift Für Bernhard Kötting*, edited by Ernst Dassmann and K. Suso Frank, 447–57. Jahrbuch Für Antike Und Christentum Ergänzungband 8. Münster: Aschendorff, 1980.

Cuneo, Terence. *Ritualized Faith: Essays on the Philosophy of Liturgy*. Oxford: Oxford University Press, 2016.

Dahlstrom, Daniel O. *Identity, Authenticity, and Humility*. Milwaukee: Marquette University Press, 2017.

Dalarun, Jacques. *Robert of Arbrissel: Sex, Sin, and Salvation in the Middle Ages*. Translated by Bruce L. Venarde. Washington, DC: Catholic University of America Press, 2006.

Dallen, James. *The Reconciling Community: The Rite of Penance*. Collegeville, MN: Liturgical Press, 1986.

Dausend, H. "Der Franziskanerorden und die Entwicklung der kirchlichen Liturgie." *Franziskanische Studien* 11 (1924): 165–78.

Dawbeny, Henry. *A Sober and Temperate Discourse, Concerning the Interest of Words in Prayer: The Just Antiquity and Pedigree of Liturgies, or Forms of Prayer in Churches: With a View of the State of the Church, When They Were First Composed, or Imposed*. London: Printed for W.A., 1661.

De Mey, Peter. "Church Renewal and Reform in the Documents of Vatican II: History, Theology, Terminology." *The Jurist* 71, no. 2 (2011): 369–400.

Delumeau, Jean. *Sin and Fear: The Emergence of a Western Guilt Culture, 13th–18th Centuries*. New York: St. Martin's Press, 1990.

*The Divine Liturgy of Our Father among the Saints John Chrysostom: The Greek Text Together with a Translation into English*. Oxford: Oxford University Press, 1995.

*Documents on the Liturgy, 1963–1979: Conciliar, Papal, and Curial Texts*. Collegeville, MN: Liturgical Press, 1982.

Douglas, Mary. *Natural Symbols: Explorations in Cosmology*. 2nd ed. London: Routledge, 1996.

Driscoll, Michael S. "Penance in Transition: Popular Piety and Practice." In *Medieval Liturgy: A Book of Essays*, edited by Lizette Larson-Miller, 121–63. New York: Garland, 1997.

Duffy, Eamon. *The Stripping of the Altars: Traditional Religion in England, 1400–1580*. 2nd ed. New Haven, CT: Yale University Press, 2005.

Durkheim, Émile. *The Elementary Forms of Religious Life*. Translated by Karen E. Fields. New York: Free Press, 1995.

Eire, Carlos M. N. *War Against the Idols: The Reformation of Worship from Erasmus to Calvin*. Cambridge: Cambridge University Press, 1986.

Évagre le Pontique. *Chapitres sur la prière*. Edited by Paul Géhin. Sources chrétiennes 589. Paris: Éditions du Cerf, 2017.

Evagrius of Pontus. *Evagrius of Pontus: The Greek Ascetic Corpus*. Translated by Robert E. Sinkewicz. Oxford: Oxford University Press, 2006.

———. *Talking Back: A Monastic Handbook for Combating Demons*. Translated by David Brakke. Cistercian Studies Series 229. Collegeville, MN: Liturgical Press, 2009.

Evans, Rachel Held. "Want Millennials Back in the Pews? Stop Trying to Make Church 'Cool.'" *Washington Post*, April 30, 2015.

Fagerberg, David W. *Consecrating the World: On Mundane Liturgical Theology*. Kettering, OH: Angelico Press, 2016.

———. *On Liturgical Asceticism*. Washington, DC: Catholic University of America Press, 2013.

———. *Theologia Prima: What Is Liturgical Theology?* 2nd ed. Mundelein, IL: Hillenbrand Books, 2004.

———. "A Theologian Is One Who Prays." *Word & World* 35, no. 1 (2015): 57–64.

———. "Traditional Liturgy and Liturgical Tradition." *Worship* 72, no. 6 (November 1998): 482–501.

Ferrara, Alessandro. *Modernity and Authenticity: A Study in Social and Ethical Thought of Jean-Jacques Rouseau.* Albany: State University of New York Press, 1993.

———. *Reflective Authenticity: Rethinking the Project of Modernity.* London: Routledge, 1998.

Feuchtwang, Stephan. "On Religious Ritual as Deference and Communicative Excess." *The Journal of the Royal Anthropological Institute* 13, no. 1 (March 1, 2007): 57–72.

Fitzmyer, Joseph A. *First Corinthians: A New Translation with Introduction and Commentary.* The Anchor Yale Bible, v. 32. New Haven, CT: Yale University Press, 2008.

Flanagan, Kieran. *Sociology and Liturgy: Re-Presentations of the Holy.* New York: St. Martin's Press, 1991.

Flannery, Austin, ed. *Vatican Council II: Constitutions, Decrees, Declarations; The Basic Sixteen Documents.* Collegeville, MN: Liturgical Press, 2014.

Flynn, Gabriel, and Paul D. Murray, eds. *Ressourcement: A Movement for Renewal in Twentieth-Century Catholic Theology.* Oxford: Oxford University Press, 2012.

France, R. T. *The Gospel of Matthew.* Grand Rapids, MI: Eerdmans, 2007.

Francis, Pope. *Magnum Principium.* September 3, 2017. http://www.vatican .va/content/francesco/en/motu_proprio/documents/papa -francesco-motu-proprio_20170903_magnum-principium.html.

Franklin, R. W. "Guéranger and Pastoral Liturgy: A Nineteenth Century Context." *Worship* 50, no. 2 (March 1976): 146–62.

———. "Nineteenth Century Liturgical Movement." *Worship* 53, no. 1 (January 1979): 12–39.

———. "Response: Humanism and Transcendence in the 19th Century Liturgical Movement." *Worship* 59, no. 4 (July 1985): 342–53.

Fry, Timothy, ed. *Rule of Saint Benedict 1980.* Collegeville, MN: Liturgical Press, 1981.

Fuller, Reginald H., and Daniel Westberg. *Preaching the Lectionary: The Word of God for the Church of Today.* 3rd ed. Collegeville, MN: Liturgical Press, 2006.

Geertz, Clifford. *The Interpretation of Cultures.* New York: Basic Books, 1973.

Geldhof, Joris. *Liturgy and Secularism: Beyond the Divide.* Collegeville, MN: Liturgical Press, 2018.

Goodwin, Daniel R. "On the Use of Lēb and Καρδία in the Old and New Testaments." *Journal of the Society of Biblical Literature and Exegesis, Including the Papers Read and Abstract of Proceedings For* 1 (June 1881): 67–72.

Grillo, Andrea. *Beyond Pius V: Conflicting Interpretations of the Liturgical Reform.* Translated by Barry Hudock. Collegeville, MN: Liturgical Press, 2013.

Guardini, Romano. "A Letter from Romano Guardini." *Herder Correspondence* 1, no. 8 (August 1964): 237–39.

———. "Personal Prayer and the Prayers of the Church." In *Unto the Altar: The Practice of Catholic Worship*, edited by Alfons Kirchgaessner, translated by Rosaleen Brennan, 32–43. New York: Herder and Herder, 1963.

———. "Some Dangers of the Liturgical Revival." In *Unto the Altar: The Practice of Catholic Worship*, edited by Alfons Kirchgaessner, translated by Rosaleen Brennan, 13–22. New York: Herder and Herder, 1963.

———. *The Spirit of the Liturgy.* Translated by Ada Lane. Milestones in Catholic Theology. New York: Crossroad, 1998.

Guéranger, Prosper. *The Liturgical Year.* Edited by Lucien Fromage. Translated by James Laurence Shepherd. Westminster, MD: Newman Press, 1948.

Guignon, Charles B. *On Being Authentic.* London: Routledge, 2004.

Haquin, André. "The Liturgical Movement and Catholic Ritual Revision." In *The Oxford History of Christian Worship*, edited by Geoffrey Wainwright and Karen B. Westerfield Tucker, 696–720. Oxford: Oxford University Press, 2006.

Hausherr, Irénée. *Penthos: The Doctrine of Compunction in the Christian East.* Translated by Anselm Hufstader. Kalamazoo, MI: Cistercian Publications, 1982.

Hays, Richard B. *First Corinthians.* Interpretation, a Bible Commentary for Teaching and Preaching. Louisville: John Knox Press, 1997.

Hervieu-Léger, Danièle. *Religion as a Chain of Memory.* New Brunswick, NJ: Rutgers University Press, 2000.

Heschel, Abraham Joshua. *The Prophets.* New York: Harper & Row, 1962.

Hoffman, Tobias. "Albert the Great and Thomas Aquinas on Magnanimity." In *Virtue Ethics in the Middle Ages: Commentaries on Aristotle's Nicomachean Ethics, 1200–1500*, edited by István Bejczy, 101–129. Leiden: Brill, 2008.

Holzherr, Georg. *The Rule of Benedict: An Invitation to the Christian Life.* Translated by Mark Thamert. Cistercian Studies Series 256. Collegeville, MN: Liturgical Press, 2016.

Irwin, Kevin W. "Authentic Worship in Spirit and in Truth." *Pastoral Music* 33, no. 1 (October 2008): 51–60.

———. *What We Have Done, What We Have Failed to Do: Assessing the Liturgical Reforms of Vatican II*. New York: Paulist Press, 2013.

Jeffery, Peter. *Translating Tradition: A Chant Historian Reads Liturgiam Authenticam*. Collegeville, MN: Liturgical Press, 2005.

John Paul II. "Papal Address on the Liturgy." *Sacred Music* 129, no. 1 (2002): 22–24.

Johnson, Maxwell E. *Praying and Believing in Early Christianity: The Interplay Between Christian Worship and Doctrine*. Collegeville, MN: Liturgical Press, 2013.

Kardong, Terrence G. *Benedict's Rule: A Translation and Commentary*. Collegeville, MN: Liturgical Press, 1996.

Kavanagh, Aidan. *On Liturgical Theology*. Collegeville, MN: Liturgical Press, 1992.

Keener, Craig S. *A Commentary on the Gospel of Matthew*. Grand Rapids, MI: Eerdmans, 1999.

Lasch, Christopher. *The Culture of Narcissism: American Life in an Age of Diminishing Expectations*. New York: Norton, 1978.

———. *The Minimal Self: Psychic Survival in Troubled Times*. New York: W. W. Norton, 1984.

Lathrop, Gordon. "New Pentecost or Joseph's Britches? Reflections on the History and Meaning of the Worship Ordo in the Megachurches." *Worship* 72, no. 6 (November 1998): 521–38.

Lechner, Robert F. "Liturgy and Contemplation." *Worship* 34, no. 7 (June 1960): 418–19.

Lehner, Ulrich L. *On the Road to Vatican II: German Catholic Enlightenment and Reform of the Church*. Minneapolis: Fortress, 2016.

Leithart, Peter J. "What's Wrong with Evangelical Theology." *First Things* 65 (August 1996): 19–21.

Lentini, Anselmo. *San Benedetto: La Regola*. 2nd ed. Monte Cassino, 1980.

Lessi Ariosto, Mario. "Rights and Duties Arising from the Nature of the Liturgy: Considerations in the Light of the Motu Proprio Magnum Principium," December 22, 2017. http://www.cultodivino.va/content /cultodivino/it/documenti/motu-proprio-/-magnum-principium ---3-settembre-2017-/articoli/mario-lessi-ariosto--s-j-/english.html.

Lindholm, Charles. *Culture and Authenticity*. Oxford: Blackwell, 2008.

*The Liturgy Documents, Volume Three: Foundational Documents on the Origins and Implementation of* Sacrosanctum Concilium. Chicago: Liturgy Training Publications, 2013.

Lot-Borodine, Myrrha. "Le Mystère Du 'don Des Larmes' Dans l'Orient Chretien." In *La Douloureuse Joie: Aperçus Sur La Prière Personnelle de l'Orient Chrétien*, edited by Olivier-Maurice Clément, 131–95. Spritualité Orientale 14. Bégrolles: Abbaye de Bellefontaine, 1974.

Louth, Andrew. *The Origins of the Christian Mystical Tradition from Plato to Denys*. Oxford: Oxford University Press, 1981.

Luz, Ulrich. *Matthew 1–7: A Commentary*. Edited by Helmut Koester. Translated by James E. Crouch. Minneapolis: Fortress, 2007.

Lynch, Gordon. *The Sacred in the Modern World: A Cultural Sociological Approach*. Oxford: Oxford University Press, 2012.

MacIntyre, Alasdair. *After Virtue: A Study in Moral Theory*. 2nd ed. Notre Dame, IN: University of Notre Dame Press, 1984.

Macy, Gary. *The Banquet's Wisdom: A Short History of the Theologies of the Lord's Supper*. New York: Paulist Press, 1992.

———. *The Theologies of the Eucharist in the Early Scholastic Period: A Study of the Salvific Function of the Sacrament According to the Theologians, c. 1080–c. 1220*. Oxford: Oxford University Press, 1984.

Mahmood, Saba. *Politics of Piety: The Islamic Revival and the Feminist Subject*. Princeton, NJ: Princeton University Press, 2005.

Mannion, M. Francis. "The Catholicity of the Liturgy: Shaping a New Agenda." In *Beyond the Prosaic: Renewing the Liturgical Movement*, edited by Stratford Caldecott, 11–48. Edinburgh: T&T Clark, 1998.

Marcus, Joel. *Mark 1–8: A New Translation with Introduction and Commentary*. The Anchor Bible, vol. 27. New York: Doubleday, 2000.

Maritain, Jacques, and Raïssa Maritain. *Liturgy and Contemplation*. Translated by Joseph W. Evans. New York: P. J. Kenedy, 1960.

Martens, Peter. "Holy Spirit." In *The Westminster Handbook to Origen*, edited by John Anthony McGuckin, 125–28. Louisville, KY: Westminster John Knox, 2004.

Martin, David, and Peter Mullen, eds. *No Alternative: The Prayer Book Controversy*. Oxford: Basil Blackwell, 1981.

Marx, Nathaniel. "Ritual in the Age of Authenticity: An Ethnography of Latin Mass Catholics." PhD diss., University of Notre Dame, 2013.

Mazza, Enrico. *The Origins of the Eucharistic Prayer*. Collegeville, MN: Liturgical Press, 1995.

McCall, Richard D. *Do This: Liturgy as Performance*. Notre Dame, IN: University of Notre Dame Press, 2007.

McGuckin, John Anthony, ed. *The Westminster Handbook to Origen*. Louisville, KY: Westminster John Knox, 2004.

*Mens concordet voci pour Mgr A.G. Martimort: à l'occasion de ses quarante années d'enseignement et des vingt ans de la Constitution* Sacrosanctum Concilium. Paris: Desclée, 1983.

Millare, Roland. "The Spirit of the Liturgical Movement: A Benedictine Renewal of Culture." *Logos* 17, no. 4 (September 2014): 130–54.

Mitchell, Nathan D. "Liturgy and Life: Lessons in Benedict." *Worship* 82, no. 2 (March 2008): 161–74.

———. *Liturgy and the Social Sciences*. Collegeville, MN: Liturgical Press, 1999.

———. *Meeting Mystery: Liturgy, Worship, Sacraments*. Maryknoll, NY: Orbis Books, 2006.

Neyrey, Jerome H. *Honor and Shame in the Gospel of Matthew*. Louisville, KY: Westminster John Knox, 1998.

Nguyen, Joseph H. *Apatheia in the Christian Tradition: An Ancient Spirituality and Its Contemporary Relevance*. Eugene, OR: Cascade Books, 2018.

Niederwimmer, Kurt. *The Didache: A Commentary*. Translated by Linda M. Maloney. Hermeneia—A Critical and Historical Commentary on the Bible. Minneapolis: Fortress, 1998.

Novick, Tzvi. "The Author and the Expert." *Commonweal* 146, no. 15 (October 2019).

O'Collins, Gerald. *Lost in Translation: The English Language and the Catholic Mass*. Collegeville, MN: Liturgical Press, 2017.

O'Meara, Thomas F. "The Origins of the Liturgical Movement and German Romanticism." *Worship* 59, no. 4 (July 1985): 326–42.

Onimus, Jean. "Péguy, la différence et la répétition." *Revue d'Histoire littéraire de la France* 73, no. 2/3 (March 1, 1973): 470–90.

Otto, Rudolf. *The Idea of the Holy: An Inquiry into the Non-Rational Factor in the Idea of the Divine and Its Relation to the Rational*. Translated by John W. Harvey. New York: Oxford University Press, 1958.

Paul VI. "Address to the Members and Periti of the Consilium," April 19, 1967. In *Acta Apostolicae Sedis* 59 (1967): 418–20. Translated in *Documents on the Liturgy, 1963–1979: Conciliar, Papal, and Curial Texts* (Collegeville, MN: Liturgical Press, 1982).

Pecklers, Keith F. "The Jansenist Critique and the Liturgical Reforms of the Seventeenth and Eighteenth Centuries." *Ecclesia Orans* 20 (2003): 325–39.

———. "Ressourcement and the Renewal of Catholic Liturgy: On Celebrating the New Rite." In *Ressourcement: A Movement for Renewal in Twentieth-Century Catholic Theology*, edited by Gabriel Flynn and Paul D. Murray, 318–32. Oxford: Oxford University Press, 2012.

Peterson, Brent. "The Science of the Sacraments: The Being and Becoming of Persons in Community." *Wesleyan Theological Journal* 44, no. 1 (2009): 180–99.

Petigny, J. de. "Lettre inédite de Robert d'Arbrissel à la comtesse Ermengarde." *Bibliothèque de l'École des Chartres* ser. 3, t. 5 (1854): 209–35.

Pine, Gregory. "Magnanimity and Humility According to St. Thomas Aquinas." *The Thomist: A Speculative Quarterly Review* 82, no. 2 (2018): 263–86.

Pius X. *Tra le sollecitudini. Motu Proprio* on the Restoration of Church Music. November 22, 1903. Translated in *The Liturgy Documents, Volume Three: Foundational Documents on the Origins and Implementation of* Sacrosanctum Concilium, 25–32. Chicago: Liturgy Training Publications, 2013.

Pius XII. *Mediator Dei.* Encyclical on the Sacred Liturgy. November 20, 1947. Translated in *The Liturgy Documents, Volume Three: Foundational Documents on the Origins and Implementation of* Sacrosanctum Concilium, 107–56. Chicago: Liturgy Training Publications, 2013.

*Plenty Good Room: The Spirit and Truth of African American Worship.* Washington, DC: United States Conference of Catholic Bishops, 1990.

Prusak, Bernard P. "Getting the History Right." *Commonweal* 134, no. 14 (August 17, 2007): 16.

Ratzinger, Joseph. *The Spirit of the Liturgy.* Translated by John Saward. San Francisco: Ignatius Press, 2000.

Reid, Alcuin. "The New Liturgical Movement After the Pontificate of Benedict XVI." *Sacred Music* 141, no. 1 (2014): 10–26.

———. "*Ut mens nostra concordet voci nostrae*: Sacred Music and Actual Participation in the Liturgy." *Sacred Music* 139, no. 1 (2012): 8–33.

Reinburg, Virginia. "Liturgy and the Laity in Late Medieval and Reformation France." *The Sixteenth Century Journal* 23, no. 3 (1992): 526–47.

Riesebrodt, Martin. *The Promise of Salvation: A Theory of Religion.* Chicago: University of Chicago Press, 2010.

Roberts, J. J. M. "Contemporary Worship in the Light of Isaiah's Ancient Critique." In *Worship and the Hebrew Bible: Essays in Honor of John T. Willis*, edited by M. Patrick Graham, Richard R. Mars, and Steven L.

McKenzie. Journal for the Study of the Old Testament Supplement Series 284. Sheffield: Sheffield Academic Press, 1999.

———. *First Isaiah: A Commentary*. Hermeneia—A Critical and Historical Commentary on the Bible. Minneapolis: Fortress, 2015.

———. "Hosea and the Sacrificial Cultus." *Restoration Quarterly* 15, no. 1 (1972): 15–26.

Ross, Melanie C. *Evangelical Versus Liturgical? Defying a Dichotomy*. Grand Rapids, MI: Eerdmans, 2014.

———. "Joseph's Britches Revisited: Reflections on Method in Liturgical Theology." *Worship* 80, no. 6 (November 1, 2006): 528–50.

Rousseau, Jean-Jacques. *Emile, or, On Education*. Edited by Christopher Kelly. Translated by Allan David Bloom. Hanover, NH: University Press of New England, 2010.

Rouwhorst, Gerard. "The Mystical Body Falling Apart? Reflections on the Emergence and Development of Eucharistic Spirituality in the Western Middle Ages." *Religion & Theology* 23, no. 1–2 (2016): 35–56.

Rutledge, Douglas F., ed. *Ceremony and Text in the Renaissance*. Newark: University of Delaware Press, 1996.

Sarah, Robert Cardinal. "Towards an Authentic Implementation of *Sacrosanctum Concilium*." In *Authentic Liturgical Renewal in Contemporary Perspective*, edited by Uwe Michael Lang, 3–19. London: Bloomsbury T&T Clark, 2017.

Saward, John. "The Pedagogy of Péguy." *The Chesterton Review* 19, no. 3 (August 1993): 357–79.

Schmitt, Siegfried. *Die internationalen liturgischen Studientreffen, 1951–1960: Zur Vorgeschichte der Liturgiekonstitution*. Trier: Paulinus-Verlag, 1992.

Seligman, Adam B., Robert P. Weller, Michael Puett, and Bennett Simon. *Ritual and Its Consequences: An Essay on the Limits of Sincerity*. Oxford: Oxford University Press, 2008.

Skublics, Ernest. "Vagaggini Remembered." *Worship* 93 (January 2019): 32–36.

Smith, Innocent. "Vagaggini and Congar on the Liturgy and Theology." *Questions Liturgiques* 96, no. 3–4 (2015): 191–221.

Smolarski, Dennis C. *How Not to Say Mass: A Guidebook for All Concerned about Authentic Worship*. New York: Paulist Press, 1986.

Sorabji, Richard. *Emotion and Peace of Mind: From Stoic Agitation to Christian Temptation*. Oxford: Oxford University Press, 2000.

Strathern, Marilyn. *The Gender of the Gift: Problems with Women and Problems with Society in Melanesia*. Berkeley: University of California Press, 1988.

Stuflesser, Martin. "*Actuosa Participatio*: Between Hectic Actionism and New Interiority: Reflections on 'Active Participation' in the Worship of the Church as Both Right and Obligation of the Faithful." Translated by Robert J. Daly. *Studia Liturgica* 41, no. 1 (2011): 92–126.

Taft, Robert. "Liturgy as Theology." *Worship* 56 (March 1982): 113–17.

———. "Structural Analysis of Liturgical Units: An Essay in Methodology." *Worship* 52, no. 4 (July 1, 1978): 314–29.

Tanner, Norman P., ed. *Decrees of the Ecumenical Councils*. 2 vols. London: Sheed & Ward, 1990.

Targoff, Ramie. *Common Prayer: The Language of Public Devotion in Early Modern England*. Chicago: University of Chicago Press, 2001.

———. "The Performance of Prayer: Sincerity and Theatricality in Early Modern England." *Representations*, no. 60 (Autumn 1997): 49–69.

Taylor, Charles. *The Ethics of Authenticity*. Cambridge, MA: Harvard University Press, 1992.

———. *Modern Social Imaginaries*. Durham, NC: Duke University Press, 2003.

———. *A Secular Age*. Cambridge, MA: Belknap Press of Harvard University Press, 2007.

———. *Sources of the Self: The Making of the Modern Identity*. Cambridge, MA: Harvard University Press, 1989.

Tertullian, Cyprian, and Origen. *On the Lord's Prayer*. Translated by Alistair Stewart-Sykes. Crestwood, NY: St. Vladimir's Seminary Press, 2004.

Trilling, Lionel. *Sincerity and Authenticity*. Cambridge, MA: Harvard University Press, 1972.

Turner, Victor W. "Ritual, Tribal and Catholic." *Worship* 50, no. 6 (1976): 504–26.

———. *The Ritual Process: Structure and Anti-Structure*. Chicago: Aldine, 1969.

Vagaggini, Cipriano. "Fundamental Ideas of the Constitution." In *The Liturgy of Vatican II: A Symposium*, edited by William Baraúna and Jovian Lang, vol. 1. Chicago: Franciscan Herald Press, 1966.

———. "Liturgy and Contemplation." *Worship* 34, no. 9 (October 1960): 507–23.

———. *Theological Dimensions of the Liturgy: A General Treatise on the Theology of the Liturgy*. Translated by Leonard J. Doyle. Collegeville, MN: Liturgical Press, 1959.

Van Dijk, Stephan. "The Liturgical Legislation of the Franciscan Rules." *Franciscan Studies* 12, no. 2 (1952): 176–95.

———. "Liturgy of the Franciscan Rules (Continued)." *Franciscan Studies* 12, no. 3/4 (1952): 241–62.

Venarde, Bruce L. *Robert of Arbrissel: A Medieval Religious Life*. Washington, DC: Catholic University of America Press, 2003.

Verheijen, Luc. *Saint Augustine's Monasticism in the Light of Acts 4.32-35*. Villanova, PA: Villanova University Press, 1979.

Vogüé, Adalbert de, ed. *La règle de saint Benoît*. Sources chrétiennes 181–86. Paris: Éditions du Cerf, 1972.

———, ed. *The Rule of the Master*. Translated by Luke Eberle. Kalamazoo, MI: Cistercian Publications, 1977.

Volf, Miroslav. *After Our Likeness: The Church as the Image of the Trinity*. Grand Rapids, MI: Eerdmans, 1998.

Wainwright, Geoffrey. *Worship with One Accord: Where Liturgy and Ecumenism Embrace*. New York: Oxford University Press, 1997.

Ware, Kallistos. "'An Obscure Matter': The Mystery of Tears in Orthodox Spirituality." In *Holy Tears: Weeping in the Religious Imagination*, edited by Kimberley Christine Patton and John Stratton Hawley, 242–54. Princeton, NJ: Princeton University Press, 2005.

Warnach, Viktor. "Mens concordet voci: Zur Lehre heiligen Benedikt über die geistige Haltung beim Chorgebet nach dem 19. Kapitel seiner Klosterregel." *Liturgisches Leben* 5 (1938): 169–90.

Wawrykow, Joseph P. *The Westminster Handbook to Thomas Aquinas*. Louisville, KY: Westminster John Knox Press, 2005.

Webster, John. "The Church as Theological Community." *Anglican Theological Review* 75, no. 1 (Winter 1993): 102–15.

William, Fr., OCD. "A Re-Examination of the Liturgical Movement in the United States." *Spiritual Life* 5 (1959): 82–93.

Witvliet, John D. "The Mysteries of Liturgical Sincerity: The Amen Corner." *Worship* 92 (May 2018): 196–203.

———. "'Planting and Harvesting' Godly Sincerity: Pastoral Wisdom in the Practice of Public Worship." *Evangelical Quarterly* 87, no. 4 (October 2015): 291–309.

Wolterstorff, Nicholas. *Acting Liturgically: Philosophical Reflections on Religious Practice*. Oxford: Oxford University Press, 2018.

Zaret, David. *The Heavenly Contract: Ideology and Organization in Pre-Revolutionary Puritanism*. Chicago: University of Chicago Press, 1985.

# Name Index

Adam of Dryburgh, 121
Aristotle, 23–24, 232–34, 236
Asad, Talal, 128–31, 197
Augustine of Hippo, 30, 92, 100–110, 112–13, 117–18, 134–35, 142, 150, 157, 166, 175, 179, 231, 235–36
Austin, J. L., 225

Barish, Jonas, 135
Barron, Jessica M., x–xi, 25
Beauduin, Lambert, 157–60, 165
Becon, Thomas, 135
Benedict of Aniane, 117
Benedict of Nursia, ix, 33, 35, 63, 107, 111–18, 207. *See also* Rule of Benedict
Benedict XVI, 192, 206–8, 213
Benson, Bruce Ellis, 209–10, 237
Bernard of Clairvaux, 118–19
Braman, Brian J., x, 27, 112, 148
Branch, Lori, 124, 126, 131, 133, 135–39
Bugnini, Annibale, 177–78, 186
Bunyan, John, 63–64, 124, 136

Cajetan, Thomas, 238
Cannizzaro, Giovanni Bruno, 177
Casel, Odo, 122, 161–64
Cassian, John, 92, 97–98, 102
Chauvet, Louis-Marie, 29
Chrysostom, John, 135, 224–26, 230, 238–39
Cicero, 93
Climacus, John, 97
Congar, Yves, 23, 153, 155, 179–85
Constable, Giles, 64, 93, 111, 117–27, 154
Corbon, Jean, 190
Cramer, Winfrid, 92–93
Cuneo, Terence, 227–29, 241–42
Cyprian of Carthage, 63, 79–84, 90, 114

Dahlstrom, Daniel, x, xiii, 142, 147–48, 231–38, 241
Dallen, James, 129–30
Dawbeny, Henry, 138

Douglas, Mary, 195–98
Duffy, Eamon, 124–26
Durkheim, Émile, 194–96

Ermengarde of Anjou, 122–23
Evagrius of Pontus, 92, 94–102
Evans, Rachel Held, 25–26

Fagerberg, David, 44, 94–95, 166, 204, 217–19
Flanagan, Kieran, 195–96
Francis (pope), 15–17, 239
Francis of Assisi, 121–22, 178
Franklin, R. W., 146, 151–52, 156–57

Geertz, Clifford, 197
Géhin, Paul, 96–97, 100
Geldhof, Joris, 157
Goodwin, Daniel R., 35–36
Grillo, Andrea, 184, 187
Guardini, Romano, xii, 17–21, 24–25, 34, 67, 71–72, 152, 155, 160–61, 178–79, 188–89, 191, 207, 215–17, 220–21, 223, 231
Guéranger, Prosper, 151, 156–57
Guignon, Charles, 103, 112, 133–34, 143–44, 150

Hays, Richard B., 58–60, 69
Hervieu-Léger, Danièle, 145–47, 212
Heschel, Abraham Joshua, 41, 44
Hosea, 41–42, 44, 49

Irwin, Kevin, 193, 242
Isaiah, 38–49, 65, 69–70, 82, 83–84, 115, 120, 168, 192

Jeffery, Peter, 10–11
Jeremiah, 41, 46, 66–67
Jesus, xii–xiii, 28–29, 37, 39–40, 46–58, 65–66, 69–70, 75–76, 80–84, 89, 114, 192, 201, 204, 239

John, Gospel of, 71, 96, 158, 200–201
Johnson, Maxwell E., 73–75

Kardong, Terrence, 33, 114–15
Kavanagh, Aidan, 31, 220, 242

Lasch, Christopher, 142, 233
Lathrop, Gordon, 203
Lehner, Ulrich L., 146, 148–49
Leithart, Peter, 199
Lessi Ariosto, Mario, 16
Lindholm, Charles, 4, 9, 27, 144
Louth, Andrew, 102
Luke, Gospel of, 28, 57, 66
Luz, Ulrich, 53–54

MacIntyre, Alasdair, 229–32
Macy, Gary, 126, 133
Mahmood, Saba, 23, 145, 221
Mannion, M. Francis, 186–87, 193
Maritain, Jacques, 170–77
Maritain, Raïssa, 170–77
Mark, Gospel of, 28, 37, 39–40, 46–50,
    69–70, 82, 120, 168, 192, 235
Marmion, Columba, 157, 159
Martimort, Aimé-Georges, 185–86
Mary, Saint, 130, 170
Matthew, Gospel of, 28, 37, 39, 46–58, 66,
    69–70, 75–77, 81–85, 88–89, 100–101,
    114, 120, 122–23, 203, 239
McCall, Richard D., 5
Millare, Roland, 165
Mitchell, Nathan, 6, 18, 72, 83, 112–14
Möhler, Johann Adam, 157

Neyrey, Jerome, 52, 54–56
Nguyen, Joseph H., 91–94, 96
Nilus of Ancyra, 98
Novick, Tzvi, 31

O'Meara, Thomas, 151
Origen of Alexandria, 84–92, 102, 113,
    122, 135, 192
Otto, Rudolf, 194–95

Paulinus of Nola, 108
Paul the Apostle, xii, 28, 36, 46–47, 52,
    56–70, 78, 86–87, 115, 123–24, 136,
    154, 157, 163–64, 192, 200–202, 240
Paul VI, 12, 15–16
Pecklers, Keith F., 146, 149, 184
Péguy, Charles, 155, 183–84, 237
Peterson, Brent, 199
Peter the Venerable, 118–19

Philo of Alexandria, 92
Pine, Gregory, 237–38
Pius VI, 149
Pius X, 152, 157–58, 162, 165, 176, 185
Pius XII, 165–71, 174
Plato, 90, 135

Ratzinger, Joseph. *See* Benedict XVI
Reid, Alcuin, 187
Riesebrodt, Martin, 194
Robert of Arbrissel, 118, 122–24
Roberts, J. J. M., 39–46
Ross, Melanie C., 200–204, 213–14
Rousseau, Jean-Jacques, 144–45, 148, 150,
    232
Rouwhorst, Gerard, 127
Ryelandt, Idesbald, 159–60

Sarah, Robert, 187
Seligman, Adam B., 24, 26, 29, 132
Seneca, 93
Shakespeare, William, 141–43
Smith, Christian, 25
Smith, Innocent, 181
Smolarski, Dennis, 234
Stewart-Sykes, Alistair, 82, 84, 90
Strathern, Marilyn, 221
Stuflesser, Martin, 32, 154–55, 185, 215–16

Taft, Robert, 146–47
Targoff, Ramie, 51–52, 139–40
Taylor, Charles, x, 27–28, 102–3, 133, 141–
    44, 148, 150, 183, 231–33
Tertullian, 75–79, 84, 135
Thomas Aquinas, xiii, 22–24, 67, 100–101,
    130, 168, 171–72, 179, 232–40
Trilling, Lionel, 141–45, 232
Turner, Victor, 195–98
Tyndale, William, 135

Vagaggini, Cipriano, 16, 171, 173–77, 181,
    185–86
Verheijen, Luc, 108–9
Vogüé, Adalbert de, 33

Wainwright, Geoffrey, 68
Ware, Kallistos, 97–98
Warnach, Viktor, 116
Wawrykow, Joseph P., 22, 24, 130
Werkmeister, Benedict, 149
Williams, Rhys H., x–xi, 25
Witvliet, John, 199–200
Wolterstorff, Nicholas, 5–6, 223–25, 229–
    30, 242

# Subject Index

adaptation, 11–13, 21, 29–30, 161, 180, 210, 235

*anamnesis*, 21–22, 42, 145–52

*apatheia*, 85, 91–102, 110, 226

asceticism, 90–97

attention, 80–82, 89–90, 96, 101, 112–17, 125, 159, 222, 242–43

audience of prayer, 5–6, 51–53, 81, 88, 91, 100, 114, 142

authenticity
  as a modern value, ix–xiii, 2–3, 24–27, 133, 137, 139–51, 155, 181–82, 188, 193, 232–234
  as a virtue, x–xi, xiii, 2–3, 23–24, 27, 31–32, 231–43
  as being real, x, 16, 19, 22, 56, 59, 62, 126–28, 131–32, 154, 160–62, 168, 171, 179–82, 210–11, 226, 232
  as being true or genuine, 4, 7–14, 18–20, 30–31, 36, 45–46, 52, 65, 75, 77, 89–91, 94–96, 103–6, 118–19, 132, 152, 157–64, 168, 177–85, 201–2, 205, 220
  as being true to oneself, xiii, 133, 141–43, 152, 232–34, 241
  critique of authenticity, ix–xiii, 24–27, 182, 193, 231–33
  genealogical authenticity, xi–xii, 4–17, 21, 25, 34, 48, 69–70, 117–18, 145–51, 155–56, 181, 186–88, 211–12, 219–21, 230
  performative authenticity, xi–xii, 4–17, 21–24, 34–35, 47–48, 67, 70, 79, 111–12, 117–19, 125, 138–39, 147–49, 155, 178, 181, 185, 188, 190, 211, 220–21, 230, 235, 241
  verification, 4, 72–73, 83, 120, 179, 211–12

authority, 4, 10, 29–30, 80, 131, 149, 163–66, 187–88, 240

awareness, 2, 32, 81, 102, 142, 155, 177, 180, 184, 191–92, 198, 231, 239

baptism, 29, 74, 76, 80, 148, 163, 167, 214, 229, 235

Benedictines, 113, 118, 124, 146, 152, 156, 177, 185

body
  as metaphor, 35, 39, 46–47, 60–69, 71–72, 130, 200
  bodiliness, embodiment, xi, 2–3, 8, 18–20, 29, 31, 46, 64–66, 76, 81, 96–101, 105, 115, 120, 130, 139, 166, 193–99, 205

Body of Christ, 2, 17, 22, 60–72, 78, 104–7, 110, 157–58, 160–69, 172, 176, 180–81, 191, 202–3, 207, 220, 223–24, 227, 231, 239, 242–44

Catholicism, 1, 10, 119, 130–35, 139–40, 144–56, 183–84, 193, 196–200, 205–13

Christ
  as head of his Body, 68, 105–6, 157, 164, 167, 169, 176, 224
  as subject of liturgical action, xiii, 2–3, 5, 17, 21, 28, 161–63, 167, 174–76, 219, 222–24
  teaching on prayer, xii, 37, 39–40, 46–58, 61, 65–66, 70, 75–76, 80–82, 84, 89, 114

church, xi–xiii, 9, 17–21, 31, 56, 67–72, 78, 132–33, 153–54, 161–70, 174–79, 188–91, 200–204, 214–17, 223–24, 242

*Comme le prévoit*, 12–15

communion
  as activity, 68, 105, 180, 230
  in Christ, 68, 71, 170, 184, 243
  of saints, 67–68, 87–88, 90–91, 105, 169,
    220, 229–30, 241
concord, *concordia*, xi, 35, 76–80, 84–85,
    93–94, 108–10, 112, 116–17, 119, 121,
    178, 185–86, 207, 231
conformity, 3, 8, 14, 26–28, 65–66, 73, 86,
    112, 118, 125–27, 142, 162–63, 167,
    174–76, 182, 207, 211
contemplation, 95–96, 102, 126, 132,
    170–76, 205, 244
continuity. *See* authenticity: genealogical
    authenticity
contrition, 46, 98, 128–30, 159, 228
cooperation
  in the Body of Christ, 68, 110, 155, 163,
    169, 180, 201, 223–24, 227, 230
  with grace/Holy Spirit, ix, 2–3, 11, 22–
    23, 88–90, 155, 207, 216–20, 223–24,
    227, 230
creativity, 14–17, 29–31, 50, 94, 135, 150,
    156, 163, 183–84, 194, 202–5, 210–15,
    234–40, 244
custom, convention, 9, 24–25, 46, 55,
    61, 77–78, 93, 118, 136–37, 145–50,
    182–83, 210, 225

dichotomy, xiii, 111, 132, 188, 200, 213–15,
    217
*Didache*, 60, 75
discernment, 9, 28–30, 43, 62–65, 69, 78,
    101, 142, 164, 187, 191, 214–16, 220,
    240–44
discipline, 69, 114–15, 128–33
discord, 45, 58–59, 74–76, 85, 109–12, 170
display. *See* performance: as display or
    show
dispositions, 2, 6–8, 11, 22–23, 61, 85, 113,
    128–31, 139–40, 159, 167, 199, 207–8,
    220–22, 232, 239
distraction, 22, 89, 96, 101, 168, 222, 228
Divine Office. *See* Liturgy of the Hours

ecumenism, 68, 181, 184, 199–200, 202–3,
    213–18
emotion, 35–36, 40–41, 85, 91–94, 98, 102,
    112, 125, 128, 130, 133, 135–38, 144–
    45, 150, 196–98, 208, 221–23
enactment, 5–7, 59, 61, 73, 83, 153, 158,
    197, 208, 220–30, 242–43
Enlightenment, 146–51

ethics, 41–42, 72–74, 78–79, 83, 120, 214–17.
    *See also* justice
Eucharist, 58–61, 73, 105–6, 123–27, 134–35,
    151–52, 166–68, 191–92, 209, 226–27,
    234, 238–39
  Lord's Supper, 29, 58–63, 69
  Mass, 1, 15, 18, 30, 123–27, 132, 135, 140,
    145, 148–49, 159, 165–69, 172–73, 179–
    82, 205–15, 239
evangelicals, x, xii, 25, 199–204, 209, 213–14
expression, 5–6, 11–16, 18, 77, 98, 105, 108,
    124–25, 141, 145, 147, 150–51, 160–64,
    182, 193, 196, 199, 205, 208, 221–23,
    242

fasting, 53–55, 77, 83, 165, 168
forgiveness, 85–86, 97, 129–30, 228
formality, 125, 136–37, 161, 204, 210, 221
formation, xi, xiii, 6–8, 14, 19–23, 31, 95, 99,
    120, 124–31, 140, 160, 165, 203, 208–9,
    214, 220–23, 243
free churches, xii, 3, 199–204, 212
free prayer, 135–39

glossolalia, 63–65, 87, 92, 115, 124

habit, 6, 23–32, 61, 81, 95, 99–101, 145, 182–
    83, 209–18, 223, 232–33, 237, 244
harmony
  of mind and voice, ix, xi–xii, 1–3, 29, 34,
    70–72, 76, 79–80, 85–86, 92–93, 98,
    108–15, 119–21, 133, 137, 152, 154–55,
    158–70, 177, 185, 204, 219–21, 230
  with one another, xi–xiii, 3, 65–72, 76,
    78–80, 85–86, 94, 103, 107–12, 116, 156,
    169, 176, 191, 221, 231, 244
heart (*kardia, cor*), 35
  as metaphor for interior, xii, 34–37, 40–
    41, 45–50, 52, 56–57, 65–68, 75, 78–82,
    92, 111–15, 120–26, 221
  as seat of emotions, 26, 35–36, 97–98,
    102, 121–26, 135–39, 144, 147, 160
  having one heart, 65, 68, 70, 75, 79,
    106–9, 116, 170, 230–31
  pure heart (*see* purity: of heart)
Holy Spirit
  dwelling in Christians, 9, 12, 67, 71, 87,
    164, 190, 201–6, 214–16, 219
  guiding the church, 9, 12, 71, 78, 163,
    178, 187–91, 201–2, 215–18, 224
  interceding, 9, 86–87, 90–91
honor, 50–57, 61–63, 88, 100–101, 123,
    233–36, 244

humility, xiii, 34, 46, 50, 57, 77, 93, 124, 128–31, 159, 200, 215–16, 225, 235–41, 243
hypocrisy, 2, 44–51, 85, 88–90, 111, 120, 123, 137–38, 168

improvisation, 73, 198, 205, 237. *See also* spontaneity
inauthenticity
  artificiality, x–xi, 9, 18, 25, 43, 77, 98, 131, 141, 145, 161, 180, 185, 210–11
  emptiness, 19–20, 34, 38, 48, 51, 70, 77, 90, 100, 119, 131, 162, 168, 171–72, 235
  theatricality, 5, 18, 20, 52, 88–89, 135–40, 168, 209
individualism, 26, 71, 142–45, 152, 159, 173, 201–2
insincerity
  deception, xi, 2, 22, 36, 40, 48, 52, 74, 82, 89, 108, 141, 236
  falsehood, xi, 9, 22, 33, 39, 41, 66, 76, 110, 124, 141–42, 147
  pretense, xi, 38, 123–24, 130, 141, 168, 227
integrity, integration, xii, 3–6, 14, 17–20, 34–39, 64–73, 84, 90, 98–99, 108–9, 150, 161–62, 199, 205, 207–8, 215–24, 231
intelligence, intelligibility, 3, 64, 87, 95, 101, 148–49, 156, 181, 193–99, 232
intention, 2, 6, 24, 49, 65–66, 82, 117–19, 134, 138, 167, 221, 228
inwardness, interiority, xii, 18, 30, 102–4, 107–9, 112–14, 120–27, 133–34, 140–45, 151–52, 154, 170–76, 185, 195–96, 231. *See also* prayer: interior prayer

justice, 38–49, 66, 79, 82–84, 214–17. *See also* ethics

knowledge, 41–46, 65–66, 86, 93–95, 99–105, 136. *See also* understanding
know-how, 194, 228–31, 241

Latin Mass, xiii, 9, 165, 187, 195, 200, 205–15, 222
lip service, 38–43, 92, 115, 137–38, 168, 174
*Liturgiam Authenticam*, 10–16
liturgical act, 6, 17–24, 34, 67, 71–73, 161, 176, 188, 199, 213–15, 220–31, 235, 237, 242–43
liturgical movement, xii, 20, 151–89, 207, 217

liturgical reform, 1–3, 10–17, 20, 117–20, 124–25, 146–56, 164–66, 177–88, 192–99, 217, 220
Liturgy of the Hours, ix, 2, 15, 33, 108, 113–14, 123, 168, 185
Lord's Prayer, 26, 51, 79–80, 84–85, 90, 203
love
  of God, 37, 67–68, 70, 72, 94, 102, 110, 114, 171–75, 192, 215, 235, 242
  of neighbor, 37, 72–74, 85, 192, 215, 235, 242 (*see also* mutuality)

magnanimity, xiii, 34, 156, 200, 215–16, 231–41, 244
*Mediator Dei*, 165–71, 174–77, 180, 185
memory, memorization, 2, 14–15, 21, 35, 103, 120, 123, 130, 145–47, 152, 212
mind (*mens*), xi, 35, 93, 103, 114–22, 177–78, 185, 207
  having one mind, 62–65, 69, 75, 79, 86, 116, 170, 190, 226–27, 230
  of christ, 31, 62–65, 69, 176, 194
modernity, x, xii–xiii, 4–5, 18–28, 36, 51–52, 71–72, 102–3, 111–12, 131–52, 161, 181–84, 193–99, 231–34
monks, monasticism, ix, 2, 92–101, 107–8, 111–31, 145–46, 151, 156
mutuality, 7, 68, 107–8, 164, 191, 226–27, 239–44
Mystical Body, 156–58, 161, 166, 172, 180, 239. *See also* Body of Christ

newness, novelty, 9, 15, 25, 60, 118, 149, 163–64, 173, 178, 188, 194, 204, 216, 237–38, 244

organic development, 7, 13, 156, 185–88, 194, 205

participation
  active participation, xiii, 1–2, 7, 11, 22, 32, 154–70, 172, 176–77, 184–88, 191–92, 198, 219, 228–29
  exterior/interior participation, 1–14, 112–13, 120, 127, 138, 154, 158–180, 185, 195–99, 208–9, 217, 225–26
peace, 76–80, 93, 106–9, 170, 226–27, 242
penance, 127–31, 134
performance
  as display or show, 5, 18–20, 24–26, 44, 51–62, 76–77, 81, 88–89, 99–100, 131–32, 135–43, 147–48, 221–22, 235–36 (*see also* inauthenticity: theatricality)

authentic performance (*see*
   authenticity: performative
   authenticity)
liturgy as performance (*see* enactment)
manner of performance, 5, 21, 80, 86–
   87, 108, 115, 151, 211, 224–31
posture, 2, 26, 50, 74, 77–78, 80–82, 85,
   167, 209, 211, 225–26
prayer, praying
   interior prayer, xii, 47, 52, 57, 91, 99,
      120–21, 124–26, 131, 144, 150, 160,
      178, 206
   private prayer, 51, 116, 122, 140, 159,
      162, 173–74, 176, 179
   public prayer, 18, 24, 33–47, 50–82,
      88–90, 99–101, 104–110, 114–21, 127,
      135–40, 143–49, 160–65, 171–76, 201,
      203, 214–17, 234, 238
   scripted prayer, 26, 73, 124, 136–37,
      143, 147, 208–9, 222
   with the mind/understanding, 63–65,
      82, 124, 136
preservation, 7–8, 11, 13, 15–16, 21, 70,
   179, 181
pride, 53, 62, 77, 93–94, 102–4, 110, 114,
   123–24, 131, 142, 144, 148, 235–36,
   240
Protestantism, 119–20, 125–26, 132–40,
   147–48, 151–53, 193–205, 212, 217
psalmody, 2, 33, 108, 113–16, 120, 124,
   175–76, 207, 242
Puritanism, 124, 138–39, 222
purity
   of heart, 36, 47, 66, 75, 78–79, 82, 94,
      106, 108, 110, 112
   pure prayer, 93–94, 96–97, 99, 101
   pure sacrifice, 73–77, 79–80, 84–85, 94,
      104, 116
   ritual purity, 45, 49–50, 73–75, 85, 93–
      94, 96, 108, 112, 118, 151, 154, 156

reform. *See* liturgical reform
Reformation. *See* Protestantism
repetition, 13–15, 91, 101, 118, 124, 137–
   38, 168, 183, 212–13, 217–18, 237–38
   recitation, 26, 37, 42, 69, 120, 124, 130
   rote, rote-learning, 39–40, 42, 70, 120,
      136, 210
   routine, 2, 25, 100–101, 124, 136, 182
representation, 89–90, 127–39
*ressourcement*, 155, 181, 184, 237
reverence, 80–81, 99, 191, 208–9, 214–15,
   237, 240–42, 244
ritual, 24–29, 72, 112, 120, 124–40, 145,
   182, 193–99, 210–14

critique of ritual, 24–28, 112, 124, 126–27,
   131–40, 143–45, 150, 161, 168, 180–84,
   193–99, 217
ritual change, 1–3, 8–17, 20, 29–30, 118–
   19, 148–49, 163–66, 178–82, 193–99,
   204–5
Romanticism, 112, 148, 150–51, 194, 222, 231
Rule of Augustine, 107, 117–18
Rule of Benedict, ix, xi–xii, 2, 33, 92–94,
   108, 112–21, 155–56, 168, 177, 185–86,
   207–8
Rule of the Master, 93, 115

sacraments, sacramentality, 7, 22–23, 104–7,
   125–32, 134–35, 174, 179–80, 200, 202,
   228–29
   sacramental efficacy, 125–33
   sacramental validity, 2, 22–23, 128, 179,
      182, 228–29
sacredness, sacrality, 168–69, 195–96, 198
*Sacrosanctum Concilium*, ix, xi, 1–3, 5–18,
   21–24, 29–30, 32, 117, 154–58, 166, 171,
   177–78, 185–88, 190–96, 198–99, 207,
   214, 216, 219, 222–24, 227, 229–30, 238
script, score, 6, 190, 224–28, 238, 242
secret, secrecy, 45, 50–57, 80–81, 88–89, 100,
   123, 134, 160
self, 26–30, 37, 102–4, 112, 128, 133–34,
   139–43, 147–48, 150, 179, 233
   self-expression, 13–14, 18, 141–42, 145,
      182, 223 (*see also* expression)
senses, 3, 89–90, 96–101, 158, 190, 193
signs, signification, 16, 22–23, 104–7,
   124–32, 139–40, 160–63, 179, 193–200
sin, 22, 26, 34, 57, 65, 85, 98, 100–101,
   128–31, 134, 167, 227, 239
sincerity
   as a modern value, 18–19, 24–25, 51–52,
      72, 112, 132–45, 147–48, 181–82, 232–33
   as a pre-modern value, 29, 51–52, 82, 93,
      98, 106, 111–12, 117–23, 232–33
   as being true to others, 141–43, 232
   contrasted with ritual, 18–19, 24–25, 29,
      51–52, 72, 112, 132–40, 144–45, 147,
      199–200
   relation to authenticity, 2, 4, 9, 112,
      139–45, 147–48, 181–82, 232–33
social science, x–xi, 4, 24–25, 27, 183,
   193–98, 221
society, 27–28, 71–72, 107, 133, 141, 143–50
spontaneity, 73, 98, 126, 133–39, 143, 147,
   160, 168, 196, 201, 205, 208–13, 221–22,
   237. *See also* improvisation
stability, 8, 12–15, 208–13, 243
Stoicism, 91–102, 110–11, 142

symbols, symbolism. *See* signs, signification

tears, 97–99
theater. *See* inauthenticity: theatricality
*theologia prima*, 31, 242
tongues. *See* glossolalia
*totus Christus*, 106–9, 157
tradition, 4–13, 31, 46–50, 69–70, 146–51,
181–84, 187, 203, 206, 212, 218, 229–
30, 237
*Tra le sollecitudini*, 152, 157–58, 176
transformation, 20–21, 28–29, 35, 44, 102,
128–31, 139, 167, 202, 206, 217, 222,
239
translation, 10–17, 30, 159, 210–11
Trent, Council of, 132–35
tune. *See* harmony
tuning adjustments, xii–xiii, 6–8, 15, 23,
29–31, 178–81, 188–222, 231, 235–37,
241–44
    inside-out, 163, 180, 188, 190–91, 199–
    205, 213–22, 235, 244
    outside-in, 97–98, 159–60, 165, 179,
    188, 190–91, 199–200, 204–22, 237,
    243–44

understanding, 2, 8, 16, 29, 35–44, 48–
50, 62–66, 70, 77, 84, 86, 91, 105–6,
115, 118–21, 124, 136, 159–60, 165,
180, 188–99, 207–8, 211–12, 229–30,
243–44. *See also* knowledge
unity, 8, 14, 59–63, 68–71, 75–80, 104–12,
116, 119, 158, 164, 166, 169–70, 190–
91, 202–3, 220, 227, 239

variety, 1, 8, 11, 30, 78, 119, 164, 169, 178,
194
Vatican Council II, ix, xi–xii, 1–3, 9–17,
20, 29–30, 32, 153–55, 170–71, 177–
78, 183–99, 216–17. *See also Sacro-*
*sanctum Concilium*
vernacular, 1, 10–17, 30, 149, 164–65
virtue, x–xi, xiii, 23–24, 26–27, 31, 85,
90, 93–95, 99, 128–33, 141–42, 168,
171–72, 175, 197, 215–16, 229–43
voice (*vox*), xi, 3, 33–35, 47, 78, 80–82,
87–88, 93, 108–11, 114–17, 121–22,
168–69, 177–78, 202

works, 55, 74, 83, 90, 104, 117, 122, 132–
39, 174